WILLIAM KENNETT LOFTUS

A 19TH-CENTURY ARCHAEOLOGIST IN MESOPOTAMIA

Letters transcribed and introduced by John Curtis

Frontispiece: See caption to plate 1.

Published in 2023 by
The British Institute for the Study of Iraq
(Gertrude Bell Memorial)
The British Academy
10 Carlton House Terrace
London SW1Y 5AH

© The British Institute for the Study of Iraq 2023

All rights reserved

Typeset in England
by Ben Plumridge, Edale, Derbyshire

ISBN 978-0-903472-41-8

Contents

PREFACE 6

CHAPTER 1: INTRODUCTION 8

CHAPTER 2: SUMMARY OF THE LETTERS 25

CHAPTER 3: LOFTUS'S LATER CAREER 40

CHAPTER 4: THE LETTERS 44

APPENDIX 230

BIBLIOGRAPHY 244

INDEX 249

Preface

This work is based on a collection of 56 letters that were written by the archaeologist, geologist and naturalist William Kennett Loftus (1820–58) from the Middle East between 29 January 1849 and 24 May 1851. They were addressed to friends and colleagues in Newcastle (pl. 4). As was customary at that time, such letters were often circulated around a group of acquaintances, and sometimes such letters were copied out. In the present case, the letters were copied into three consecutive notebooks by, to judge from the different styles of handwriting, a number of different people (pl. 3). On the opening page of the first volume is a note by the railway engineer John Addison (1820–1903), of The Castle Hill, Maryport, Cumbria, dated March 1890, saying that the three books contain 60 [sic] letters of which six were sent directly to his brother-in-law Mr Benjamin Green. Benjamin Green (c. 1811–58) was a well-known railway architect based in Newcastle upon Tyne who was evidently a close friend of Loftus. It seems likely that after Green's early death the notebooks passed into the possession of his brother-in-law John Addison. This would imply that the letters were copied soon after receipt and probably before the death of Green in 1858. The notebooks now belong to Luke Tredinnick, a descendant of Benjamin Green, and I am grateful to him for permission to transcribe the copies and to publish them here.

The letters were transcribed during the Covid-19 lockdown of 2020–21. As explained above, the copies are by different hands, some child-like, and spelling mistakes and misrepresentation of names are commonplace. Where these are obvious I have corrected them as I went along. There is also inconsistency in the spelling of place-names, which may well have been present in the original letters. I have tried to standardise these spellings, and where possible and practical I have followed the spellings given in the text of Loftus's book *Travels and Researches in Chaldea and Susiana* (1857) or in the map accompanying that book. In other cases I have followed well-established and familiar modern usage. There has been no attempt to adhere to a particular transliteration system.

I am also most grateful to Elizabeth Frances Radford for lending me papers relating to the Loftus and Radford families, and I am indebted to her for several stimulating conversations about W K Loftus. I have transcribed a number of letters amongst these papers relating to W K Loftus (see Appendix), and I have made use of other information in the text of this book where appropriate.

Although I have attempted to contextualise and evaluate Loftus's archaeological work in the introduction to this work, and in chapter three I have described his career in the period after that covered by the letters, this does not purport to be a biography of Loftus. That would be a major undertaking far beyond the modest scope of the present endeavour, and should also involve an assessment of his accomplishments in the fields of geology and natural history. Rather, it is hoped that the contents of the previously unpublished letters and the related commentaries will shed further light on the life and achievements of a remarkable and underrated Victorian traveller-scholar.

I am grateful to the publications committee of the British Institute for the Study of Iraq and its chair Rosalind Wade Haddon for agreeing to publish this book, and to Gareth Brereton who has copy-edited it and made a number of helpful suggestions. The book was designed and typeset by Ben Plumridge, and best thanks are due to him for his efforts.

CHAPTER ONE

Introduction

William Kennett Loftus (1820–58) was primarily a geologist who was attached to the Turco-Persian Frontier Commission that was set up to adjudicate on the disputed frontier between the Ottoman Empire and Persia (pl. 6), with Commissioners and their teams from Turkey, Persia, Britain and Russia. He was born in 1820 in Kent while his army officer father was stationed there, but the family hailed from Newcastle upon Tyne and he was brought up there and educated partly at the Royal Grammar School. In 1840 he went up to Cambridge and studied geology but he did not take a degree. He was, however, elected to the Geological Society of London in 1842. On returning to Newcastle he was active in the Natural History Society and the Literary and Philosophical Society.

He evidently made a name for himself in this period, as at the end of 1848 he was invited to join what is commonly known as the Turco-Persian Frontier Commission. The long border between the Ottoman Empire and Persia, from Mohammerah [Khorramshahr] in the south to Mt Ararat in the north, had been a source of contention between the two powers for decades, and border incidents in the 1830s and 1840s had nearly resulted in war. This was averted by the Treaty of Erzurum, signed on 31 May 1847, which had provided for a Commission to determine the exact boundary. The members of this commission were to be Turkey and Persia, and the two colonial powers who had vested interests in the area, Britain and Russia. At the end of 1847, Lieutenant-Colonel W F Williams, who had previously been involved in the negotiations leading to the Treaty of Erzurum, was appointed as the British Commissioner (Ateş 2013: 142). Austen Henry Layard, who had achieved great distinction with his excavations at Nimrud and Nineveh between 1845 and 1847, and had travelled in some of the disputed area (Layard 1887), was to join him on an equal footing (Waterfield 1963: 180–81). In September 1848, however, Layard wrote to Foreign Secretary Lord Palmerston and Sir Stratford Canning, British Ambassador in Constantinople, asking to be relieved of the appointment, ostensibly because of illness and his publishing commitments (Waterfield 1963: 188; Harbottle 1973: 198). Palmerston then wrote to Sir Henry De la Beche, head of the Geological Survey, asking him to recommend a geologist who could join the British team, and on Sir Henry's recommendation Loftus was offered the post at a salary of £200 per annum. On 3 January 1849 the Foreign Office wrote to Loftus informing him that 'although Lord Palmerston has no desire inconveniently to hurry him, His Lordship thinks it as well he should be apprised that a Steam Vessel will leave Southampton direct for Constantinople on 29th of this month' (Harbottle 1973: 199). On 5 January Loftus accepted the appointment, and as suggested sailed from Southampton on 29 January 1849. By this time the other members of the Commission had already left, and Loftus caught up with them in Mosul. The involvement of Lord Palmerston himself in Loftus's appointment may now seem extraordinary, but is an indication of the importance that was attached to British involvement in the Frontier Commission and the promotion of British interests in the region. It is also testimony to the hands-on approach of Palmerston, who guided British foreign policy for a large part of the 19th century.

During his time in Mesopotamia and Persia and while with the Commission Loftus also undertook archaeological excavations, and it is for these that he is chiefly remembered. Loftus's life and activities have been fairly well researched (see for example Boulger 1893; Welford 1895; Harbottle 1973; Barnett 1987; Smail 2004; Ermidoro 2020), and he himself wrote accounts of his travels and archaeological work (Loftus 1854a; 1855a; 1856; 1856–57; 1857; 1859). Nevertheless, it has seemed worthwhile to transcribe and put into the public domain copies of 56 letters that have recently come to my attention. They were written by Loftus to friends and family in Newcastle upon Tyne, and contain information and comment that will not be found in the other sources. In addition, being informal letters they have an immediacy and a fluency that makes them very readable. It should be stressed that this work makes no pretence at being inclusive. There are, of course, other unpublished letters of Loftus in various collections such as the British

Museum,[1] the Royal Botanic Gardens, Kew,[2] the Natural History Society of Northumberland,[3] the Royal Geographical Society,[4] the Institute of Geological Sciences[5] and no doubt elsewhere. This collection should not therefore be seen as an attempt to collect together all Loftus letters, and nor does this work make any pretence at serving as a biography of Loftus. Rather, it is hoped that the presentation here of new information about Loftus will be of service to anybody contemplating making a new and comprehensive assessment of this remarkable man.

There are 56 letters in this collection covering the period 29 January 1849 to 24 May 1851. The first letter is written from Southampton while waiting to set sail for Constantinople, and the last letter is written from the mountainous town of Kerend in Iran. During this time British Commissioners proceeded in a leisurely way to Baghdad, which had been agreed as the rendezvous point for the four teams. They waited in or near Baghdad until late December 1849 when they left for Mohammerah [Khorramshahr], the southernmost

---

1 In the Trustees' Papers there are two letters addressed to the museum secretary, the Rev Josiah Forshall, written from Mohammerah and dated 1 and 4 May 1850, concerning antiquities which are being sent in the ship 'Apprentice' (Original Papers, vol. XLIII, Nov 1849–May 1850). Loftus is also referred to in letters sent by Sir Henry Rawlinson to the Principal Librarian Sir Henry Ellis (e.g. letters of 5/11/1853, 16/12/1853, 10/2/1854, 25/3/1854).
2 There are 17 letters dated between 18 April 1853 and 29 November 1856 to Sir William Hooker (1785–1865), Director of Kew Gardens, mainly dealing with botanical matters.
3 In the archives of the Natural History Society of Northumberland are copies of eight letters written by Loftus between 1847 and 1849 in his capacity as secretary, mainly thanking people for donations of natural history specimens. There is also a letter of 26 December 1849 sent by Loftus from Baghdad accompanying a list of natural history specimens that he is donating to the Society, and a letter of 4 April 1856 sent from Norwood to Joseph Blackstock, the Secretary, offering to donate a collection of antiquities to the Society. I am most grateful to Andrew Parkin of the Great North Museum Hancock for information about these letters. The last two letters have now been transcribed and published by Ermidoro (2020: 248–9, Figs 1–2). Ermidoro also refers (2020: 249, n.21) to four letters in the Society archives written by Loftus to Albany Hancock; one dated 20 May 1849 is presumably Letter no. 12 here and Letters 16 and 40 may also be in Newcastle.
4 See Harbottle 1973.
5 See Harbottle 1973.

INTRODUCTION

point on the disputed frontier line. They were in Mohammerah from late January until June 1850 when they decamped for the mountains near Dizful, staying there until September 1850. They then went on a lengthy excursion taking in Khorramabad, Kermanshah, Hamadan, Isfahan and Shiraz before returning to Mohammerah in early 1851. They left again for the mountains in April. During this long period Loftus visited and excavated at a number of archaeological sites including Warka and Susa.

Twenty-one letters (3–4, 10, 13, 15, 18, 21, 28–29, 31, 35–36, 39, 42–43, 46–47, 49, 52–54) are to his cousin James Radford;[6] eleven letters (5–6, 22, 24, 27, 30, 32, 34, 44, 50–51) are to Edward Mather; six letters (1, 7, 17, 19, 33, 55) are to the railway architect Benjamin Green;[7] three letters (12, 16, 40) are to the naturalist Albany Hancock;[8] three letters (23, 38, 56) are to Joseph Blacklock, the treasurer of the Natural History Society of Newcastle upon Tyne; three letters (8, 9, 11) are addressed to 'dear affectionates', namely James Radford, Edward Mather and John Gray; two letters (25–26) are to the physician and antiquary Dr Edward Charlton;[9] two letters (20, 45) are to 'My dear artist Coz', the artist James Radford;[10] one letter (37) is to the

---

6   James Radford (1806–93) was a solicitor who managed the coaching business in Newcastle and was much involved in the management of the Newcastle Racecourse. See appendix for further information.
7   Benjamin Green (1813–58) was principally a railway architect, and he is credited with designing all the mainline stations between Newcastle and Berwick upon Tweed. His father John Green (1787–1852), also an architect, built the Literary and Philosophical Society Library in Newcastle in Greek revival style.
8   Albany Hancock (1806–73) was a distinguished naturalist specialising in zoology. See *Dictionary of National Biography* (1885–1900), vol. 24. The Hancock Museum in Newcastle upon Tyne is named after Albany Hancock and his brother John (1808–90), also a naturalist, principally interested in ornithology and taxidermy.
9   Dr Edward Charlton (1814–74) was a physician who in 1872 became Professor of Medicine in the University of Durham. He had wide-ranging antiquarian interests and published widely in that field.
10 This is the artist James Radford, not to be confused with the solicitor James Radford (n. 6). James Radford the artist (1810–94) was born in Salford, Lancashire, the son of Joseph Radford and Elizabeth Caroline Harvey. He was a landscape painter, based in London, and exhibited in all 15 works at the Royal Academy of Arts. At a late stage in his life he was Fine Art Master at Westminster School (information from Elizabeth Frances Radford). See also *Bryan's Dictionary of Painters and Engravers*, vol. IV.

geologist Thomas Sopwith;[11] one letter (2) is to John Gray; one letter (41) is to the secretary of the Farmers' Club, Newcastle upon Tyne; one letter (14) is to 'friends at Newcastle'; and one letter (48) is to an unknown recipient.

The letters do not contain any great revelations, but they are of interest on a number of fronts. First and foremost they make clear the difficulties and danger of travel in the Middle East in the mid-19th century. Even to get to Mosul, where Loftus met the other members of the Commission, entailed a horrendous journey. He and a companion crossed the Taurus Mountains on horseback in mid-winter, and then floated down the Tigris to Mosul on a raft. In Mesopotamia and Western Iran, conditions were harsh. Fresh water and food were often difficult to come by, fever was ever present, and summer temperatures sometimes reached 120°–125° Fahrenheit (49°–52°C). In addition, local tribesmen were often hostile. These difficulties were compounded by the need to be away from friends and family for lengthy periods. In his first trip to the Middle East, Loftus was away from home for nearly four years, leaving behind a pregnant wife and two children. There are a few passing references to them in the letters, and we must presume he kept up a separate and constant correspondence with his wife (Letters 31, 34). We learn here that at one stage the children were seriously ill with whooping cough (Letters 19–20), and there is reference to his wife's confinement in Letter 19, but there is no subsequent report of the birth of the baby.[12] It might be thought that by travelling to the Middle East Loftus was making a great sacrifice, but it was an unforced decision and he was clearly an ambitious man in search of fame and fortune. He writes in one letter (15) that 'it certainly is a severe trial to be separated so long from my wife and children, but we both believe it to be for our good'.

Then, the letters provide some information about the Frontier Commissioners which may not be easily found in official accounts or in the history of attempts to define the Ottoman-Persian border by Sabri Ateş (2013). Thus, Loftus makes observations about the Russian Commissioner

---

11 Thomas Sopwith (1803–79) was a mining engineer, geologist and local historian. He became a Fellow of the Royal Society in 1845. See *Dictionary of National Biography* (1885–1900), vol. 53.
12 This is his third child, William Kennett Loftus, born in 1849 (see Appendix).

INTRODUCTION

Colonel Tcherikoff (Letter 7), the Turkish Commissioner Dervish Pasha (Letter 19) and the Persian Commissioner Mirza Jafar Khan (Letter 45). We learn that the members of the British delegation were the Commissioner Colonel William Fenwick Williams,[13] the head of the team, who later achieved distinction at the siege of Kars, and of whom Loftus immediately formed a very good impression, Lieutenant A G Glascott, Royal Navy, the surveyor,[14] Mr Algernon Wood, the secretary and interpreter, who died in the mountains near Dezful on 15 September 1850,[15] 'a Frenchman named Garey', who was 'the provender and clerk', Henry A Churchill,[16] interpreter, artist and budding diplomat, and Joseph Olquin, the doctor.[17] There were periods when the delegation had little to do, and in those quiet times hunting was a popular recreation. Shooting francolins (common game birds in Mesopotamia) and spear-hunting boars were the preferred activities. Aqar Quf and Ctesiphon were favoured locations for the latter (Letters 26–27). Hunting boars actually

---

13 Major-General Sir William Fenwick Williams (1800–83) (pl. 8) was appointed British Commissioner for the settlement of the Turco-Persian boundary in 1848. During the Crimean War (1854–56) he commanded Turkish troops in the valiant but ultimately unsuccessful defence of Kars. For this he was created 1st Baronet of Kars. Later he was Governor of Nova Scotia, and died in London in 1883. See *Dictionary of National Biography* (1885–1900), vol. 61.

14 Lieut. Adam Gifford Glascott, RN (1805–71). Glascott was born in Drogheda, County Louth, Ireland, and by this time had had extensive surveying experience in South America, the Mediterranean, Kurdistan and elsewhere. See http://www.ocotilloroad.com › geneal › glascott1, and also Ateş 2013: 142, Layard 1853: 76 and Barnett *et al.* 1998: n.12 on p. 19.

15 See Letter 43. Algernon Wood was first attaché to the British Embassy at Constantinople, and secretary of the Commission. Loftus pays fulsome tribute to him in his book (1857: 332, note) and writes 'His abilities as a linguist, and knowledge of oriental character, rendered his death a great loss to the Commission'. He is mistakenly referred to as Almeric Wood by Waterfield (1963: 188).

16 Henry Adrian Churchill (1828–86) (pl. 9) was an accomplished artist and linguist who was appointed secretary and interpreter to the Commission after the death of Wood. In the Crimean War he joined the staff of Major-General Williams and took part in the defence of Kars in 1855. Thereafter he held various diplomatic posts in the Balkans, Syria, Algeria and Zanzibar.

17 Joseph Olquin, Fellow of the Royal College of Surgeons of England. He engraved his name on a relief at Taq-e Bustan in 1850: J Olquin FRCSE. Before joining the Turco-Persian Frontier Commission he was a surgeon on board the ship 'Erin'.

resulted in a serious injury for Loftus; while chasing after a herd of boars near Susa his horse stumbled and fell on top of him, causing severe internal injuries (Letter 38). On another occasion, while hunting a hyena near Gherrara (Letter 20), the ground gave way beneath his horse and both horse and rider fell into the hyena's den (Letter 20).

For historians (or critics) of the British Empire, there is interesting information about the grand style in which the Resident of the East India Company, Major Rawlinson,[18] lived in Baghdad. He was attended by a guard of honour and had the personal use of a steamer moored alongside the residence. Fifteen servants dressed in their native costumes waited at the table, and the guests wanted for nothing, including every kind of alcoholic drink (Letter 11). The birthday of Queen Victoria on 24 May 1849 was celebrated in grand style, with salvos of guns, all the most important residents of Baghdad coming to pay their respects to Major Rawlinson, and enjoying a sumptuous dinner (Letter 14).

It is tempting for those who are mainly interested in archaeology to think of Loftus as primarily an archaeologist. For example, the excellent article by Harbottle (1973) is titled 'W.K. Loftus: an archaeologist from Newcastle'. However, he was much more than this. He originally joined the Turko-Persian Boundary Commission as a geologist, and his appointment was recommended by Sir Henry De la Beche, the Director of the Geological Survey of Great Britain. There are passing references to geology in the letters, and a particularly interesting discovery seems to have been the fossil footsteps of a large cat, probably a cheetah or leopard, in sandstone near Dezful (Letter 56). Although the opportunities for geological research were limited in the great alluvial plain of Mesopotamia the surrounding mountainous areas were rich sources of information, and in Letter 48 Loftus says he is 'occupied incessantly in … making geological notes'. He purports to be annoyed that an extract of a letter to De la Beche has been published without his permission (Loftus 1851) but he is evidently quite gratified (Letter 53). Two much more

---

18 Major-General Sir Henry Creswicke Rawlinson (1810–95) is mainly remembered for his role in the decipherment of cuneiform. This was facilitated through the copies he made of the great trilingual cuneiform inscription at Bisitun in Iran.

substantial articles on the geology of the Zagros Mountains appeared in later volumes of the *Journal of the Geological Society* (Loftus 1854–55). Loftus was also a naturalist, and an enthusiastic member of the Natural History Society of Newcastle upon Tyne. In letters to the distinguished naturalist Albany Hancock (12, 16, 40) he refers to making collections of shells, scorpions, snakes and many species of insects.[19] These specimens are to be offered to the British Museum, with duplicates or unwanted material to be sent to Newcastle. He writes of stuffing birds himself and of teaching servants how to do it (Letters 8, 12, 19, 30). His collecting activities earned him the sobriquet 'father of insects' from the Arab chief Suttum (Letter 9). He also collected plants and seeds, and was in correspondence with the Royal Botanic Gardens in Kew.[20] In addition to all these activities, Loftus helped Glascott with his surveying and map-making (Letters 42–46, 48–9, 52, 55), and comments in his letter (42) from the summit of Mungerrah: 'I assist him and he gives me the benefit of his work for my geological sections'. In view of all his other commitments, it is remarkable that Loftus should have found any time at all to do archaeological work.

His first archaeological enterprise seems to have been at Babylon in September 1849 when he and Churchill dug out the partly buried Lion of Babylon (pl. 10), an iconic stone sculpture probably dating from around the 8th century BC, and were able to establish that it indeed represented a lion standing over the prostrate figure of a man (Letter 25). In January 1850 he and Churchill spent several days at Warka, making a plan of the site and excavating a glazed pottery coffin which was sketched by Churchill (pls. 15–16). The plan of the 'Ruins of Warka' that was later published in Loftus's book (1857: opp. p. 160) is jointly signed by Loftus and Churchill. Warka (Biblical Erech) is now celebrated as one of the world's earliest cities, mostly dating from the 4th–3rd millennia BC. In the later Parthian period it became an important necropolis.

Loftus returned to Warka alone on 4 February 1850 and in the course of about three weeks his workmen dug up many glazed pottery slipper

---

19 In his monumental book on the fauna of Iran, Eskandar Firouz refers to Loftus collecting on the Irano-Turkish frontier (Firouz 2005: 4).
20 There are plants collected by Loftus in the Herbarium at Kew Gardens.

coffins of Parthian date, often containing jewellery and terracotta figurines. He also collected bricks with cuneiform inscriptions and tablets (Loftus 1857: 207–29). Most of the coffins disintegrated on discovery. He next made excavations at the nearby site of Sinkara (ancient Larsa), where he found burials, terracotta figures and pottery mostly dating from the Old Babylonian period (early 2nd millennium BC). The antiquities were sent to Basra, and there he was joined by Churchill who sketched them before they were shipped to England.[21]

In May 1850 Loftus and Churchill attempted to start excavations at the famous site of Susa in south-west Iran but such was the hostility from local religious leaders and Arab tribesmen that they could do nothing more than make a plan of the ruins. This was eventually published (Loftus 1857: opp. p. 340) under the name of Churchill. They returned in January 1851 with the whole of the British Commission team after their lengthy perambulation through Western Iran. This time they were armed with a *firman* from the Shah, and were able to dig. On the Apadana mound Colonel Williams uncovered three column bases belonging to the Palace of Darius (522–486 BC), while Loftus opened a few trenches on the Acropolis mound. A year later, from February to April 1852, Loftus and Churchill were able to undertake more major excavations at Susa, but this is beyond the scope of the collection of letters being considered here.

The letters do not really provide any new insights into the results of Loftus's archaeological work, which are fairly well known (Loftus 1854a; 1855a; 1856–57; 1857; Moorey 1971; Curtis 1979; 1993; 2018), but they provide a lot of contextual information about the circumstances in which the excavations were conducted. What sort of reputation does Loftus have nowadays as an archaeologist? Larsen has written (1996: 282) that 'Loftus' activities [at Warka and Sinkara] can hardly be seen as anything other than a hasty raid', but this is rather unfair. One might say exactly the same about Layard's activities at Babylon, Nippur, Tell Arban and various other sites, but scholars would not

---

21   Churchill's drawing of objects from Warka and Sinkara are now in the British Museum, bound in a volume entitled *Drawings in Babylonia by W.K. Loftus and H.A. Churchill*.

nowadays dismiss Layard's efforts as frivolous. First and foremost, Loftus deserves great credit for venturing into a dangerous and unexplored part of Lower Mesopotamia and excavating at sites such as Warka, Larsa and Tell Sifr. The results at Warka in particular were significant, and yielded a cone mosaic from the end of the Uruk period (late 4th millennium BC), cuneiform tablets and material remains of the Parthian period, including glazed slipper coffins. Julius Jordan, who conducted German excavations at Warka from 1912 onwards, paid tribute to his work in the following terms: 'In ... Loftus we possess already an outstanding presentation of the first ample excavation in Warka ... the observations gathered by [him] are of such versatility and so brilliantly presented that we felt solid ground under our feet from the very beginning of our work' (North 1957: 190; Harbottle 1973: 216).

It is clear from the letters that Loftus himself believed his greatest contribution to have been the discovery and initial excavation of Warka, but he failed to appreciate the significance of his work at Susa which eclipses the results in Babylonia. Here, he seems to have been unduly influenced by the views of his contemporaries. Thus, Rawlinson, who was interested in cuneiform inscriptions and Assyrian reliefs to the exclusion of everything else, wrote to Layard in July 1852 that Loftus had 'turned the mound of Susa topsy-turvey without finding much' (Harbottle 1973: 205). In fact, Loftus was able to establish correctly the plan of that part of the Palace of Darius at Susa that consisted of a massive columned hall (Loftus 1857: 366), and he uncovered many fragments of columns and column capitals that were later taken to the Louvre in Paris.[22] Among other discoveries were terracotta figurines and fragments of alabaster vases with trilingual inscriptions of Xerxes (486–465 BC). Amongst the excavators of Susa, therefore, he has a distinguished place. It is clear, however, that at both Warka and Susa Loftus benefited greatly from the help of Henry Churchill who drew the finds and collaborated with surveying and planning. In fact, the published plans of Warka and Susa (Loftus 1857: opp. pp 160, 340) are very considerable

---

22 It is ironic that the column capitals from Susa are now one of the highlights of the Ancient Near Eastern displays at the Louvre, while their interest and importance were not at the time appreciated by the British Museum.

achievements and can be consulted with advantage to this day. One of the plans is ascribed to Loftus and Churchill jointly, the other to Churchill alone. The extent to which Loftus was dependent on Churchill is made clear in letters (45, 54) in which he says that although he has a *camera lucida* he finds it very difficult to work with and as Churchill sketches so beautifully there would be no need for it. In Letter 54, however, he asks his cousin to send a camera for making Talbotypes or Calotypes as he would very much like to experiment with it.[23] We do not know if and when this arrived, but Harbottle records (1973: 206) that when Loftus delivered his Susa report to the Trustees of the British Museum in April 1853 it was accompanied by 'photographic representations' of some inscriptions. It is not known if these are still extant.

It emerges from the letters that Loftus always saw himself as being in competition with Layard.[24] He viewed Layard as a rival, and is keen to compare his work with that of Layard. This is a position that is hard to understand as at the beginning of 1849, when Loftus arrived in the Middle East, Layard had already made a name for himself with his pioneering excavations at Nimrud. Their first encounter, at a dinner party at the British Embassy in Constantinople, was not propitious. Loftus wrote rather disparagingly (Letter 5) that he 'is not more than 26 [in fact he was 31] and just as unlike the author of a work [on Nineveh] as can be well conceived'. Subsequently (Letters 5–6), Layard helped him in advising what he needed for his onward journey, and recommended that he should buy a gold band for his cap to give himself some air of authority; interestingly, Layard is pictured by the artist Frederick Cooper supervising his excavations at Nineveh wearing a peaked cap with just such a gold band (Curtis 2010: pl.13). A little later he writes, with a hint of condescension, 'you will be surprised when I tell you that Layard cannot speak either Arabic or Persian and very little Turkish, tho' he certainly manages them well' (Letter 18). After his discoveries at Warka, he was keen to compare them with those of Layard: 'I do not envy

---

23 For the use of cameras on early excavation in Mesopotamia, see Larsen 1996: 308–9.
24 Sir Henry Austen Henry Layard (1817–94) had achieved international fame through his pioneering excavations at the Assyrian capitals of Nimrud and Nineveh between 1845 and 1851.

Layard his works at Mosul as I conceive that my discovery [at Warka] will create as much sensation as even his. With the means, I could at Warka astonish even him' (Letter 31). And then, continuing in the same vein, 'if I have half the luck of my friend Layard I shall afford more food for the wonder and astonishment of the antiquarian' (Letter 32). Loftus perceived excavation at Warka to be a greater challenge than digging in Assyria: 'Layard had even less difficulty to encounter than I may have. He was near a great centre of civilization [Mosul] while I shall be nearly 200 miles distant from the world. If I succeed, so much more credit will be due to me' (Letter 32). And then, when he has discovered the glazed clay coffins: 'Layard has never been able to fall in with them [the graves of what Loftus believed to be the Babylonians] but here they are one on the other, like herring in a basket' (Letter 32). Writing at the end of the third day of excavations at Warka he says: 'I hope to procure many [more] valuable articles to illustrate the domestic life of the Babylonians or Chaldeans. Layard has looked in vain for such, and here it has been my luck to find them in 3 days' (Letter 33).

In various letters (33, 37, 40, 46) he worries that Layard is intending to dig at Susa, and he also fears that Layard has aspirations at Warka and other sites in Babylonia (Letter 52). It was with a sense of relief that Loftus noted on 7 March 1851 (Letter 52): 'Layard had gone off to Mosul before my arrival as he has not been successful in Chaldaea. He starts for England I understand directly, so the field is yet open for me, and if I don't again attack Warka it shan't be my fault.' If Loftus was rather reluctant to give much credit to Layard, by contrast Layard was unstinting in his praise of Loftus, acknowledging that he was the first to explore the most important mounds in south Mesopotamia and noting that he obtained for the British Museum a 'highly interesting collection of antiquities from Wurka [Warka]' (Layard 1853: 544–5).

Apart from Layard, Loftus was not averse to making snide comments about other colleagues. Thus, in relation to Hatra he writes: 'Ainsworth in his researches has committed some most egregious blunders in his description of these ruins. He will, I have no doubt, be shortly put right' (Letter 9).[25]

---

25 William Francis Ainsworth (1807–96) was the surgeon and geologist attached to the Euphrates Expedition of 1835–37. Later, he visited Hatra with Christian

He is also very critical of Chesney's book[26] – 'it is a most decided failure, exceedingly incorrect and his maps as far as I can judge, humbug!' (Letter 53). Yet for Sir Henry Creswicke Rawlinson, the East India Company Resident at Baghdad, he has nothing but praise. He refers to him familiarly as 'my learned friend' (Letter 55) and anticipates that the announcement of his cuneiform discoveries in London 'will create as much if not more excitement even than Layard's' (Letter 18). After his arrival in London he writes: 'Rawlinson is playing the devil among the people of London we hear. He is a first rate fellow and will meet with all the credit his learning and researches deserve. No doubt he will be knighted' (Letter 34). At a number of sites Loftus collected inscriptions for Rawlinson, and was very pleased with the recognition accorded him by the Colonel (see for example Letter 53). However, their relations deteriorated when Loftus later worked under the nominal supervision of Rawlinson, first working for the British Museum and later for the Assyrian Excavation Fund (Harbottle 1973: 209–213; Larsen 1996: 327, 331).

What of Loftus the man? There are mixed views. His biographer, Stephen Harbottle, wrote: 'One is bound to admire the breadth of his interest and the uninhibited confidence with which he would move from collecting plants to digging up ivories, from drawing geological sections to administering rough justice among his Arab workers' (Harbottle 1973: 216). His critical opinion of Mesopotamia and its inhabitants was, in Harbottle's view, 'well suited to contemporary English views' (op cit: 200). By contrast, Mogens Trolle Larsen, in his comprehensive book about early discoveries in Mesopotamia, writes

---

Rassam, A H Layard and E L Mitford on 22–23 April 1840. He described the site in a paper he wrote in the *Journal of the Royal Geographical Society* vol. 11 (1841), pp 1–20, and in his book *Travels and Researches in Asia Minor, Mesopotamia, Chaldaea, and Armenia* (London 1842), vol. 2, pp 162–75. It is not clear why Loftus is so dismissive of Ainsworth's description. It is true that he is mistaken in supposing the original foundation of the site to be 'Chaldaean', but he is correct in dating most of the buildings to the Romano-Parthian period.

26 General Francis Rawdon Chesney (1789–1872) was in charge of the expedition sent to investigate the navigability of the Rivers Euphrates and Tigris in 1835–37. Reference is being made here to his newly published account *The Expedition for the Survey of the Rivers Euphrates and Tigris 1835–37*, 2 vols (London 1850).

that he was 'a deeply traditional man without much imagination' who had 'an extremely violent temper' (Larsen 1996: 282). Which of these divergent views is closer to the mark? As usual, the truth would seem to lie somewhere in between. To start with, it required a good deal of imagination and even vision to travel overland through the uncharted territory of Southern Mesopotamia and undertake excavations at places like Warka and Sinkara. Even Rawlinson regarded Loftus as 'active, intelligent, and thoroughly in earnest' (Harbottle 1973: 205). With regard to Loftus having a violent temper, this does not come across from the letters. He seems to have got on well with all his colleagues in the boundary commission team, and with others with whom he came into contact such as his early travelling companion Dodson[27] and the celebrated surveyor of the East India Company, Capt Felix Jones.[28] The French archaeologist Victor Place recorded that he had 'excellent relations' with Loftus (Larsen 1996: 317). According to a writer in the *Newcastle Courant* of 13 April 1889, 'in Newcastle he was greatly esteemed for his winning manner, kind and amiable disposition'.[29] The charge that he was contemptuous of the local people (Larsen 1996: 282) has more substance. He was certainly fiercely patriotic, to the extent of being chauvinistic, and some of his remarks smack of bigotry, jingoism and xenophobia. These views were fuelled by the fact that he did not adjust well to life in the Middle East. He did not like the food (see for example Letter 39), and he makes frequent reference to the squalor of the housing. This dislike of the environment extended also to what he called 'the natives'. He wrote that 'all Orientals are most unqualified liars' (Letter 18), and was shocked by what he saw as widespread bribery and corruption. Like some of his countrymen in the early 20th century, however, he did have some admiration for what he regarded as the noble Arabs of the desert.

---

27 John George Dodson (1825–97) entered parliament as a Liberal politician in 1857 and later served in several Gladstone administrations. He was created 1st Baron Monk Bretton in 1884.
28 See *Dictionary of National Biography* (1885–1900), vol. 30. His maps of Mesopotamia are a mine of information. See Curtis and Reade 1995: no. 238.
29 Perhaps drawing on the same source, in his *Men of Mark 'twixt Tyne and Tweed*, Welford records that 'those who enjoyed Mr Loftus' friendship concur in ascribing to him a kind and amiable disposition, and a winning manner that attracted everyone who came under its influence' (Welford 1895: 72).

He was sceptical of Layard's command of the local languages (see above) but it is unclear how proficient he himself became. He refers several times (Letters 18–19) to starting to learn Persian, but we don't know how much progress he made. What is clear from the letters, however, is that most of the servants accompanying the members of the Commission could speak a number of languages even if a dragoman was not present. Underlying all this is an unshakable belief in the superiority of England and Englishmen (see for example Letter 20). Finally, we have the fulsome tribute of General Sir William Fenwick Williams who in a letter of condolence to surviving friends wrote: 'A better man, a more zealous and faithful public servant, never lived'.[30]

Loftus was clearly very ambitious, and very much intent on making a name for himself. He was seeking fame and adulation. It comes across from the letters that he was desperate to win the approval of the Commissioner, Colonel Williams, and also of his mentor, Sir Henry De la Beche. In Letter 51 to Edward Mather he quotes from a letter he has received from Sir Henry De la Beche:

'It has been with no slight interest that I have heard of your progress, not only from such letters of yours which have reached me, as from other sources. I have heard much of you, always with great credit for you, from Major Rawlinson…You have done right good service in various ways and have deservedly had credit for it in this country'.

Loftus quickly realised that the fame and praise that he craved was more likely to be forthcoming through archaeological discoveries, and of course he could see the adulation that Layard was getting. He therefore found the reaction to his discoveries at Warka very gratifying. He wrote (in Letter 35): 'The Colonel and all our party are very much pleased with the paper [on Warka]…Col. W. has written a most flattering despatch to Sir Stratford Canning,[31] representing my perseverance and conduct among the Arabs in very high terms of

---

30 As reported in the President's Address in the *Transactions of the Tyneside Naturalists' Field Club* for 1858.
31 Sir Stratford Canning, 1st Viscount Stratford de Redcliffe (1786–1880), was the long-serving British Ambassador in Constantinople.

approval…You will, I am sure, be surprised when I tell you that Warka and your humble servant were the subjects of conversation at the Queen's dinner table!'. Or in Letter 45: 'Of course you are aware that I am blushing under the honours and being the first Kafir[32] who ever ventured to penetrate the Chaldaean deserts to the birthplace of Abraham'.

Has posterity accorded him the sort of adulation that he craved? He is remembered nowadays as an archaeologist who excavated at Warka, Sinkara, Susa and Nineveh. He walked in the shadow of Layard, and certainly cannot be regarded as his peer. Nevertheless, amongst 19th century archaeologists he has a distinguished place. At Warka and Sinkara he was a pioneer, and at Susa his contribution was much greater than he himself realised. At Nineveh he found a hoard of ivories in the Burnt Palace (see below). Above all, we should remember that his entire archaeological career spanned a period of less than six years, and for at least part of that time he was engaged in other branches of research. To have excavated at four major sites, to have made so many discoveries, to have written one substantial book and a number of articles, and all before his early death at the age of 37, is a remarkable achievement.

Lastly, it is important to note that in recent years there has been increasing interest in the role of 19th and 20th century archaeologists as agents of an imperialist agenda (see for example Malley 2012). In this case, it is certainly true that the Turco-Persian Frontier Commission to which Loftus was attached was a creation of the two imperial powers that had an interest in the area, Britain and Russia. However, there is no reason to assume that the Commission was created in order to discover more about the geology, natural history and archaeology of the region. Rather, it was the other way round. The Commission was created for reasons of political expediency, but once it had been established advantage was taken of its existence to discover more about the history and characteristics of the region. It might be argued that the acquisition of such knowledge, ultimately with the aim of owning that knowledge, underpinned by the possession of artefacts that support that knowledge, was (or is) a form of colonialism in its own right. I will not attempt to defend or deny Loftus's role in this; he was a product of his time,

---

32 An Arabic term for an unbeliever.

and he was working within well-accepted parameters. It would be foolish to judge him by the ethical standards of the present day. As for Loftus, his main concern was making a name for himself, and this could best be achieved by publishing the results of his discoveries and by sending artefacts that he discovered back to the British Museum. This may seem reprehensible to some in the early 21st century, but was *de rigueur* in the middle of the 19th century.

CHAPTER TWO

Summary of the letters

Loftus left Southampton on 29 January 1849 on the ship 'Erin' and reached Constantinople on 16 February, a voyage of some 19 days. They sailed via Gibraltar and Malta, and after leaving Malta ran into a violent storm in the vicinity of the Greek Islands. On board, passengers lived in the lap of luxury (Letter 3). In Constantinople (Letters 5–6) he stayed in Missier's Hotel, otherwise known as the Hotel d'Angleterre, said to have been the best hotel in the city. He dined a number of times at the British Embassy with the Ambassador Sir Stratford Canning and his family, who made a very favourable impression on him, and he helped the Ambassador's private secretary Count Pisano to prepare dispatches. He also met Layard for the first time. Loftus did some sightseeing in Constantinople but was shocked by the general squalor, a feature of life in the Middle East which he never got used to and refers to frequently in his letters. His initial impression of the Turks was similarly rather jaundiced. When he arrived in Constantinople the other members of the Turco-Persian Frontier Commission had already left, and there had been reports that the roads eastwards were practically impassable in the winter. Canning advised him to wait until spring but a report was received from Colonel Williams in Harput that the roads were better than expected. Loftus therefore took the opportunity to set off with the intention of catching up with the party at Mosul. He was accompanied by a Mr Dodson who had travelled in Egypt and Syria and was keen to go to Baghdad.[1] Loftus engaged the services of a multilingual Greek servant from Corfu by the name of

---

1 See Ch. 1, n. 6. Dodson stayed with the members of the Commission until August 1849 when he left for Damascus by way of Hit and Palmyra (Letters 20, 21).

Georgio Phillippo, while Dodson was attended by an Egyptian servant. They left Constantinople on 7 March 1849, with Loftus having stayed there for just under three weeks.

They travelled by boat to the Black Sea port of Samsun, and stayed for a short time there with the British Consul, Frederick Guarracino. On 14 March they departed for Diyarbakır, a journey via Amasya, Tokat, Sivas and Harput that took 16 days. On leaving their party consisted of Loftus and Dodson with their two servants, two local guides, and nine horses, three for carrying the baggage. The difficulties of crossing Eastern Anatolia at this time of year were horrendous. The first part of the journey was marred by heavy rain, and after Sivas they crossed the high Taurus Mountains. Around Deliktaş at 6,340 feet[2] they had to contend with freezing temperatures and fight their way through deep snow drifts. They had a series of disasters in the deep snow before reaching Keban Madeni where they crossed the Euphrates in a ferry boat. From Harput to Ergani Madeni conditions were even worse as their journey took them over a snow-covered pass with the road having in places a 45% gradient. From Ergani Madeni it was a relatively easy ride to Diyarbakır. Apart from the difficulties with the weather, Loftus describes the houses they stayed in during their journey from Samsun as being unbelievably filthy and swarming with vermin; he also took a violent dislike to the Turkish inhabitants. The diet on the journey was very monotonous – coffee and a biscuit at the start of the day, and chicken and rice every evening. At a khan in the village of Yenihan, between Tokat and Sivas, they had what could have turned into a very serious incident when Dodson got involved in a fight with a Turkish soldier. On a happier note, at Harput they caught up with and overtook the Russian party and Loftus found the Russian Commissioner Colonel Tcherikoff very agreeable. They then spent a day in Diyarbakır while a *kellek* [raft] was made for them to float down the Tigris to Mosul. Loftus gives an interesting description of the vessel: It was made of 63 inflated animal skins supporting a wooden platform on which was erected a tent of black cloth and it was steered by two Kurdish oarsmen.

---

2 *Geographical Handbook: Turkey, Naval Intelligence Division* (1943), Vol 2, p. 458.

The journey by *kellek* down the river from Diyarbakır to Mosul took six days and was made extremely uncomfortable by heavy rain. At Mosul they caught up with the other members of the British delegation who were waiting there for Loftus and whom he met for the first time. They were Colonel William Fenwick Williams, the head of the team, of whom Loftus immediately formed a very good impression; Lieutenant A G Glascott, Royal Navy, the surveyor; Mr Algernon Wood, the secretary and interpreter; 'a Frenchman named Garey', who was 'the provender and clerk';[3] Henry A Churchill, interpreter, artist and budding diplomat; and Joseph Olquin, the doctor. Everybody ate at the house of the British Vice-Consul Christian Rassam and his wife Mathilda. By contrast with the rigours of the journey across Eastern Turkey here they were very well catered for. Loftus apparently stayed with the Rassams, while Wood, Olquin and Garey lodged elsewhere in a private house.

When Loftus arrived in Mosul, Colonel Williams, Glascott and Churchill, were camping on Kouyunjik, one of the mounds marking the great Assyrian capital of Nineveh. Here they were making excavations and drawings.[4] Churchill was copying reliefs showing the assault on a walled city and its capture,[5] and his drawings were soon to be sent to Layard in Constantinople. On 12 April, a week after Loftus's arrival in Mosul, the whole party embarked on an excursion, starting at Kouyunjik where Glascott made a rough survey of the site, after which they proceeded to the Yezidi village of Basheikhah, where they stayed the night. The next day they visited Khorsabad, the site of the Assyrian city founded by Sargon (721–705 BC) and saw the sculptures and other debris left behind after Botta's excavations,[6] of which Loftus was very

---

3   Letter 8.
4   For the excavations of Colonel Williams in Sennacherib's Palace, see Turner 2001. Glascott was making a trigonometrical survey.
5   Churchill drew a number of sculptures found in the Southwest Palace of Sennacherib (Barnett *et al.* 1998: 16); it is difficult to identify with certainty which sculptures Churchill was copying at this moment, but the sculptures in Room XII showing an attack on a walled city are a possibility (*ibid*: pls 151–5). See also Turner 2001: 109–17.
6   Paul-Émile Botta (1802–70) was the French consul at Mosul who excavated at Khorsabad between 1843 and 1846.

critical. They then went via Basheikhah to Karakosh, where they stayed in the Chaldean church. Next morning they visited the Assyrian city of Nimrud, where Layard had been recently excavating. On looking round, Loftus noticed that several sculptures had been recently damaged. The party then returned to Kouyunjik, on the top of which, Loftus noted, were the crumbling ruins of a Yezidi village, whose inhabitants had been exterminated by 'the celebrated Beder Khan Bey'.[7] They spent the night at Kouyunjik in tents, and returned to Mosul on the morning of 16 April.

The next excursion on 17 April was to the ruins of Hatra, the centre of a Parthian-period Arab kingdom (3rd century BC – 3rd century AD), in the desert some 133 kilometres/83 miles to the south-west of Mosul. The British contingent was accompanied by Vice-Consul Christian Rassam and an escort of about 30 soldiers, provided by the pasha. Their guide was Suttum, the Arab chief of the Shammar tribe. It had been intended to stay away for about ten days, but shortage of drinkable water obliged them to return after about a week, having spent just two days at the ruins. As well as buying horses from the Shammar tribe it had been hoped to undertake some excavations, but this proved to be impractical. Loftus provided a very brief description of the site, and is very critical of Ainsworth's description of Hatra, saying 'Ainsworth in his researches has committed some most egregious blunders in his description of these ruins. He will, I have no doubt, be shortly put right'.[8] On this excursion and afterwards Loftus got to know Suttum quite well, and formed a great admiration for him. He wrote: 'He is a fine fellow and is delighted with the English'.[9]

On 28 April 1849 the party left Mosul for a leisurely voyage down the Tigris on four *kellek*s each made of 600 animal skins. They reached Baghdad just over a week later on 5 May, having stopped many times to visit sites such as Hammam Ali, Nimrud, Qala't Sherqat [ancient Ashur], Tekrit and Samarra. At Baghdad they rowed straight up to the Residency of Major Rawlinson. The Residency was evidently not large enough to accommodate everybody,

---

7 Letter 8.
8 Letter 9. See Ch. 1 (Introduction), footnote 24.
9 Letter 9.

so Loftus and Glascott lodged at the house of Dr John Ross which was also on the riverside. Dr Ross unfortunately died soon after, and was buried on 19 June 1849. Everybody ate at the Residency where Rawlinson lived in grand style. Major Rawlinson made an instantly good impression on Loftus: 'The major is a first rate Eastern scholar and works hard the whole day long. We shall no doubt have the results of his researches shortly before the public'.[10]

On arrival at Baghdad the River Tigris was very high and there were fears that the city might be flooded as it had been in 1831, but the disaster was averted by the hasty erection of a bund around the city. Although he thought Baghdad was 'a most wretched place' (Letter 20), in the Residency they had 'all the luxuries of India … without its disagreeables'. He speaks of a pampered and privileged existence, attended to by numerous obsequious servants. While other members of the Commission relaxed, however, Loftus was busy ordering his botanical and zoological specimens. We learn that the birthday of Queen Victoria on 24 May 1849 was celebrated in grand style, and we are informed that a colossal stone Assyrian bull that they had seen in the excavations at Khorsabad was now in front of the Embassy waiting to be taken to Basra and on to the British Museum.[11]

Baghdad had been agreed as the rendezvous of the Commissioners (Loftus 1857: 4), but although the Russians had arrived on 28 May there was no sign of the Turkish Commissioner, Dervish Pasha, who was still at Mosul claiming that he had received no instructions from his government. Meanwhile, the Persian Commissioner, Mirza Jafar Khan, had gone on pilgrimage to Karbala. On 12 June 1849 the British party together with Colonel Tcherikoff steamed down the Tigris on the EIC[12] vessel the 'Nitocris' to visit the ruins of Seleucia-on-the-Tigris, founded by Alexander's former general Seleucus in about 305 BC, and the nearby Sasanian capital city of

---

10 Letter 13.
11 This is one of the gigantic winged bulls from Khorsabad that is now in the British Musuem (BM 11808, 11809). They were left behind after the excavations of Botta and having been obtained by Rawlinson were floated down-river to Basra, whence they were taken to London (Gadd 1936: 159–60).
12 East India Company.

Ctesiphon.[13] Of Seleucia, he says 'only the remains of the outer wall are visible'.[14] He briefly describes the great Sasanian arch at Ctesiphon, 3rd–7th century AD, and refers to a former Pasha of Baghdad having pulled part of the monument down to procure bricks for building Baghdad. The party returned to the Nitocris at sunset, and early next morning (13 June) were deposited at the village of Gherrara, about four miles south-east of Baghdad. They had decided to set up camp here to escape from the heat of Baghdad and there was also fever in the city.

At Gherrara they lived in a house built of bricks that had been removed from the ruins of Ctesiphon by Colonel Taylor (Letters 20, 25). The Mesopotamian summer had now set in with a vengeance, and temperatures were recorded of 113–117° Fahrenheit (45–47° C) in the shade and 130–136° Fahrenheit (54–58° C) in the sun (Letter 24). The group and their retinue were also badly affected by fever. The Turkish Commissioner Dervish Pasha and his suite eventually arrived on Thursday 28 June, but it was by now too hot to proceed to Mohammerah [Khorramshahr] as planned and too hot to cross the desert to get to the mountains. On 16 July 1849 he visited the nearby site of Tell Mohammed, and left there a sailor from the Nitocris who 'found an urn and other antiquities'[15] soon after his departure. He also refers (Letter 20) to mounds behind the house at Gherrara in one of which 'some very curious relics have been lately found, so interesting in fact that Major Rawlinson is about to make excavations in it'.[16] He talks in Letter 24 about intending to join Captain Jones of the Nitocris on 10 September for a week to help him complete his survey of the Nahrawan Canal, but this seems never to have happened.

Between 14 and 23 September 1849 the British party made a 200-mile excursion, starting with the celebrated ancient city of Babylon, capital of the law-giver Hammurabi (*c.* 1792–1750 BC) and later the seat of the Neo-Babylonian empire (612–539 BC). They first inspected the Mujelibè, otherwise known as Tell Babil or the 'Summer Palace of Nebuchadnezzar' in the

---

13 Neither seems to be described in Loftus 1857.
14 Letter 17.
15 Letter 19.
16 Letter 20.

extreme north part of the site. His description of this mound does not add anything to other contemporary accounts, but it is interesting that 'one of the party found a small onyx cylinder or bead',[17] presumably a cylinder seal. After visiting some other parts of the ruins Loftus and Churchill separated from the main party and focused on what Loftus thought were 'the most interesting part of the ruins, the Kasr or Palace',[18] the site of the Southern Palace of Nebuchadnezzar. It was near here that the stone sculpture now known as the Lion of Babylon (pl. 10), probably dating from the 8th century BC, had been found. Loftus refers to some doubt as to whether it was a lion (as per C J Rich) or an elephant with its trunk broken off (as per the officers of the Euphrates expedition). It seems that at this time the sculpture must have been still partly buried, as at midday Loftus and Churchill returned with 'four pickers and miners, servants and sketch-books' to make 'a thorough examination'.[19] This revealed there was no doubt it was a lion, standing over the prostrate body of a man. Loftus records the dimensions and also notes there was a hole in the middle of the side into which he supposes iron or copper had been inserted to clamp it to a doorway, leading him to believe, understandably but surely erroneously, that it occupied 'the same position as the bulls and lions at Nineveh, viz. the entrance'.[20] Churchill made a sketch. He also attempted to obtain some inscribed bricks from the Kasr, but was not able to retrieve any intact. From Hillah they went on to Birs Nimrud [ancient Borsippa] which Loftus notes had been incorrectly identified as the Tower of Babel.[21] He observes that Rawlinson has from the site an inscribed brick of Nebuchadnezzar (605–562 BC). Near Birs Nimrud, just before reaching the large mound of Ibrahim al-Khalil, they passed a small rise entirely covered with 'pieces of vitrified brick, having all the appearance of a glassworks slag'. From Birs Nimrud they proceeded along the edge of the marshes to Keffil where they inspected the Tomb of Ezekiel, which is fully described in Loftus's

---

17   Letter 25.
18   Letter 25.
19   Letter 25.
20   Letter 25.
21   The surviving brickwork at the site is the remains of a ziqqurat.

book.[22] From Keffil they travelled by boat though the marshes to Nebbi Yunus, and then rode on horseback to Meshed Ali [Najaf] via Kufa.[23] At Najaf they visited the Mosque of Imam Ali, and observed the Shia practice of bringing bodies to the shrine for burial.[24] From Najaf they rode across the desert to Karbala, but here were not allowed in to visit the mosque of Imam Hossein.[25] From Karbala, they made their way back to Gherrara.

From 29 September until 8 October they stayed at Ctesiphon on a hunting trip, but although francolins were plentiful wild boars and lions proved to be elusive. They were joined for a few days by Rawlinson. Then, between 19 and 24 October 1849 Loftus went on a boar-hunting expedition with Captain Jones, camping near Aqar Quf, the ancient Kassite city of Dur-Kurigalzu, mostly 15th–12th century BC. They failed to find any boars, but Loftus paid two visits to the ruins which is not recorded in his book (1857). He describes Aqar Quf as a solid mass of sun-dried brickwork about 120 feet (*c.* 37 m) high made from bricks about 12 inches (*c.* 30 cm) square fixed together with mud mortar and with a layer of reeds every seven courses. He describes there being a large hole on the east side of the monument (now known to have been a ziqqurat) about 40 feet (*c.* 12 m) above the ground but they were not able to get into this to inspect it. He notes that like Birs Nimrud the structure is pierced with small square holes on all sides 'to ventilate and dry the bricks'.[26] On 25 October they are still at Gherrara awaiting orders to proceed to Mohammerah where the commissioners will convene. There is then a break in the letters from 25 October to 4 December, but it is clear that sometime during this period they moved back to Baghdad and were living in the house next-door to the Residency. Also during this time Loftus made an eight-day excursion with Captain Newbold. They camped at Babylon close to the Kasr mound, and were able to examine the ruins undisturbed. Attempts to prise

---

22 Loftus 1857: 34–36.
23 For a description of Kufa see Loftus 1857: 47–8.
24 For a description of the mosque and the burial practices see Loftus 1857: 51–58.
25 See Loftus 1857: 59–68.
26 Letter 27.

loose a complete inscribed brick were not successful, and Loftus also failed to buy one in Hillah. They also visited Birs Nimrud, Karbala and Aqar Quf.

They left Baghdad towards the end of December and after a journey of 25 days reached Mohammerah on 21 January. Colonel Williams had given permission for Loftus and Churchill to travel on the east side of the Euphrates 'through the land of Chaldea'[27] while the rest of the party went by steamer to Basra. During this time they visited Tell Hammam (pl. 11),[28] where they collected fragments of a stone statue of the Sumerian ruler Gudea (c. 2144–2124 BC), Tell Ede / Yede (pl. 12),[29] and then, for the first time, Warka, ancient Uruk, Biblical Erech. This is now known to have been a great urban centre as early as the 4th millennium BC that was reoccupied in the Parthian period (1st–2nd century AD). On this occasion they stayed several days making a plan of the ruins, and excavating a glazed pottery coffin which was sketched by Churchill (pls. 15–16).[30] At Mugayer [Ur of the Chaldees] (pl. 20)[31] the Sumerian city later made famous through the excavations of Leonard Woolley between 1922 and 1934, they collected inscriptions for Rawlinson, miscellaneous antiquities and 'found a broken statue, and an altar with an inscription'.[32] They could see Abu Shahrain [ancient Eridu] 'about 8 miles to the south-west',[33] but were not able to visit the site.

After a brief stay of around a week in Mohammerah, Loftus was able to return to Warka via Basra to conduct excavations with the encouragement of Colonel Williams, who had undertaken to finance the excavations himself if Sir Stratford Canning and Lord Palmerston were unwilling to do so from the public purse. He arrived at Warka on 4 February, and set up camp about six miles from the ruins. Later, because of the rising water level in the Euphrates, he was obliged to move to Duraji [Kalaat Debbi], about nine miles from

---

27   Letter 30.
28   British Museum 92988. See Loftus 1857: 113–17.
29   Loftus 1857: 117–20.
30   Loftus 1857: 123–5.
31   Loftus 1857: 127–35. Shortly after Loftus's visit to Ur, John George Taylor excavated there in 1853, 1854 and 1858.
32   This is in Letter 38.
33   Letter 38.

Warka.[34] Loftus tells us that he rose at daybreak, worked all day at the site, rode back to camp often in the dark, and usually did not get to bed before 2.00 am for a few hours' sleep. In the course of about three weeks his workmen dug up about 100 glazed slipper coffins but most disintegrated on discovery. With great difficulty, however, he succeeded in salvaging three complete examples which were taken to Basra for onward transportation to the British Museum. Loftus was convinced that he had found the main burial-ground of the Babylonians, but conceded (Letter 34) that there were arguments for their being of Sasanian date.[35] In addition to the coffins he collected cuneiform tablets, inscribed bricks, inscribed cylinders, terracotta figurines, jewellery, pottery and lamps.[36] The miscellaneous antiquities included 'a fragment of ivory carving'[37] and a piece of tridacna shell with incised decoration showing galloping horses.[38]

On completion of the excavations at Warka he followed the Shatt el-Nil to Sinkara (Larsa, an Old Babylonian site) where he found burials within vaults and terracotta figures and pottery (pl. 21).[39] Also at Sinkara, he observed a type of drainage system that had only recently been adopted by farmers in Britain. He wrote to the Secretary of the Farmers Club in Newcastle upon Tyne about this (Letter 41).[40] He arrived back at Mohammerah on 7 March 1850 and soon after this returned to Basra with Churchill who sketched the antiquities[41] before they were packed for shipment to England. They were back in Mohammerah by 7 April.

For the next month, until about 8 May, Loftus was in Mohammerah with the rest of the British team. During this time he finished his paper on Warka,

---

34   See also Loftus 1857: 151.
35   By the time of the publication of his book he had reverted to the now standard view that the glazed slipper-coffins are of Parthian date (1857: 203).
36   For these excavations at Warka see Loftus 1857: 207–29; Loftus 1859a; and Curtis 1979.
37   Letter 34.
38   BM 117997.
39   For the excavations at Sinkara, see Loftus 1857: 240–73.
40   The letter was read at a meeting of the Newcastle Farmers' Club and reported in *The Newcastle Journal* on 9th November 1850 (Ermidoro 2020: 247).
41   Four of Churchill's exquisite watercolour sketches have been included in Curtis 1979.

which was sent to England together with Churchill's sketches. Loftus is scathing about Mohammerah which he describes as a 'miserable place of reed huts within a mud wall, governed by an independent sheikh'.[42] Meanwhile, there had been bad flooding in Baghdad and their former house at Gherrara had been washed away.

Loftus left Mohammerah on about 8 May and, accompanied by Churchill, proceeded via Ahvaz to Shushtar, following the course of the River Karun. Here they were received by the governor of Ahvaz, Mirza Sultan Ali Khan. They inspected the Sasanian hydraulic works (c. 3rd century AD) which Loftus says had been well described by Rawlinson and Layard. From Shushtar they proceeded to Dizful, which they found to be flourishing owing to the recent introduction and exploitation of the indigo plant, and on to Susa, the main object of their journey where Colonel Williams encouraged them to make some small scale excavations. It was thought that the great mounds at Susa were likely to produce sculptures and other treasures similar to those found by Layard at Nimrud and Nineveh. At Susa, Loftus and Churchill met with a lot of hostility from 'the Seyyids and Arab sheikhs'[43] who tried to prevent them from excavating, and on this first visit they were not able to do more than make 'a careful plan of the ruins'.[44] He remarks on the abundance of lions in the thick foliage along the banks of the River Kerkah, and notes that 'the obelisk mentioned by Major R. still exists on the slope of the mound'.[45] He was able to copy the inscription, which was of the Elamite king Shilhak-Inshushinak I (c. 1150–1120 BC). Although he acknowledges that Susa obviously has great potential, his first impression is that it is not to be compared with Warka. While at Susa, Loftus had a serious accident. When out riding with Churchill on 29 May they came across a herd of wild boars and could not resist chasing them. Loftus's horse stumbled and fell on him, injuring his right side and apparently causing internal injuries that troubled him thereafter. He was obliged to go to Dizful for some days to recover.

---

42 Letter 34.
43 Letter 37.
44 Letter 37. See Loftus 1857: 328.
45 Letter 37.

CHAPTER TWO

In a letter of 18 June 1850 Loftus reports that he and Churchill are waiting at Dizful for the arrival of the rest of the party as Colonel Williams has decided that to escape from the murderous heat of Mohammerah they will all spend the summer in the cooler mountains of Mungerrah near Dizful. The group left for the mountains, 3 days' travel from Dizful, on 2 July. On 3 September 1850 (Letter 42) he reports that for the last fortnight he has been camping with Glascott on the summit of the Mungerrah range where they have been 'making a panoramic view of the surrounding mountains'.[46] He helps Glascott with his surveying work and Glascott helps him with his geological work. Their camp is 8,245 feet above Mohammerah and 3,140 feet above the base camp. The work was interrupted for a few days when they were obliged to come down from the summit of Chaouni to the base camp on 12 September as Algernon Wood was dangerously ill and died on 15 September. He was buried on the same day. The work of the Commissioners was now further delayed by a dispute about Mohammerah which by the terms of the Treaty of Erzurum was supposed to have been ceded to Persia, but the Turks refused to do this. Colonel Williams therefore decided that the British group should go on a lengthy excursion while this matter was being resolved.

They left Mungerrah on around 23 September 1850 and arrived in Kermanshah on 10 October after a journey across the Zagros Mountains via Khorramabad. At Khorramabad they were received by Prince Ardeshir Mirza and stayed in a palace of the late Prince Mohammad Ali Mirza, both sons of Fath Ali Shah. At Khorramabad, Loftus 'with Churchill's assistance'[47] copied a previously unrecorded Kufic inscription.

At Kermanshah they stayed in a once magnificent summer palace of Mohammad Ali Mirza, now in a sad state of disrepair but still boasting walls with painted and gilded decoration, coloured glass windows, and attractive gardens.

From Kermanshah they travelled to Hamadan, arriving there on 22 October 1850 and visiting en route Taq-e Bustan, Bisitun, Takht-e Shirin,

---

46   Letter 42.
47   Letter 45.

and Kangavar. In Letter 48 he provides a brief description of the Sasanian rock reliefs at Taq-e Bustan, correctly identifying two of the kings depicted there, Shapur II (AD 309–379) and Khusro II (AD 591–628), and rightly expressing the view that the floral decoration and the winged female figures holding diadems on the facade of the great *ayvān* of Khusro II are of oriental workmanship and not Greek workmanship as was sometimes supposed at that time. It is not stated in the letters, but the presence of the British party at this time is attested by their engraved signatures on the back wall of the great *ayvān* (pl. 29).[48] At Bisitun, apart from the monumental trilingual inscription of Darius (522–486 BC) high up on the mountainside, he notes the relief at the base of the cliff showing the satrap Gotarzes together with a Greek inscription, as described by Rawlinson.[49] They made a detour to Takht-e Shirin to inspect a great slab of white marble that was supposed to be inscribed, but found it to be plain.[50] Finally, before coming to Hamadan, they visited the Temple of Anahita at Kangavar, probably mostly of Sasanian date.

They rested in Hamadan from 22–26 October, visiting on 24 October the trilingual inscriptions of Darius and Xerxes at Ganj Nameh. He describes the site of Ecbatana as 'a heap of mounds and rubbish to the east of the town'. After a journey of 15 days from Hamadan they arrived in Isfahan, by way of Khomeyn, Golpayegan, Khansar and Najafabad, on 9 November. Like all travellers before him and since, Loftus was overwhelmed by the beauty of Isfahan and wrote in awe of the splendour of Chehel Situn (where they were accommodated), Ali Qapu and the mosques of Shah Abbas, Sheikh Lotfollah and Madar-e Shah. He was particularly impressed by a 'smaller palace'[51] [Hasht Behesht?] that had such beautiful stained glass windows that he commissioned painted copies both of the windows and 'the pattern of the roof

---

48 Colonel Williams R.A., 1850, J. Olquin FRCSE, H.A. Churchill, W.K. Loftus. – These graffiti are between the back legs of the horse on which Khusro is mounted. Other graffiti on this wall are H.C. Rawlinson, A. Hector, 1847.
49 Rawlinson 1839: 114–15.
50 See Rawlinson 1839: 111.
51 Letter 49.

and cornice of the same chamber'.[52] In Isfahan they met up with the Russian delegation that on 13 November proceeded north.

On 4 December 1850 the British party arrived in Shiraz, having visited the great Achaemenid Persian sites of Pasargadae and Persepolis, and spending two days at the latter. While there, Loftus, Olquin and Williams engraved their names in the Palace of Darius and the Gate of All Nations respectively (Simpson 2005: 39–40, 50, 65–6, figs 14, 22, 30). Loftus comments on the Grecian (fluted columns) and Egyptian (doorways) influence that he sees at Persepolis. At Naqsh-e Rustam they climbed the cliff by means of ropes and entered the tomb of one of the Achaemenid kings which was '60 feet [*c.* 18 m] long and contained three recesses, each with three sarcophagi'.[53]

There is then a break in the letters between 6 December 1850 (Shiraz) and 4 March 1851 (Mohammerah), but we know that in January 1851, the whole of the English Commission team camped at Susa intent on undertaking excavations, armed with a *firman* from the Shah. In the course of a month's stay, before they were recalled to Mohammerah, a few trenches were opened on the Acropolis mound and Colonel Williams uncovered three column bases on the Apadana mound (Loftus 1857: 333–4, 349–55; Harbottle 1973: 203; Curtis 1993: 2–5). These belonged to the Palace of Darius. We learn from Letter 52 that Christmas 1850 was spent 'in pouring rain in the desert of Ram Hormouz',[54] perhaps en route between Isfahan and Dizful.

By 4 March 1851 the whole party was back in Mohammerah, with the Commissioners having been summoned back there following an apparent breakthrough in the Frontier negotiations. Loftus has been busy helping Glascott map the area between Mohammerah and Susa, and charting the courses of the Rivers Hawizeh and Karkheh. At the same time he is still in pain following his riding accident at Susa nine months earlier. By 26 March 1851 he was staying in the British Residency in Baghdad, having come to Baghdad to get a medical opinion from Dr Hyslop[55] at the Residency. Hyslop's

---

52   Letter 49.
53   Letter 50.
54   Letter 52.
55   Dr James McAdam Hyslop was in the service of the East India Company and at this time was Assistant Surgeon in the Baghdad Residency.

view was that he 'must have received a severe crush on a portion of the bowels near the liver' but the liver itself does not appear to be injured. On 24–25 March Captain Kemball organised a picnic at Ctesiphon for those people staying in the Residency. On 7 April 1851 Loftus is still in Baghdad, and by now has consulted Dr Ballingale the doctor on the Nitocris who 'thinks that the diaphragm and probably some of the integuments of the liver have received a severe strain'.[56]

Loftus arrived back at Mohammerah on 16 April, and on the next day, 17 April, the whole British party left for the mountains to escape the increasing heat. They travelled along the banks of the Karun and then of the Karkheh, and going via Susa and Dizful, they eventually arrived at Kerend on 17 May. Among the sites and monuments visited en route were the Sasanian bridge at Pol-e Dokhtar, and Sirwan [Siravand] in Luristan which Rawlinson had identified as the ancient Celonae referred to by Diodorus (Rawlinson 1839: 54–5).

The last letters in this collection are written from Kerend-e Gharb, now in Kermanshah Province, Iran, on 24 May 1851. He says he does not know how long they will be at Kerend, but 'however long it may be Glascott and myself have enough to employ ourselves with, for all our map making has to be gone thru' as well as my rough geological notes to be put in order'.[57] The last letter, Letter 56, is to Blacklock, informing him that he has sent on the Brig 'Fortitude', a large box of antiquities addressed to Newcastle Museum. Dr Charlton has apparently asked about the possibility of sending sculptures for the 'Antiquarian Society', but Loftus is anxious to know how the costs would be covered. Lastly, he reports that he has discovered fossil footsteps in the sandstone near Dizful, probably 'a cheetah or hunting leopard, at any rate of some large feline animal'.[58]

For a summary of Loftus's activities after 24 May, see chapter 3.

---

56   Letter 54.
57   Letter 55.
58   Letter 56.

CHAPTER THREE

Loftus's later career

The last letter in the series printed in this book is dated 24 May 1851. In that same month, Loftus received a letter from Rawlinson asking whether, as Layard was leaving the country, he would be willing to continue excavations on behalf of the British Museum. Loftus replied that he assumed Layard was not returning, in which case he would be 'happy to undertake the task but if it is required of me merely to act in Layard's absence I should of course decline altogether having anything to do with it' (Harbottle 1973: 204). By January 1852 Loftus had been given leave of absence from the Boundary Commission, and under Rawlinson's nominal supervision he worked briefly at 'a palace of Nebuchadnezzar about ten miles distant from Baghdad' (Gadd 1936: 79),[1] and then at Susa from the middle of February 1852 until the middle of April 1852.

This time, the work at Susa produced important results (Loftus 1857: 364–415; Harbottle 1973: 204–5; Curtis 1993, 2018) and Rawlinson's assertion that 'Loftus had turned the mound of Susa topsy-turvy without finding much' (Barnett 1976: 8, n. 11) was totally unfounded. By finding further column bases he was able to determine the plan of the main part of the Palace of Darius and Churchill was able to reconstruct in sketches the columns with their double-bull capitals. Amongst the small finds were a group of some 200 figurines of naked women, glazed bricks, some with masons' marks, a hoard of Umayyad coins and fragments of alabaster vases with cuneiform and hieroglyphic inscriptions (pls. 22–27).

---

1 Gadd adds "This place (wherever it was) yielded nothing but small antiquities of the late period" (Gadd 1934: 79).

He then re-joined the Commission which shortly thereafter finished its work. After consulting Rawlinson in Baghdad, he determined to return to England, after which things took an unexpected turn. On his way home in October 1852 he met by chance Hormuzd Rassam at Cizre in southeast Turkey, and was surprised to discover from him that he had been appointed in June 1852 by the Trustees of the British Museum to continue the excavations in Assyria. He continued his journey and was back in London by middle of December 1852, having been away nearly four years (Harbottle 1973: 206).

Loftus was now a free agent, the work of the Boundary Commission having finished, so when the independent Assyrian Excavation Fund was established in London in July or August 1853 he was an obvious person to be appointed as its excavator. Consequently, he left England again on 5 October 1853 (Harbottle 1973: 208), having been back home for just nine months. On arrival in Mesopotamia, Loftus, now accompanied by the artist William Boutcher, was steered by Rawlinson towards Babylonia as Hormuzd Rassam was already in Assyria digging on behalf of the British Museum. Loftus and Boutcher worked at Warka between January and April 1854 (Loftus 1857: 154–207, 229–39).[2] The chief discoveries at this time were a wall with cone mosaic decoration in an inner courtyard of the Late Uruk period Eanna Temple, *c.* 3200–2900 BC, a group of Seleucid period tablets with interesting seal impressions (Mitchell and Searight 2008: 18) and pieces of architectural stucco of the Parthian period (Thompson 1979). They also cleared the façade of a building with semi-engaged columns on the mound called 'Wuswas'. A basalt stele of the Late Uruk period showing a figure wielding a spear, found on the surface, was sketched by Boutcher (Loftus 1857: 185–6; Curtis 1986). On the whole, however, one gets the impression that the previous campaign at Warka with Churchill had been rather more fruitful.

While leaving Boutcher in charge of the excavations at Warka, he also worked at Sinkara [ancient Larsa] and Tell Sifr in March and April 1854. He had previously visited Sinkara in 1850, and on the basis of what he saw then

---

[2] The work at Warka is also described in the First Report of the Assyrian Excavation Fund, reproduced in Barnett 1976: 71–73.

CHAPTER THREE

believed there was the possibility of discoveries like those recently made by J G Taylor at Ur.[3] In the event, the Sinkara excavations produced cuneiform tablets, inscribed barrel cylinders, stamped bricks and terracottas (Loftus 1857: 240–62). At Tell Sifr he found cuneiform tablets and an important hoard of bronze tools from the Old Babylonian period (Loftus 1857: 263–72; Moorey 1971; Moorey *et al.* 1988).

Meanwhile, things in Mosul had not gone according to plan for the British Museum; the artist Charles Doswell Hodder had fallen ill in January 1854 and Rassam was obliged to stop work at the end of March 1854 when the British Museum's funds ran out. The coast was now clear for Loftus and Boutcher to proceed to the north. Boutcher arrived at Nineveh in early April and Loftus in June having waited at Aqar Quf for the arrangements to be formalised. From then onwards they worked in Assyria. At Nineveh they made further excavations in the North Palace of Ashurbanipal, and Boutcher copied many of the beautiful relief sculptures found therein (Barnett 1975: 16–21; Curtis 1992; Brereton 2021).[4] At Nimrud, initial results were disappointing apart from the discovery of a 2nd millennium tomb under the SE Palace with a bronze axe-head and dagger and glass beads (Curtis 1983: 74, 80, fig. 2, pls VIIB, VIII),[5] but on 11 February 1855 Loftus was able to report to Rawlinson that he had found in the SE Palace a chamber full of ivories (Barnett 1975: 23). This is the important collection of Syro-Phoenician ivories now known as 'the Burnt Palace ivories'.[6] Curiously, in his 1857 book Loftus does not describe his excavations in Assyria, and makes only fleeting references to them (1857: 198, 380, 397).[7] If he had included a report in

---

[3] Letter to the Directors of the Assyrian Excavation Fund dated 10 February 1854.
[4] Recent publications with information about Loftus' excavations at Nineveh, which I have not yet had an opportunity to consult, include Turner 2021 and Reade 2022.
[5] For a report on the work at Nineveh and a mention of the tomb at Nimrud, see the Second Report of the Assyrian Excavation Fund, reproduced in Gadd 1936: appendix, and Barnett 1976: 73–75. The tomb is also mentioned in Loftus 1857: 198.
[6] A new publication of the Burnt Palace ivories is presently being prepared by Dr Georgina Herrmann.
[7] Presumably he was intending to produce another volume.

the book, with some of Boutcher's exquisite drawings, his reputation as a pioneering archaeologist of the Victorian era would have been assured. Loftus worked in Assyria until the end of March 1855, and by July 1855 he was back in England (Harbottle 1973: 212).

He left again, now as it was to transpire for the last time, about 12 December 1856 (Harbottle 1973: 214), having accepted an appointment as an assistant with the Geological Survey of India. He took up his post at Calcutta on 3 February 1857. In the next 18 months little seems to have been achieved, partly because the Indian Mutiny broke out on 10 May 1857 and partly because Loftus himself was not in good health. In November 1858 he was given sick leave and died at sea on 27 November 1858, the day after embarking for England. The cause of death is said to have been an abscess of the liver (Harbottle 1973: 214). One suspects that a contributory, or perhaps the primary cause of this, was the riding accident at Susa some eight years previously when his liver had apparently been damaged.

Sadly, Loftus left behind a widow and five young children ranging from two years to thirteen years in age (see genealogical chart, pl. 32). His widow, Charlotte née Thurlbourne, died just four years after him. Apart from the Assyrian reliefs (see Appendix) and various antiquities which he donated to the Literary and Philosophical Society, memorials to Loftus in the Lit and Phil included a photographic portrait (pl. 1), donated by James Radford,[8] and a bust by the sculptor John Henry Foley. This was presented to the Society by his daughter Fanny Loftus.[9] As noted in an article in the *Newcastle Courant* for 13 April 1889, the bust shows Loftus with a fulsome beard and the writer remarks that 'he at length returned home (from the east) with a beard of raven hue, very silky and much admired'. The present whereabouts of this bust is unknown and it is suggested that it might have been destroyed in a fire at the Lit and Phil on 8 February 1893.[10] Fortunately, an engraving of the bust (pl. 2) was published by Richard Welford in his *Men of Mark 'twixt Tyne and Tweed* (1885: 69).

---

8   Information from Karen Loftus in letter of 3 March 2008 to Frances Radford.
9   Information from Karen Loftus in letter of 28 March 2008 to Frances Radford.
10 Information kindly supplied by Carole McGivern of the Literary and Philosophical Society, Newcastle.

CHAPTER FOUR

The letters

Letter 1, Southampton, 29 January 1849

My dear Green

I had hoped to reply to your very kind letter sooner, but my time was so taken up in London that I had not a moment to lose. I now write to you on the point of sailing. You were I am sure not more disappointed than myself at our not having met before my leaving Newcastle. I only feared you might have thought <u>me</u> neglectful in not calling on <u>you</u> but I had not a single moment to spare in Newcastle. I was kept till 6 o'clock in town before all <u>Turf</u> matters were settled and was obliged to be packing all night. With regard to <u>that</u> matter[1] I am perfectly satisfied in my own mind that I have been most effectually <u>done</u>, but I go away with the conviction that I have acted honourably throughout, and that, should anyone dare to cast imputations on me in my absence, I shall be nobly defended by you and other kind friends who have exerted themselves so energetically on my behalf. I cannot express my thanks to you for your exertions in words sufficiently, but believe me, that your kindness shall never be effaced from my memory, and that I shall exert myself in the discharge of my duties in such a way that you shall never repent having expended such labour and trouble on my affairs as you have done. I am not a man given to say things which I will not act to, but believe me when I say I shall not give you cause to think me ungrateful.

---

1 It is unclear what problem is alluded to here.

You would hear from my cousin of my movements and of the handsome manner in which Sir Henry has behaved. I believe I have placed myself on a good footing with him, and from his account, with the Foreign Office too as I am entrusted with valuable despatches for our Ambassador Sir Stratford Canning[2] at Constantinople. I am H.M.'s Courier for the time being, armed with a most formidable passport-

"Mr William Kennett Loftus, en service de sa Majesté Britannique allant à Constantinople, chargé de dépêches", calling on Kings and Potentates to aid & forward him with his "hardes & baggage".

Sir Henry[3] has got me put into formal communication with him, and he has undertaken to render me his best assistance. Anything I want, or anything he thinks I may want he will send me under the power of his big seal of office. I am to report myself on arrival to Sir S. Canning who is to provide me with funds and what is requisite to forward me to the head seat of the Commission. Where [they] are God knows, whether at Mt Ararat, Erzerum or Nineveh? By the bye we are certain to visit the "Great City" and I believe Mr Layard is to bear me company or rather vice versa – I really think I am a lucky fellow and that the card has turned at last in my favour. Tho' the pain of parting from those most dear to me is great, yet I bear myself up with the reflection that I am doing my duty. I leave in good spirits because I feel that I shall return safely with honour and advantage. Danger I do not fear, tho' I don't intend to expose myself rashly.

Adieu, my dear fellow, and pray let me often hear from you and I will not fail to reply as often as may be.

Faithfully ever yours,

Wm Kennett Loftus

P.S. I told Gray to give you the broken part of the decanter, have you got it?

---

2   Sir Stratford Canning. See Ch. 1, n. 28.
3   Sir Henry De la Beche (1796-1855), Director of the Geological Society of Great Britain.

CHAPTER FOUR

Letter 2, Off Cape Trafalgar, 3 Feb 1849

Dear Gray,

As I had not an opportunity of writing you a few lines at Southampton before leaving England I feel myself bound to write to you first. (Six o'clock) I began this letter when the vessel was rolling at such a rate that I was obliged to stop. We have now arrived at Gibraltar after a very pleasing passage and I understand a short one. Our party is but small, in consequence of the Governor of Gibraltar not having come out with us in the "Erin" as expected. He means to start in the "Montrose" from Southampton the day after us. Amongst the officers I have made acquaintance with is a Capt. Topham,[4] who has travelled a good deal in Persia and Turkey, and from whom I have got a good deal of valuable information. The captain of the "Erin" is well acquainted with Col. Williams[5] and I am led to expect in him a most agreeable commanding officer. Col. Williams is on his way to Baghdad where I suppose I shall have to join him! How I am to get there I gave no idea as the distance is enormous. Before I go any further I must beg of you to excuse all mistakes as my head is rolling as if still at sea! Of course I can send you little news: after leaving Southampton we sat down to a capital dinner, but few remained to finish it. I however continued till after tea when I fell sick like the rest, tho' not so bad as most – all day I continued in bed, but looked up the following evening and have since been well and can bear the rocking with the best of them. Time is spent in much the same way I presume as most of sea voyages. Dinner appears to be the great point of attraction: reading, talking and sleeping fills up the remainder of our time. We just arrived here in time, too late to have a good view of the famous rock and Sir Charles Napier's[6] squadron which is lying in the harbour. I presume we shall

---

[4] This is possibly Capt W Topham of the 7th Regiment of Bengal Native infantry who died at Ahmedabad on 18 May 1851 (*The Indian News*, 30 June 1851, p. 290). The 'Erin' was probably en route to India.
[5] Major-General Sir William Fenwick Williams. See Ch. 1, n. 13.
[6] At this time, Sir Charles Napier (1782-1853) was Commander-in-Chief in India.

see all tomorrow [but] we cannot land, much to the disappointment of all on board as we [are in] quarantine on a/c of the cholera in England. Will you be good enough to tell my cousin and Mather that I have written to you and that as I told you before you must consider a letter to one of you as for you all jointly. Their letters I got by sending to the P.O. at Southampton just in time to [save] me as we were actually moving from the quay at the Docks when they were thrown on board. Pray thank them both for the contents as they were very acceptable and cheering [when] parting and leaving England. My cousin says you have been exerting yourself on my behalf. That I am sure you have done – and I am sure I scarce shall know how to repay the kindness of you all. As we have received notice that letters must now be enclosed I must bid you adieu for the present. I shall write to some of you again from Malta on arrival. By the bye the Capt. tells me that Col. Williams has engaged the surgeon who was aboard the vessel during her last voyage, as surgeon to attend the Commission. This I am glad to hear as we are all liable to attack of fever etc. in such unknown countries. There will be about 150 of us altogether when assembled at Baghdad or elsewhere. The Russians muster strong. Tell my cousin that the heat has already turned me brown and with my beard a little longer I shall be a Persian or Turk at once. Give my kind remembrance etc. and believe me

Wm Kennett Loftus

Letter 3, Off island of Pantelleria, 8 Feb 1849

My dear Cousin,

As we expect to reach Malta early tomorrow morning, and as I wish to see as much as possible during the little time we stop there to take in coals, I sit down to scribble a few lines to announce progress tho' it is no easy matter to write as the vessel moves. I presume that Mr Gray would duly receive my letter despatched from Gibraltar on Sunday. There we had an accident which delayed us several hours. The Erin broke away from her moorings at the coal station and drove broadside against the bowsprit of a large merchant vessel, smashed our lifeboat and did sundry and divers damages to our ropes etc.

CHAPTER FOUR

This however gave me the opportunity of seeing the St Vincent 120[7] and Sir C. Napier as we passed immediately under the stern of this splendid vessel. We got away from Gibraltar about 6 pm on Sunday and got a good pitching all night and the next day along the coast of Spain which is exceedingly bold and picturesque. We could discern with the glass many of the old Moorish towers with which the coast is covered. For the last three days we have been going along at the rate of 11 miles an hour with a fair wind. The climate appears to be delightful. I have never worn a great coat since leaving Cape Ushant, even late at night. But I suppose I shall have to feel the cold severely at Constantinople. On Wednesday morning we hope to arrive there if the weather is at all favourable. I am the only passenger on board for the City of Palaces. All the rest leave us at Malta – the greatest part for Bombay – the system on board is excellent, and every delicacy provided, wines including claret and champagne with dessert, green peas at Gibraltar, and in fact everything one can desire. Everything is exceedingly clean and the servants extremely attentive. I don't know that I can say much more as to our voyage. All is going on as well as can be wished, and I find myself a capital sailor, and enjoy every incident. I do not know that I mentioned to you my having three letters of introduction to Mr Layard, whose small book I got before leaving at the recommendation of Mr Hammond. I think you would be rather amused if you could but see the cut I am. My face and hands are turned dark brown, and my beard is grown to a strong stubble! I shall be quite a Persian before my arrival on the borders. Be kind enough to tell Mather I shall write to him when I arrive at Constantinople and have delivered my despatches and know further of my movements.

Remember me kindly to him as well as to Mrs Radford, Gray, Geen, etc., etc., and believe me, my dear Cousin,

Yours ever sincerely,

Wm Kennett Loftus

I hope you found the deeds all right.

---

7 HMS St Vincent 120 Guns.

THE LETTERS

Letter 4, Hotel d'Angleterre, Constantinople, 16 Feb 1849

My dear Cousin,

We are arrived here this morning at seven o'clock. After breakfast I set off with my despatch bag for the palace, and delivered letters of the 27th ult. before those of the 19th from England. His Excellency was exceedingly kind, and I dine with him today at seven when I shall most likely hear more as to my journey. Capt. Williams and all the party have set out for Baghdad. They last were heard of from Tokat. I shall have to follow them Tatar[8] I presume.

I just have time to scribble these few lines to save the Post, which leaves at two today, as I know you will be anxious to hear of our safe arrival. After leaving Malta we encountered a terrific gale of wind, which lasted for three days. At night it was perfectly awful. We lost our gib boom, sprang the foremast and had our decks regularly swept. After driving about among the Greek islands unable to make out our latitude, we gained the south coast of Mytilene where we lay to in a snug little bay on Wednesday afternoon and night – the gale abated early in the morning so that we gained the Dardanelles just in time to save pratique[9] last night. The sail was most beautiful along the coast of Mytilene and past the Plains of Troy.

The scene here is a most strange one. I will not attempt to describe it, but the streets! What streets! Just walk up the lane at the back of the stand[10] after months [of] rain, and imagine a row of houses on each side nearly touching each other! The filth is horrible, but thank God, there is no cholera or any appearance of it.

As the Erin returns on Monday I shall take advantage of the opportunity and write Mather a lengthy despatch, which may probably arrive before this – she is a fast sailor. We passed a steamer this morning eleven days from Malta.

---

8   'Messenger Tatars' were postmen in the Ottoman Empire who rode long distances in the shortest possible time. Tatars sometimes also acted as guides.
9   Permission for a ship to enter a port after quarantine.
10 The grandstand at Newcastle racecourse.

CHAPTER FOUR

Kind remembrance to all my good friends in England. Excuse haste.

Believe me, my dear cousin,

Yours ever sincerely,

Wm Kennett Loftus.

I wrote you from Malta.

Letter 5, Missiri's Hotel d'Angleterre, Constantinople, 18 Feb 1849

My dear Mather,

You will I fear think my promised letter long in appearing, but I hope that the length of the contents will gain me forgiveness, if I have even to ask it. I wrote my cousin on Friday as to our rough passage, which therefore need not be repeated. I also mentioned my having to dine at the English Palace at 7 that evening. A little before that time, I sallied forth under the guidance of a big-breeched [?] Turk and lanthorn with three candles – no one after dark may go out without a light – my legs and lower clothing enclosed within two immense boots, borrowed for the occasion, to shield me from the mud; necessary articles, I assure you, as Sandgate, Gallowgate, Castle Garth Stairs *et hoc genus omne* of streets in Newcastle are perfect Regents Streets in comparison with the main streets of Constantinople. There is just room for two horses laden to pass each other, and you may look out for yourself. The houses are all of wood with the windows of the upper stories all but meeting across the streets – but to proceed, I was received very kindly at the Embassy – the dinner party consisted of Sir Stratford, Lady & Miss Canning, Mr Allison the foreign interpreter, Count Pisani,[11] the private secretary, Mr Layard, the author of the work on Nineveh, Sir Godfrey Webster, the Commander of one of HMS at present here,

---

11   Count Alexandre Pisani had been made head of chancery by Stratford Canning in 1841; see R A Jones, *The British Diplomatic Service 1815-1914* (Waterloo, Ontario 1983), n. 24 on p. 92. Reference found online.

and myself. Sir Stratford is exceedingly like my father in profile, Lady C is a very pleasant woman; in fact I was at home with them immediately. Layard, whom I had letters for, is not more than 26[12] and just as unlike the author of a work as can be well conceived – he has undertaken to assist me in procuring such requisites as are necessary for the journey. Sir Stratford wishes me to stay until the winter is over or nearly so, as Col. Williams gives but a very sorry account of the weather and roads. They have been frozen on one side, and roasted on the other, and travelling up to their horses' chests in mud. I heard yesterday of Colonel Williams having written last from Sivas – Sir S. thinks I shall be able to overtake the Russian party before reaching Baghdad, even should I leave a month hence. The English party en route consists of Colonel W., Lieut. Glascott, R. N.,[13] Mr Olquin[14] the surgeon who is a Spanish Mexican, and formerly on board the "Erin", Mr Wood,[15] an attaché at the Embassy, a young man called Churchill[16] and another. They are supplied with all sorts of necessaries and luxuries (!) having 80 horses and 20 camels to convey their traps [?] etc. Feb 19 – I have just returned from a call at the Palace, and have been assisting to write dispatches for them for three hours, which will shorten your letter I fear, as I may be wanted again tomorrow for the same purpose. They were hard up for hands, and on the point of sending for me when I fortunately arrived – I think you will conclude as I do that all is going on well and that luck may yet be in store for me. A great friend of Col. Williams called on me yesterday, Mr Redhouse,[17] but I was out. After attending service at the Embassy Chapel, I returned the call this morning, and am going to get tea there this evening. Everyone appears extremely attentive and anxious to assist me, to the best of their power. I think I told my cousin that I shall have to travel alone till I reach the party which probably will not be till they arrive at Baghdad, 1000 miles; to Samsun by steamboat is about 300 so that I shall have probably to ride

---

12 In fact, Layard (b. 5th March 1817) was 31 at this time.
13 Adam Gifford Glascott. See Ch. 1, n. 14
14 Joseph Olquin. See Ch. 1, n. 17.
15 Algernon Wood, secretary and interpreter. He died 15 September 1850. See Ch. 1, n. 15.
16 Henry Adrian Churchill. See Ch. 1, n. 16.
17 Sir James Redhouse was the author of a celebrated Turkish Dictionary.

CHAPTER FOUR

700 on horseback. Alas! for my leather, but I have a stock of plaster in case of accidents! It is not unlikely that I may go down the Tigris from Mosul on a raft. There is a young Englishman staying at Missiri's called Dodson[18] who has been travelling in Egypt and thinks of going to Baghdad. I hope he may be inclined to join me, he is a very nice fellow and company would be agreeable as I shall have to rough it rather if I travel Tatar, as I hope I may, leaving my luggage to follow more slowly. Baghdad is 40 days by the ordinary mode of travelling, but only 10 or 12 Tatar from Samsun. I suppose you are anxious to know what I think of the "City of Palaces". As I always have been disappointed when led to expect anything extraordinary in the sightseeing line, so I was on first beholding this immense city. It is certainly a most beautiful sight and entirely different from anything I have before seen when entering the Golden Horn. But the sun was not shining and consequently I did not see it to advantage; yet I had expected something more, but impossible to say what it was, any admiration one feels at viewing the exterior is alas immediately dispelled on setting foot on shore. The streets are as I have said before deep in mud and narrow and the people filthy in the extreme. Their costumes are most picturesque and strange, but filth, filth, filth meets the eye at every step. I will not say that the nose is offended, it is confounded entirely, and I think I shall shortly lose its sense altogether; perhaps it would be an excellent loss – at least for the time being Pera is bad enough, but what should I say of Stambul! I went on Saturday to see the bazaars and found the streets nearly knee deep but was delighted in the sight of the bazaars, one can almost fancy the days of the Thousand and One Nights returned again, you have no idea of the variety and value of the goods exposed for sale. The various costumes, the mixture of riches and filth – Newcastle Butchers' Market is a pygmy compared with the great Bazaar. It is not difficult to lose oneself it is so immense. To describe the scene it is quite impossible and I am quite sure that no description can convey to you any idea. There are goods from every country under the sun. Imagine what a Babel! Cottons and clothes from England and France, glass from Bohemia, carvings (?) from Switzerland, silks and satins from Persia and Syria, shawls etc from Cashmere, furs from Russia, perfumes, diamonds and precious stones

---

18   John George Dodson. See Ch. 1, n. 25.

from God knows where, I don't, works most exquisite in gold and silver, arms of all description, drugs innumerable and most curious these are in a bazaar by themselves called the Egyptian. The perfume is most delicious in walking through. In the bazaar you meet costumes of every nation – Turks, Jews, Greeks, Armenians, Persians, Egyptians, Russians, French, English, etc, etc. The fox dogs are swarming in the streets but may not be killed, and their howling is most hideous at nights. Of all things the costumes of the women are most strange. The Turkish only expose their noses, tho' they don't stand on ceremony as to their knees. They wear short socks and yellow (bright) boots and cloaks of all forms. The Armenians cover their mouths and noses and leave their eyes visible. They are all ugly and it is quite as well that they do cover up. The Greeks wear a sort of wreath and are better looking, many very English in appearance. I have not yet seen the Sultan. He is visible on Fridays on going to [the] Mosque. His time I hear is entirely spent in his Harem among his 7 wives and 300 ladies! A few days ago he attended the opera at Pera. He had a day performance to <u>himself</u> and as his Box faces the stage, no one may turn his back on him. He gave £1200 to be divided amongst the company – £200 each in snuff boxes to the manager, lessee and Mr Smith the Architect. The opera was only opened last November for the 1st time. Imagine the sultan going to the opera! Does it not appear absurd! I hope however that it may be the means of rendering the Turks more civilized. [It] will be long before they can be classed as Europeans, tho' the soldiers have adopted the European dress. This hotel is the best in Constantinople and is the place where parties connected with the government, not attached to the Embassy, reside. A Russian prince has half of the house. Our dinner party consists of a Swiss, a Belgian count and secretary to their embassy and who is constantly jabbering French and talking of his boots, his coats and his cane; and myself, a Mr Joseph who returns with the Erin and Mr Dodson. Yesterday Sir Godfrey Webster dined with us. I met him at the Palace. We have very classic food here. Honey from Mt Ida,[19] and wines from Zenedoes [?]: for fires we have charcoal burners, which are placed in the middle of the room, but make my head ache desperately, tho' I am getting more accustomed to them. My bedstead is a light iron one covered by a fine green net

---

19   Probably Mt Ida in Crete.

instead of curtains which is close all round and has to be crept under to reach the bed. If I am called to the Embassy tomorrow I shall not be able to write to Lancaster as I intended doing. Of course I must not fail to do my utmost to gain favour at the Palace. Count Pisani expressed himself as much obliged to me and was pleased with my style of writing which by the bye was very different from this. He is a very nice fellow. Remember me, etc.

W.K. Loftus

Letter 6, Missiri's Hotel, Constantinople, 5 March 1849

My dear Edward,

This is the last letter I shall write from here. The Post leaves tomorrow for England and I on Wednesday for Samsun. I should not have started as early, but as Col. Williams had arrived at Harput on the 5th Feb and reports the roads as being in a better state I am anxious to get on and join him if possible at Mosul. I have, you will all be glad to hear, found a travelling companion; a young Englishman from Oxford who is going to Baghdad and stayed here some days before my arrival with the Russian commissioner Colonel Tcherikoff.[20] Dodson has been travelling all last year on the Nile and thro' Syria and is an exceedingly nice fellow. He is equally glad of company as myself. We have been for the last few days busily employed and preparing provisions, etc. – tea, coffee, sugar, biscuits, tongues, brandy, etc. which are not to be procured and to which we shall often be obliged to have resource to when grub is not otherwise to be had. Dodson has a clever Egyptian in costume as his servant and I have engaged at HBM's expense a fine athletic Greek from Corfu as mine – he speaks English well and also Turkish, Arabic, Greek, French, Italian, and in fact is a regular walking and living dictionary. He was recommended to me by the character he bears from his last master who was taken extremely ill of fever at Cyprus where Georgio Phillippo attended him like a brother. He has

---

20   Yegor Ivanovitch Tchirikof; see S Ateş, *The Ottoman-Iranian Borderlands: Making a Boundary 1843–1914* (Cambridge 2013), passim.

since broken his collar bone, in doing a kind action; and from enquiries I have made, I believe I have secured a valuable servant. May he prove so! We have supplied ourselves with immense grekos [snow boots], saddle bags, firmans, teskere's,[21] and all that is likely to facilitate our passage over the snowy ranges to beyond Diarbekir [Diyabakir]. After reaching the plain at Nisibin, we expect to be burnt in our shoes – but never mind, come what may I can bear it all, and thank God, I am well in health and long to proceed. The accounts which all the party have sent to their friends here are pleasing to hear – they speak of their cold journey as full of interest and there is not one of them who would now turn back. With regard to the treatment I have experienced in Constantinople, you cannot conceive how everyone has endeavoured to aid and assist me – I came amongst them a perfect stranger, and I think I know everyone with acquaintance in Pera. At the Embassy Sir Stratford and Lady Canning have been hospitable beyond measure – I have dined there 4 times, besides having the offer of Lady C's box at the opera when I please. I have promised her Ladyship a collection of plants for her garden, should I meet with any worthy [of] her acceptance. She is very anxious to have a good series of eastern species, and has undertaken to raise plants from the seeds I may send. This will form a nice nursery and halfway house for Kew Gardens. Look in Wolff's [?] [xxxx] you will see Mr Redhouse's name mentioned as forming one of the Erzerum Commission[22] I believe. He has lately written a work on the Turkish language, and is one of the best Turkish scholars extant, and interpreter to the Porte. He called on me shortly after my arrival and has been very attentive. He is Col. Williams' intimate friend. Of Constantinople I have not seen much, as I have been engaged in preparations for our formidable journey. What I have seen is anything but favourable to the Turks, who are the biggest set of rascals you can conceive. They have no hesitation, in fact it is the custom, to demand more than double the value of every article they sell. The other day at Layard's recommendation I went to the bazaar to purchase a gold band for my

---

21 Probably a corruption of the Arabic word 'tadhkir' (colloquial taskir) meaning 'ticket' or 'pass'.
22 James Redhouse was a member of the commission that drew up the Treaty of Erzerum in 1847 dealing with the boundary between the Ottoman Empire and Persia. The reference to Wolff is obscure and the next word is unclear.

CHAPTER FOUR

cap to give the inhabitants of Asia an imaginary idea of our importance – after bargaining for a while I got two for 15 piastres, which they asked 40 for! Every article from Western Europe is excessively dear, and I only wish I had known what I required when in London and I should have saved something. The only thing which makes the place tolerable is the kindness of the English and the picturesque beauty of everything which meets the eye – what scenes there are for the brush of the artist, for brush it must be since the pencil cannot express the brightness of the colours of the dresses. I quite agree with Murray, that the costumes of the European ladies here is hideous. Imagine their wearing light pink and blue bonnets, trimmed with bright flowers. Last week Count du Val de Beaulieu (!) Dodson, N.S. [?] Maudslay the engineer of Lambeth and myself crossed the Bosphorus to Scutari and climbed the hill above that quarter. The day being fine we had the most lovely view around us. The Sea of Marmora with the Prince's Islands on the west, Constantinople, the Golden Horn and the Bosphorus on the north, the windings of the Bosphorus on the east and sea and lofty mountains covered with snow. The view was certainly lovely – but give me the bold and rugged scenery of Switzerland. Perhaps I shall be glad to get a peep at a few mud huts. I got an unaffected introduction to Mr Smith the geologist and mineralogist to the Porte, who has only just returned from a tour of the emery works of Asia Minor. He has given me a few valuable hints as to what I [should] look out for on our route to Mosul. By the bye, let me mention it when I think of it, you may send letters and papers by the Embassy bag which leaves London the 17th I think [xxxx][23] must have forgotten this date, as there is a despatch bag sent off every month of that date. Tell my cousin that I only got the paper of the 3rd from the Embassy a day or two ago. It only then came by the French mail. I shall not have time to write to him today, but say that Mr Barker's cousin is here after travelling thro' Persia and the east. He intends I believe publishing a work. I have given him my card with my cousin's address as he is on his way to England. He is an exceedingly rum fish. Tell Gray I shall write to him from Samsun. Mr Guarracino,[24] the consul,

---

23   Blank space in manuscript.
24   Frederick Guarracino was the British Vice-Consul at Samsun 1846–55, and Consul 1855–60.

was here staying for a week with his wife and child on his way from Malta and we are to take up our quarters with them immediately on our arrival there. He will procure us horse[s] and start us on our way. Should you see any Nat. Hist. friends, pray give my best remembrance to them. I have had no time to get anything here as the weather is cold, but on my return I hope [to] make a collection of the fish of the Black Sea and Bosphorus (I have just this moment got another invitation from Lady C. to dine at the Embassy). The fish here are the most strange and beautiful I ever saw and I imagine are scarcely known beyond the Dardanelles, as soon as I have anything worth writing about I shall give Albany Hancock a few lines and I hope he will write me to say how the new arrangements succeed at the Museum.

Remember me most kindly to Ellen, to my cousin and to Mrs Radford, Mr and Mrs Gray, Mr Beckwith, Mr Whitfield Kay and all the rest of my good friends in the coally [sic] town. Tell them all that letters are soon written, postage is cheap and letters from England, few and far between, not to say most acceptable when they do arrive. My paper is now full, so I must conclude with every assurance of friendship and thanks of

My dear Edward,

Yours most sincerely,

Wm Kennett Loftus

Letter 7, Diarbekir, 30 March 1849

My dear Ben,

I wrote Mr Gray from Samsun promising to tip you a stave [sic] on arrival at Tokat or Sivas and to say a few words about the Mosque of St Sophia at Constantinople. Our journey has been such a rapid one that I have never had an opportunity of performing this promise. Of the mosque I shall however say nothing but leave that till we meet again years hence. In this letter I shall give you a short account of our journey from Samsun – of course you have heard from Mather or my cousin of my former proceedings and that I had set

CHAPTER FOUR

out with a young Englishman named Dodson,[25] travelling for pleasure in the East – I do not know who he is but he directs his letters to Lady D., Spring Fields. We agree very well. Mr Stevens[26] H.M.C. [at] Trebizond having arrived at our host's, Mr Guarracino, we left at 12 o'clock on the 14th for Kavak, as we thought we were intruding and occupying too much of Mr G.'s house and time. D. had been unwell, rather feverish. At 12 then we started with 9 horses, two for ourselves, two for our servants and 3 with the baggage: the other two for our Surajees[27] or guides. We travelled post. Posting rate is a quick walk or a hard jog trot. Post horses are horses gathered together by the post master (who often turns Surajee in hopes of receiving "backsheesh") by the force of our Firmans & Teskere's and seized for our special benefit and misery. For our post horses, often mules, we pay 2 ½ piastres per hour, and many an hour have we paid for that we never rode. Arriving late at Kavak we applied at the Governor's for a night's lodging. It was granted and the occupants of 3 sides of the guest chamber turned out in their shirts for us to take their places. In a short time a splendid Turkish repast was set before us, consisting of pilaf or rice and bad oil or tallow, soup of extraordinary looking beans, the meat boiled in it, and fried eggs in oil. So far so good and we lay down, but not to sleep. I was shortly roused by a host of little black fleas and glad was I when morning dawned. Finding the Governor's House so infected I have since taken to my mosquito net of Sevinges [?] invention into which I crawl thro' a hole and tie myself in and the vermin without. The only inconvenience from using this is that I am obliged to undress entirely which is rather a bother when we wish to make an early start. The 2nd day we got to Amasia, 14 hours ride! We were deceived by our suragees who told us there was a village at 10 hours and we were obliged to proceed. To add to our discomfort it rained in torrents and we travelled 3 hours by the river side in utter darkness. On reaching the town we lost the way, Dodson's horse fell and rolled upon him in the street and we were obliged to procure a light before he could be extricated

---

25 J G Dodson (1825-97). See Ch. 1, fn 25.
26 Francis (Frank) Iliff Stevens (1817-77), British Vice-Consul at Trebizond 1841-56, Consul 1856-67.
27 Surajee (or Surijy) is a Turkish postilion, a person who rides the near lead horse in order to guide a team of horses.

from his perilous situation, fortunately not hurt. The rain poured in pails full from the house tops and we were thoroughly soaked to the skin, even my large boots were no protection. To conclude this wretched night we arrived at length at a khan where we with difficulty procured a dirty room, without a fire, about 10 feet square, whose furniture consisted of a filthy matting full of fleas! The only result of this adventure was a very bad cold for us all. Amasia to Tokat 2 days. Nothing particular took place. Tokat has a Genoese castle in ruins most picturesquely situated on a lofty and pointed rock. We had now commenced to rise [up] the Taurus [mountains] and our next day's journey took us into the snow. The 2nd day from Tokat we had an adventure at a khan in the little village of Yenihan. D[odson] was warming himself at the fire, his servant Achmet cooking, & myself writing my journal when a soldier walked in, and threw his pipe in one place, his gloves in another, and walking straight to the fire pushed D. nearly over. D. in a great passion jumped up and speaking Turkish bestowed a <u>very polite</u> epithet on the gentleman, who had the impudence to draw his sword & strike D. with it, on which he received a good English blow on the face which nearly sent him sprawling & I don't know what might have been the result had we not all interposed and I got the fellow pushed out of the door. I got my hand slightly cut with his sword which was most infernally sharp. We forthwith donned [our] caps [with] gold bands and firman in hand applied to the Governor who summoned the rascal but could not punish him. He promised to give us a letter to the Pasha of Sivas but his captain begged for him and undertook to inflict punishment if we insisted on it. Having got out of him an apology we took no more notice of the matter. Sivas next day. Next to Deliktaş the highest point of this range of the Taurus, 6000 feet above the sea. You may imagine that as we rose the air got colder and the snow deeper. We had to make our way through furious drifts of snow and drifts up to the breasts of our horses. The wind now blew keen and cutting and not all the clothing we had on could keep its piercing blast from freezing every muscle in our skins. We sat on our horses stiff and cold as statues. You remember the Gemmi.[28] That was bad enough but the cold was nothing there in comparison. I had often heard of the nose being bitten off by

---

28   The Gemmi Pass in Switzerland.

CHAPTER FOUR

the frost. I really thought I should have lost mine. It broke out in a large blister at the end and became so rigid I could scarcely move it. The sun shone now and then in the intervals of the storm and his rays were so hot on one side that we could scarcely bear our cloaks, etc, while the other side was freezing with the cold wind. This you cannot well comprehend and it is difficult for me to describe the sensation, suffice it to say that from the freezing and cooking I had not a particle of skin left upon my face and my new pallor [?] is a swarthy old Arab colour. You no doubt wish to know what sort of lodging we had on our route? The dwellings are generally built of mud and straw, and raised about four feet from the ground. The streets are filled with mud and dead animals, and the stench is most horrible. High above the tops of the houses rise mounds of horse dung, which are the only objects visible in the distance to point out that human dwellings are near. If such be the exterior, what must we expect within? Thro' a low doorway we enter the common ante room by an inclined plane [?] to the stables and sleeping [?] room unswept, unwashed since the days of the foundation of the building! The walls, the floor, the roof, all are mud. Leuk[29] was bad enough, but many a time have I envied our night even there! What would you have done in our case? I think I see disgust and horror depicted on your face. But worse and worse, the places swarm with vermin: rats, mice, cats, bugs, fleas, lice, ticks! In myriads! I do not jest. The house I am now writing from is swarming with lice of immense size and I tell the truth when I say that I found several in my drawers this morning. But this is nothing when you're used to it! In the last 16 days I have scarcely got myself washed, 1st because we had not time, 2nd because basins were not to be had, and lastly because it would have been no use as we should have been unlike our neighbours. Glad was I today to have a Turkish bath. Never did I more need one and never did I get a more thorough and luxurious scrubbing. It was happiness intense tho' the first instance was overpowering. Some people have praised the Turks beyond measure as fine [?] fellows. I have found them rascals, liars and filthy dirty. They take the most solemn oath to the greatest lie; instance our host this very evening who tells that Queen Victoria is very fond of him [and] that he went to London all the

---

29   Leuk in canton Valais, Switzerland.

way on horseback! They wash often in their baths, but of what use is it [when] they put on their lousy clothes again. From Deliktaş to Keban Madeni we had a series of disasters in the snow: losing our way when the path was snowed up; horses falling and rolling over the baggage in the drifts; repacking in the driving snow. At the latter place we crossed the Euphrates in a ferry boat. The celebrated river is about 40 yards wide and a turbid, rapid stream, much finer in idea than in reality. The silver mines are unworked. At Harput we overtook the Russian Commissioner who left Constantinople a week I think, if not three, before I arrived there. We dined with them and found Col. Tcherikoff a very nice fellow. From there to Ergani Madeni is a terrible journey over a most extraordinary pass covered with snow. It was a very difficult and tedious [journey]. We were obliged to take six guards to support our horses up roads at 45° angle and to carry the baggage in the awkward places. Yesterday we came 11 hours over the uninteresting plain starting by lantern light at ½ past 3. Today a kellek has been bargained for and made. Tomorrow at 6 we start on our sail down the Tigris. Our vessel is composed of 63 inflated skins, tied together, on which are laid a few rough timbers very slight and a platform roughly put up of rougher boards 12ft by 8ft for our tent of black cloth 4ft high. The whole length of the raft is not [more than] 18 feet and width 10 feet. It is guided by two Kurds and two oars. By this we hope to reach Mosul in 6 days. Col. W. will not have arrived there yet. You will therefore conclude that we have made a very quick journey and that I have had no opportunities of working. I have however got an insight into the geology of the Taurus. I could say a great deal more but my paper bids me stop and time says "go to bed". I must beg your kind indulgence for the manner in which this is written, as altho' I have learned to drink Turkish coffee I cannot yet manage to write on my knees. Tables and chairs we have none, I fear, left far behind, and ottomans are not the most comfortable seats to write on. Will you be kind enough to let my cousin Mather and Gray see this and with my best remembrance to all our mutual friends.

I remain my dear Ben

Sincerely yours

Wm Kennett Loftus

CHAPTER FOUR

Letter 8, Head Quarters of the Commission, Mosul, 15 April 1849

My dear English affectionates,

Here I am at last, the long wished for goal is as at last arrived at. At Diarbekir [Diyarbakır] I wrote to Mr Benjamin Green giving him a short account of our movements up to March 30. He would no doubt let you see my letter. The following morning we went on board our raft of skins and floated down the Tigris. For two days we got on very well after which it rained almost incessantly, the river became swollen and rushed furiously down its channel carrying us frequently 12 miles an hour down the rapids where we swung round & round at a most extraordinary rate, the water rushing in first at one side, then at the other, sometimes in front, sometimes behind, and not infrequently from below. We prevented the rain from coming in from above by fastening my poncho over the top of the kellek. This saved us for a time tho' we were at last obliged to sleep on our wet carpets and rugs and in this state arrived at Mosul on the 5th inst., none the worse for our wetting but glad to escape from our cage. All our packages were soaked from the continual splashing of the water from below, Our Vice Consul Mr Rassam & his wife received us in his own house & introduced us to Wood, Olquin & Garey who were in Mosul at a private house tho' they grubbed at Mr R's. The Colonel, with Glascott and Churchill, were at the mound of Kouyunjik making excavations & drawings. Their tents were visible from Mosul. On the next day, Good Friday, I went across to pay my respects to my future commander. Our meeting was in the ancient palace of an Assyrian king between two enormous bulls shortly before uncovered from the accumulated rubbish of centuries. He received me most cordially and told me that he did not expect my arrival so soon, tho' he was aware of my having left Constantinople. He purposed waiting at Mosul till I might arrive. He is a fine handsome fellow, about 40, and was dressed in a fez, a drab loose coat with black braid, corduroy trousers & chamois leather shoes with a pipe in his mouth. He looked the picture of work and was evidently heart and soul in his occupation. The sculptures excavated are smaller tho' much more beautiful than those in the British Museum. The figures of the horses with which the walls were covered are evidently the work of a first rate artist and would shame many a one of the present day. The strange looking figures of the men beside them are evidently the work of a less accomplished hand. A double row of subjects is represented on the slabs, the attack & taking of a walled city. Young Churchill has copied the whole most correctly & beautifully & the drawings will be sent tomorrow with this to Layard at Constantinople. The weather continued very wet until Wednesday when a change took place for the better and a trip was arranged to view the other ruins of Nineveh. On Thursday at eight o'clock the Mosul party preceded by 3 cavasses who cleared the way, walked from Mr Rassam's to the ferry, by which we crossed and took horse at the other side. At the foot of the mound of Kouyunjik we were joined by the colonel & party, Glascott proceeded to make a rough survey of the great city. He was joined by Churchill & myself. We went direct to the Yezidi village of Basheikhah, while the rest took the road to Khorsabad where Mr Botta made such a large excavation for the French government. They joined us in the evening. We went to Basheikhah in expectation of seeing a Yezidi feast but it proved not to be due till next Friday. However, after dinner in the garden of our host Sherriff Bey under the bright blue sky we were entertained with Turkish dances, graceful and disgraceful! After a night of visitation from fleas our division started at 5 am for Khorsabad which we reached in 2 ½ hours. The immense winged bulls are lying about broken in every direction, mixed with fragments of inscriptions and figures in great quantities. There seems to have been no order or system in Botta's plan of operation and he does not appear to have excavated low enough. There is much to be yet discovered here. The freshness of the sculpture of the marbles after having lain such a length of time is most remarkable. One can almost imagine them to have been finished but yesterday. I have an idea that the bulls will prove to be the ornaments of the top of the palace or of a terrace. They are I think on a level with what appears to be such. I have little doubt that the style of architecture of these palaces has been very similar to the dwellings of the upper classes of Mosul of the present day. The rooms are narrow & lofty arched and much adorned with carved marble inside as well as out. I should not be surprised if they discover chambers below like the cellars of Mosul which are used for protection from heat in the summer time. We returned to Basheikhah & followed the other party to a place called Karakosh where we were today lodged at the church of the Chaldean Christians. All the inhabitants were out to see the arrival of the English beys! Fearing fleas even in the sacred edifice, a party of us took up our abode for the night on the highest part of

CHAPTER FOUR

the roof, but alas! It was of no use. They tormented us even there. Where they came from God knows, but very little sleep did we get. Next morning we all started together for Nimrud which we reached in 5 hours and rambled over the innumerable chambers of the various palaces, wondering more and more at the skill and power displayed in the sculptures yet to be transported to the British Museum. The sooner this is accomplished the better, as the Arabs have evidently very lately defaced a beautiful figure with the fir cone and basket. Two heads of lions buried for safety have been again exposed and alas damaged. Lions here appear to supply the place of the bulls of Khorsabad. After seeing all that is visible we set out on our return for Kouyunjik which we reached at 8 o'clock, slept all night in our tents on the top of the mound and returned to Mosul this morning. I have therefore as you may see performed the three days journey round the great city and seen sights only yet enjoyed by four Europeans besides our party! What would not many a one give to see what we have seen? Though the mounds of Nineveh are not conspicuous objects from the distance to arrest the attention, yet they must have been the wonder of many from their peculiar form and for their great number. We passed very many which without doubt contain many most interesting remains to be yet brought to light. The palaces appear to have been built at the angles of immense squares or courts enclosed by a raised wall or surround of bricks or earth. All the villages of the present generation are built in the immediate vicinity of these mounds. No doubt that the accumulation of rubbish upon the ruins is caused by successive villages which have each in turn been swept away. On the top of Kouyunjik even now may be seen the crumbling ruins of a Yezidi village, the inhabitants of which were exterminated by the celebrated Beder Khan Bey. Today we spend in letter writing & tomorrow in preparing for an excursion into the desert of Sinjar to visit the ruins of Al Hadhr [Hatra].

This excursion was planned also for another purpose – to purchase horses of the Arabs of Shammar for our journey and work in the mountains as we have all hitherto had hired horses. We had thro' Mr Rassam secured the services of one of their chiefs, but a circumstance has happened which will defeat one of the ends of our journey. The Pasha of Mosul has imposed a tax of 2 ½ piastres a load on Arabs with grain leaving the town which has so offended the Shammar that they are about striking their tents to proceed [to] plunder all the villages on the NE side of their desert in the direction of Nisibin, Mardin, Jezirah etc. When I tell you that this tribe numbers 15,000 tents you may conclude that the Pasha has put his finger into the fire. As we are not going to be done out of our journey to Al Hadhr we start [on] Tuesday armed to the teeth with 40 soldiers in case of attack from other wandering tribes not friendly to the Shammar. Our chief was very anxious to join his tribe, but Mr Rassam has succeeded in prevailing on him to stay. At Al Hadhr I hope to procure a couple of the wild ass for the Zoological Gardens. They have never yet had one and are only known to Report in Europe. It is possible we may be making some excavations at the ruins which 6 centuries ago was a place of some importance, tho' I am not sure such will be the case. We shall most likely return to Mosul in a week or 10 days and within three weeks from this time be in Baghdad. I imagine our stay will be short on our first visit and we shall likely make off for the mountains and remain in camp with our friends the Russians until the Turks and Persians shew fight. They are very shy in coming to the scratch! The sun is now shining brightly and it is much hotter than our English summer. During our three days ride I have gone thro' the process of having my hide tanned most effectually [sic]. I shall not want any more gloves as my hands are of a most beautiful brown colour. I have succeeded in getting some very nice things during our ramble thro' Nineveh, insects, land shells, fresh water malanopes [?] and nerites, land crabs, serpents, tree frogs & plants & I have tried my hand at stuffing some falcons and a beautiful green and blue jay shot by the Col. at Kouyunjik. Ask Albany Hancock what he thinks of a naturalist riding about collecting on horseback. It does appear very absurd, but the heat is most overpowering. When I have anything worth communicating I intend writing to him and shall be glad if he will favour me with any Nat. Hist. chit chat. You will probably desire to hear of our party. Col Williams is exactly what I expected him to be from all I had read & heard of him. He is a very great favourite and quite the father of the party. He now and then gets a little out of temper when dirty ditch water is drank [sic]! Instead of finding Lieut. Glascott a very swell officer, I find a raw bon'd Irishman with very red hair, a broad brimmed white felt hat and much worn inexpressibles.[30]

---

30   Tight-fitting trousers which left nothing to the imagination.

CHAPTER FOUR

Wood the Secretary and Interpreter is decidedly the swell of the party. He is very fair and has a white beard and a rather queer temper, wears a white felt broad hat, black velvet shooting coat with an infinity of black braid about the breast; a red silk belt round his waist; a black glazed belt over his shoulder & a small sword. Churchill is a very young fellow who sketches well. Olquin is the Dr & a Frenchman named Garey is our Provender & Clerk. But this I must say, a nicer party could not have been formed and I am quite satisfied that I should have been a great ass to have declined my appointment. The opportunity of seeing these countries at all is sufficient to induce me to accept such a chance, independently of my having to pursue those studies most pleasing to me. I would not now have missed this on any account. We are everywhere treated with the greatest respect and every reasonable wish gratified. The Colonel will not allow me to exert myself much in case I should be laid up and has desired me to look out on arrival at Bagdad [Baghdad] for a sharp fellow whom I can instruct in skinning birds and dig up plants and do the heavy work. I have my servant besides. You will therefore see that there is every possible disposition to assist me shewn by all parties with whom I have held communication on the matter. Nothing can be more pleasant than to work under such circumstances. I hope to astonish a few with the collections I shall bring home.

In case you should wish to follow my course on the map during my journey from Samsun to Mosul I send you a list of our stations with the distances in hours:

			Post hours	Performed in
Mar	14	Samsun to Kavak	8	8
___	15	Amasia	14	14
___	16	Harinalskoi [?]	7	6 ½
___	17	Turhal & Tokat	13	11 ¼
___	18	Ischerfuss [?]	6	5 ½
___	19	Yenihan	6	5 ½
___	20	Sivas	9	8
___	21	Deliktaş	10	10 ½
___	22	Alacahan	9	10 ½
___	23	Hasançelebi & Hekimhan	11	10

	24	Argowan [?]	8	7
	25	Keban Madeni	10	9
	26	Harput	10	10
	27	Kejahinchan [?]	9	9 ½
	28	Ergani Madeni	9	11
	29	Diarbekir	14	10 ½
	30	Rest one day to make kellek		
	31	From Diarbekir		
Apl	5	to Mosul		

To procure anything but bread except at the large towns was a difficult thing and our canteen was often called into requisition. Fowls were pretty plentiful, our one meal per diem was devoured on arrival at our day's journey (as a fingal[31] of coffee and a biscuit at starting cannot be called a meal). It consisted of a pilaf of rice and a roast fowl. The first dish was varied by chicken broth & the boiled chicken. We calculate that about 100 fowl were demolished by us. I think I shall never be able to enjoy a fowl again after such a surfeit but we have now got into the bosom of Mr Rassam's family, a land of plenty flowing in everything: Kymac [kaymak], the cream of buffalo milk used for butter is most delicious and is celebrated at Mosul, one third of the milk turns to a most rich cream or butter. I wonder [why] the animal has never been tried on the rich pastures of old England. Yahourt (sour milk) [yogurt] is not bad. Fresh milk is boiled with a little sour and left to stand overnight & a sort of custard is produced in the morning and is the general food of the Turks. The Turkish sweetmeats are very good, especially rahatlakoun [rahat lokum] (morsel of comfort) and helvas (sweet thing), this is a mix [?] of bruised [?] sesame seed and sugar or honey.

I have now written you a long letter and must conclude. Remember me most kindly to all your good ladies and fail not to give my best remembrance to all enquiries. You may tell them that a letter from old England is fit subject now for a month's contemplation, and did they know how anxiously post

---

31 al-fingal is an Arabic coffee cup.

days are looked forward to, they would I am sure endeavour to afford pleasure to the absent.

Believe me, my dear Cousin, Mather & Gray,

Your most affectionate and obliged friend,

Wm Kennett Loftus.

Letter 9, Mosul, 24 April 1849

My dear affectionates,

Safely returned from the Desert of Sinjar I sit down to write you for the last time from this place, and to give you a short description of our excursion. On Tuesday morning last, all due preparations having been previously made we issued from the gates of Mosul, a most formidable looking party and as motley a group as ever an artist would wish to see. Nearly all the rabble of the place was on the walls to see us depart staring with all the eyes they had got (by the bye, many had no eyes at all but still the blind man came out to see) upon the principle I suppose that one fool may look at another. Our cavalcade was headed by 30 irregular troops of the Pasha's led on by their band of music which consisted of a Kettle Drum & a squeaking clarionet [sic]. These were all fully armed with muskets, pistols & swords ready to resist the attack of any party of wandering Arabs who might feel disposed to shew fight. Behind these followed our guide Suttum, the Arab chief of the Shammar with his black slave, mounted on his splendid dromedary. This group was the admiration of us all. Next came our party led on by our Vice Consul and Col Williams, dressed in such costumes as best suited the fancy of each as most likely to keep off the flaying heat of the sun. The V. Consul wore his silver banded cap & European dress. The Col in a nankeen[32] suit with broad brimmed hat & large color'd handkerchief floating over it and his shoulders. Wood in a loose green frock

---

32   Nankeen is a type of yellow-coloured cloth originally made in Nanking (Nanjing), China.

of his own design, broad hat, sword and glazed belt. The Dr in his blue and white striped trousers without straps, and white jacket might have passed for a Sailor had it not been for the bright color'd head dress & Camels hair tie on the Top in imitation of the Arabs. Churchill dressed in white with 2 pieces of white cloth for his head dress. Dodson in his usual travelling costume. Glascott could not go as he was not well. Over my own red fez or skull cap I wore a genuine Arab head dress. The long kerchief of red wool & yellow silk with innumerable streamers, surmounted by the rope of camel's hair. I was pronounced to be a capital Arab if I had no spectacles. Behind us followed our servants, cavasses, cooks, scullions, water carriers, with their horses. 30 camels with our tents, tables, chairs, grub, wood for firing, and other requisites for the sojourn of our party for 10 days if requisite in the desert. Around the whole flitted a host of wild Arabs on their beautiful steeds, javelins in hand. Our road lay for three hours over rich fields of grain, without a single speck [?] in the whole to meet the eye. Corn is produced around Mosul of the first quality from land yielding every other year without any manure whatever! After passing a sulphur spring in a chasm 100 ft deep on the summit of a low range of hills of marble we came upon the desert not of sand but of flowers of every hue. On the dead flat [desert] over which our route lay I had innumerable opportunities of collecting and I have brought back many interesting insects, plants, snakes, etc. We all suffer much from thirst and glad were we to rush to a muddy ditch where the water tasted either bituminous, salt, or of decayed vegetation. Not once did we get good water and the consequence was that we were all attacked with bowel complaints. After sleeping in our tents for 2 nights we reached the ruins of Al Hadhr [Hatra] on the 3rd day at mid-day. There we had expected to find a spring of sweet water, but it could not be discovered altho' the Arabs themselves resided here for some time past. They however knew nothing about it as their women are their water carriers. Our disappointment was severe as we had been led to expect such a treat. Instead of sweet water we had stinking pond water, the refuge of thousands of water fowl from the surrounding desert. Al Hadhr is truly a most remarkable ruin standing as it does amidst the dreary desert, a relic of nations long since extinct, the Parthian and the Roman. Ainsworth in his researches has committed some most egregious blunders in his description of these ruins. He will, I have no doubt, be shortly put right. The ground occupied is about 3 miles in circumference [circumstances written]

CHAPTER FOUR

& many of the vaulted chambers of the palace are as perfect and the surface of the stone as smooth as when first erected. Not a single soul was to be seen and we wandered about among the old halls & galleries for 2 days. The water being so bad we determined to return to Mosul on the 3rd day. All preparations having been made & we were sitting about 8 o'clock quietly enjoying our tea in the cool shade of the ruins when Suttum brought tidings that several Arabs had just been seen outside the mounds & that there was consequently every probability of an attack after midnight. Then what a commotion took place. The Arabs and our "Royal Guard" put out all the fires; scouts were posted at regular intervals, guns & pistols loaded, all the servants in a mortal funk, while we enjoyed the scene most amazingly, none of us believing the report[s]. At 9 we quietly went to bed to start early, but no one had got undressed when a volley of musketry was fired from the ruins on our left & the wild cry [?] of the Arabs mixed with their still wilder music caused us to assemble in the large tent. The shouts from the walls were answered by similar ones from our tent guard followed by more firing and an Arab war-song! All together it was a most strange affair, but nothing came of it! Whether the enemy ever appeared or not none of us can make out, but the same row was kicked [?] up the whole blessed night, and very little sleep was the consequence. We reached Mosul on the second day from Al Hadhr, starting at 12 at night so as to avoid the awful heat. We had no water for 14 hours, i.e. 'fit to drink', & I was so exhausted on arrival that I have felt fatigued ever since. So ended our trip to Al Hadhr which has been visited by only 4 Europeans before, viz. Ainsworth, Layard, Dr Ross[33] & Mr Mitford. Mr Rassam our Vice Consul is a native of Mosul & was one of the Euphrates expedition. He married an English lady. They have no children. It has been raining in torrents since our journey to Al Hadhr & we have been amusing ourselves with Suttum the Arab chief. He is chief of about 2000 tents & allowing 15 to each, he has 30,000 under his command! He is a fine fellow and is delighted with the English. We told him that the Russians' party would wish to see Al Hadhr, but he said "When the Russians become English they

---

33   John Ross had at this time been the East India Company surgeon to the British Residency at Baghdad for 17 years. He died in June 1849 and was buried in Baghdad on 19th June 1849.

shall see Al Hadhr, but not till then". He has promised to get me two wild asses of the desert & send them to Mr Rassam who will forward them for me to Beirut to be shipped for the Zoological Gardens. They are very rare and have I believe never been seen in Europe.

We did not see any. Suttum christened me "Father of insects" when he saw me collecting. Of snakes he was much afraid and would not come near even a dead one. He wanted us to make treaty with the Arabs against the Turks! We are all truly interested in him. He is now gone to join his tribe in their plundering expedition and it is likely that his end will be similar to his kinsman's Sofuk[34] betrayed and murdered. Poor fellow, I hope not. I believe that our visit has paved the way for any Englishman among the Shammar Bedouins. The Russian party has not yet got here & nothing has been heard of either Persians or Turks so we start tomorrow, if the weather clears up, on our voyage per kellek down the Tigris to Baghdad, taking it very quietly & visiting all the ruins of antiquity by the river side. We have 4 kelleks prepared of 600 skins each. On arrival at Baghdad we take up our abode at Major Rawlinson's at the Palace of the East India Company. We hear that the heat is there so intense that they have already taken to living in the cellars & sleeping on the roofs. So we have rather a hot prospect before us.

Yours ever

Wm Kennett Loftus

Letter 10, Mosul, 26 April 1849

My dear Cousin,

I have given you a short description of our trip to the Desert & I only wish I could amuse you by it, as I was amused by the reality. I have little time for letter writing as my time is quite occupied with my collections, making notes

---

34 For an account of the death of Sofuk, sheikh of the Shammar tribe, see Layard 1849: I, 111–14.

on what I gather, cleaning and preserving some, sketching the perishable ones, etc, etc. This is quite enough to take up all my time. With the Colonel I am delighted, and indeed who would not be so. I hope he will be equally well satisfied with me. Letters from yourself & Mather awaited my return from Al Hadhr [Hatra] and were very acceptable as you may imagine. I also got one from Blacklock enclosing a vote of thanks from the Soc. of which I am sure there was no need. As soon as I possess anything of interest to communicate I will let him hear from me, but we have not yet got to our working ground. I am however busy enough & the only busy one of the party. I am glad you were pleased with my letter tho' I am sure I do not remember its contents. Your list for the Plate is not so good as could have been wished but it looks well compared with Manchester. I am sure you are all doing your best on my behalf and I know not how sufficiently to evince my gratitude. I got thro' the country well enough without any sword or pistol loaded and I am quite convinced that no one will molest us if we behave ourselves, especially when we come armed with all sorts of powers. It is possible we may be detained at Baghdad all the summer, if as I think the Col. will encamp somewhere in the nearest mountain range to escape the heat. The Turks and Persians are very slow in their movements. Give my best regards to Mrs R & to all friends not forgetting Mr Gray.

Yours ever,

Wm Kennett Loftus

Letter 11, Baghdad, 9 May 1849

Dear Affectionates,

"Here we are" as the clown says, safely arrived after a delightful float down the Tigris. Leaving Mosul on the 28th we got here on the 5th. The journey has been so well described by Rich in his work on Koordistan & Nineveh that it leaves me little to say as regards the places we visited, as, of course, we took matters very quietly and saw all that was to be seen. We stopped at the bitumen spring and baths of Hammam Ali,[35] had another peep at Nimrud and its remains, from which we rode back to our kelleks on bare backed Arab mares, reminding us of the style of riding represented in the sculptures, Toprak Kalesi or Kalaa,[36] Tekrit & its old castle & moat, Imam Dour,[37] probably not far from the spot where in the plain of Dura all nations were summoned "to fall down and worship the golden image which Nebuchadnezzar the king had set up",[38] Eski Baghdad, Samarra & its Babel like tower, Kadesia [Qadisiyyah] & its ancient glass work ruins, Syndia [?], Dokhala [?] were each in turn examined – each highly interesting in itself but the wonder excited by any of them is a nothing when we look at the innumerable traces of ruins which are everywhere to be seen. It really almost appears incredible. From Mosul to Baghdad, on each side of the river, as far as the eye can reach traces of ruins can be seen: – in fact it must have been one dense mass of dwellings containing an enormous population.

The whole distance the banks consist of an alluvial deposit of great thickness, and rich description. Imagine this river in the days of old, and as it is now! Scarcely a town of more than 400 families while the soil is an uncultivated desert, occupied at this time by roving tribes of Arabs. On arriving near Baghdad, the graceful date palm reared his head from the surrounding desert and formed a pleasing change to the treeless route from Tokat and even Samsun. The Pasha sent his state out some distance to meet us and we rowed up to Major Rawlinson's at the Residency in solemn state style by 20 rowers. The Major received us most kindly and is doing the honours of hospitality in most prince like style I can assure you. There not being accommodation at the residence for the whole party Glascott and I are lodged at the house of the celebrated Dr Ross, the discoverer and describer of Al Hadhr [Hatra]. This is much quieter and more snug and we both prefer it. Of course we grub with the rest at the Major's. Baghdad is so connected with India that it is quite

---

35   Layard had opened some trenches here – Layard 1853: 465.
36   It seems Loftus is here referring to Kalah Shergat (Assur), which they certainly visited at this time – Loftus 1857: 4.
37   The Shiite shrine of Imam al-Dur is 20 km N. of Samarra. The shrine was destroyed by Daesh in 2014.
38   Daniel, Ch. 3, v. 5.

CHAPTER FOUR

different from any Turkish town I have yet seen, and the character of the place and appearance of the people is Indian. At dinner 15 servants in their native costumes are in attendance to obey your every nod: – Turks, Negros, Indians, Persians. It is a more complete Babel than Constantinople. What a table the Major keeps, port, sherry, claret, hock (Johannesburg), champagne & beer flow in abundance. He has a guard of honour in their English dress, and a small steamer is always stationed at his disposal. In fact we are in first rate quarters, and likely to continue in them for some time as altho' the Persian commissioner[s], much to our surprise, arrived here a week before us, the Russians had not reached Mosul when we left, and we have heard nothing whatever of the Turk. Even when all the party is collected, the weather will be so hot that no human being can exist in the heat of the sun. For 5 months the people of Baghdad have to live in their cellars (serdabs)[39]:- at Busrah [Basra] it is still hotter, and fevers most abundant. To proceed to the hills will be equally bad, as there are many unhealthy spots in our route. I shall be able to tell you better of our plans in another post or two. I think the idea of visiting Babylon is given up for the present on account of the hot season coming on. The thermometer is now standing night & day at 80° in the shade – in a short time we shall sleep on the roof. I shall however have plenty to do, as this part of the world has never been examined at all. The birds are most beautiful & I am about to commence collecting them as I cannot get any geology. We are now almost devoured with flies. On the river we were attacked by swarms of mosquitoes, which have disfigured the beauty of our faces [?] to an incredible extent. Lizards are running all over the ceilings and in a short time we shall be amused by an influx of fleas and of black scorpions 5 inches long.

Large hornets are buzzing about in every direction so I need never be idle. We arrived here at a very critical period; the river from the continual rains had risen 22 ½ feet, which is higher than has been known since the great inundation of 1831 when 7000 houses were destroyed. Fears were entertained for the safety of the place & the whole of the population had been turned out to raise a mound round the walls, which was just finished as we arrived.

---

39 Serdab is a Persian word (lit. 'cool water') for cellar or underground room.

The water rose to 2 feet of the top. Had the mound burst, or any of the foundations of the houses next [to] the river given way Baghdad would have been no more.

The Major's and Dr Ross' houses overlook the river, and are built on higher ground than the interior of the town. The waters have flowed into the serdabs in both houses 3 feet deep! The flood is now subsiding & we shall be able to get out in a few days. There is little doubt that the city will be entirely washed away in a few years, as they have very inconsiderately dug canals up the river which is making terrible havoc on its mud banks. The very highest rise of the spring floods is very seldom 18 feet which is considered extraordinary, therefore I leave you to consider what a fright the natives must have been in.

I can scarcely believe that I have found my way to Baghdad, the old city of the Kalifs – the scene of the tales of the Arabian Nights! Can I have followed the example of the sleeper, and slept for the last three months – All that I have passed appears but a dream, from which I have wakened to a pleasing reality. Notwithstanding the heat which is frequently in shade 125°, I understand it must be a delicious place of residence. The serdabs are cool, then in the evening a strong breeze sets in and cools the heated skin. All the luxuries of India are here without its disagreeables. The Major's garden is the most delicious place you can conceive. It is one vast shade of vines, oranges, lemon, lime & pomegranate, fig, apple and pear trees. Sheep are to be had for 4/- each & oxen proportionately cheap. Fruit is to be had for a mere trifle and house rent a nonentity! I am getting some calico coats and trousers made at the rate of 1/6 each – a person may live like a prince for £100 per year, and keep his horse and two servants into the bargain. In Persia I understand it is still cheaper living. We had on Saturday the Prince of Oude to dinner, some years ago he made some stir in England in endeavouring to obtain the throne of his father by intercession of our government. He lives here and lives in great style with an income of £8000 a year. He is a fine old fellow, very stout, talks English & wears the European dress with a Persian cap. He has just lost his wife, a granddaughter of the great Tippoo Saib.[40] The Pasha has been very

---

40   Tipu Sultan (1750–99) was the ruler of Mysore in South India.

polite to the Colonel, returning his call by the present of a very handsome Arabian mare. They would have saluted us on arrival, but feared for the safety of the walls of the town.

And now having nothing more to communicate I must conclude with kind remembrance to all friends.

I remain dear affectionates,

Yours sincerely,

Wm Kennett Loftus.

Letter 12, Baghdad, 20 May 1849[41]

Many, many thanks to you, my dear Hancock, for your kind and most welcome letter – the more welcome because unexpected. You expected it would reach me before leaving Constantinople for Mt Ararat. It has oddly enough overtaken me at another of the mighty cities of former days – the city of the Kalifs – the scene of the tales of witchcraft and wonder which make such an impression on the schoolboy's mind – Baghdad! How strange it sounds! Five months ago I should have laughed at the idea of visiting Baghdad, yet here I am. Mr Radford has most probably informed you of my proceedings up to our arrival here. And I therefore shall not repeat what I have previously written. With regard to our stay here, I can give you no idea, as nothing can be done until the four Commissioners meet. The Russian is now at Mosul and will be here probably next week but we have no news of the Turk. Unless he comes very shortly we shall not be able to move from Baghdad for four months on account of the heat. To go to Mohammerah,[42] one of the disputed

---

41 The original letter is apparently preserved in the archives of the Natural History Society of Northumberland, together with 3 other letters from Loftus addressed to Albany Hancock (Ermidoro 2020: 249, n. 21). These probably include Letters 16 and 40.
42 Now Khorramshahr.

points, below Busrah [Basra], would be certain death, while the journey to the mountain of Zyohab [?] is formidable also on account of the unhealthy swamps in the neighbourhood. No matter, I have plenty to amuse me here in my department; we are in good quarters at the Consul's and the heat is not yet intolerable. In the shade it is now from 80° to 85° night and day, and we have not yet begun to sleep on the house tops, nor have we yet descended to the serdabs or cellars during the middle of the day. In fact I much doubt if we shall be able to take up our quarters there at all on account of their having been overflowed by the inundation. The day is spent by most of the party in a most eastern manner, lolling on sofas, sleeping, eating and smoking. We generally rise soon after day break, take a ride, which cannot be extended beyond the mound outside the walls as the waters are still out. I generally manage to pick up something. After breakfast I arrange and work on my acquisitions and receive what any one has procured for me, take an hour's snooze at midday, ride again, or go to some of the date gardens and enjoy the luxuriant shade there, dine at sunset and go to bed when I like. And now to say a few words on our favourite subject, Nat. History. Up to this time I have had few opportunities of procuring many specimens; of shells I have found but few, 11 sp[ecimens] of Helix etc., 2 Melanopsis, 1 Neritina, 2 [gap] & 1 Cyrena; the water is yet too high for me to get many river and canal species, but I hope to add to this list shortly. I think of going down the river to Busrah in the EIC[43] steamers [sic] stationed here, and which sails to bring up the Indian letters about the 28th and returns in about a week. I am getting a dredge made for our future wanderings. In the stagnant waters are innumerable shoals of a species of Cypris & a Linulus [?] 2 inches long. I did not know before that the Linulus or sub-genus of Linulus inhabits fresh (i.e. stagnant) water. I should like to know if I am correct in this supposition and if there are many species. The scorpions of Baghdad are large black fellows and for the first time I got 2 yesterday, one about 5 inches. They are so common that for a punishment, the sailors are made to bring a dozen on a string before dinner! These and the centipedes are just beginning to appear – of insects I have about 70 species chiefly Colcoptera. We were too late for the butterfly season. The mole cricket

---

43   East India Company.

is perhaps one of my most strange looking brutes. We have here the carpenter bee in abundance, and hornets in myriads. Night lizards are running all over the ceilings and walls after sunset. Of snakes I have about 5 species. I am now about to work among the birds and fish which are both curious. Of the former I have a few specimens and am now endeavouring to teach a young fellow to take the skinning etc. of birds off my hands. Of plants I have also procured a few species, so you see that I am not idle. You ask how I like my vocation, nothing can be more delightful. Col Williams is a most capital fellow, and a great favourite everywhere; we have only to ask for what we want and there it is supplied immediately – our party is a very agreeable one. We of course are treated everywhere as the HBM's Commissioners should be treated. Nowhere do we move without the respectful salaams of the natives attended by [gap] and servants. We are in fact revelling in the luxuries of India in the residency. All this is very well in its way but I am longing to be off to more active service in the mountains, to hammer at my favourite rocks, and see nature unseen by European eye before. On all sides, however, discontent and rebellion are rife. The Kurds have beaten the Turkish troops near Rowanduz and decamped to their mountain castles, carrying with them the cattle of the surrounding country: the Arabs near Hillah (Babylon) have revolted from their chief set over them by the government and troops are being poured from here into the desert to overcome them but there is little probability of their being able to reach the Arabs, as the country between Hillah and Baghdad between the two great rivers is one vast lake! Never has such an inundation been known. In Persia [there is] rebellion at Shiraz and the post has arrived this morning with the news that the Shah has refused to ratify a treaty entered into by his father[44] with the French & that the Frenchman has hauled down his flag and sold it (!) and left the kingdom with a threat that a French fleet shall shortly be at Bushire. Pretty work! Yet amidst all these commotions, in the midst of so many nations, the Englishman is sacred, and for my own part I should not fail to travel alone anywhere in these regions. English influence is fast increasing in the East, while French is on the decline. The Turkish Empire is however in a very tottering state and it would be no great source of regret to its subjects

---

44   Mohammad Shah Qajar, r. 1834–48.

were it to cease to exist. The extortions of its rulers are most barefaced and disgraceful. The Pasha here is robbing the country in every direction, taxing everything 'ad libitum' till it actually is of no use for the inhabitants to till the ground. This year without doubt he will buy up all the corn and when prices have risen to an exorbitant extent, he will open his granary and make an enormous profit: when the Col. made his formal call on him he received an Arab horse as a present. The Col. as is the custom made a handsome present to the servant who brought the horse. We heard the next day that the Pasha had taken the money from the servant and borrowed [?] it for his own especial use! The horse is a bad one and he will probably charge the Sultan with 10 times his value! Isn't this precious government? All the boats in the river were seized the other day to pass the troops over the river, without any remuneration to their owners. The towns and villages throughout the Empire are becoming heaps of ruins and everything going to decay. It is most pitiful to see such a rich and valuable country so utterly destroyed by its rulers! Here, the soil is capable of producing 3 and 4 crops a year with little or no manure. You ask when the Commission will be finished and I shall return to my own dear home? The Col. thinks in about 2 years from this, tho' the general impression is that the matter will not be finished for 5 or 10 years! In fact it is at present impossible to say. As I hope to be for some time on the shores of the Persian Gulf I shall not forget you, the Nudibranches or the boring sponges. I have a few shells now given me from the mouth of the Indus with "borers" [?] for you. I am sorry to hear so bad an account of the Roy[al?] Soc. & your work. With regard to Bowerbank[45] I am sorry to say that I had no opportunity of seeing him before I left England and should you be writing him I shall feel obliged by your telling him how disappointed I was. Of course I cannot give you any information about Catherina Georgia! [?] Classic (nonsense) indeed! At Mosul I received a note of thanks from the Soc. for my supposed services – I feel highly obliged by their remembrance of me and I commission you to return them my best thanks tho' I fear I little deserved theirs for what I had done. That I entertained every wish for the prosperity of the Society you are I am sure well aware, and tho' absent I hope I shall able to add to the stores.

---

45   James Scott Bowerbank, FRS (1797–1877), British naturalist and palaeontologist.

CHAPTER FOUR

The collections I make are to become the property of the public, and after the British Museum is supplied, the Co. is at liberty to dispose of the remainder as he thinks best. The disposal he has left at my discretion and you may therefore rest assured of the Newcastle Museum's not being forgotten. I was sure the penny admission would answer and I think you may calculate on more than 70 or 80 £. Your account of the success of the reading of papers is not so satisfactory. I was in hope that this would have assisted to raise an interest in the Society and I would gladly have lent my aid towards so good an end, by scribbling now and then for your amusement, a paper on the wanderings in the eastern counties or any natural phenomena which I thought would prove of interest to you; I hope you will let me know the result of Mr Alder's attempt. I should much like to see your paper on the Cliona, as it may direct my attention to something at the Gulf or in some of the salt lakes of the north. I am not aware that I have got anything new; at the same time I may soon obtain something, but I am rather in a fix, as not having any book to refer to I might send off specimens to the British Museum, and others might claim the honour of discovery. In what way do you think I may prevent this, as of course I should in this case like to claim the reward of my own labours. Any hints on this point will be a favour. I am now endeavouring to procure a brace of maneless lions of Busrah for the Zool' Gardens tho' I fear I shall not succeed this year as the cubs are getting old. I expect daily to hear that my Arab friend Suttum the Chief of the Shammar has caught for me a couple of the Hamar-el-Wasb [sic] or wild ass of Sinjar. It will be acceptable in Europe as it is I believe different from the wild ass of Persia. I hear of two or three strange animals in the Kurdish Mountains, and I do not doubt that I shall be able to send home something new & interesting. I have seen a few fossils from these mountains, which strike me as being very similar to those sent off by Dr Valimar and Capt. Cautlay from the Himalaya Mountains. It will be interesting if the same beds can be traced along the boundary line of Persia. Thursday next is the Queen's birthday, and great preparations are making [sic] to celebrate the occasion in grand style. A levee will be held in the morning, all the officials in full dress. Our dinner party at 5 will consist of all the English now here to the number of 30. At sunset is the grand gathering when the Baghdad ladies muster on the Major's terrace, having first laid aside their hideous black horse hair masks & large wrappers in which they appear in the streets. Then take[s] place no end of firing salutes, illuminations and feasting till midnight. Large VR's, stars, crowns, etc. are being fixed up in the courtyard. This day week we breakfasted with a celebrated character called here the Nawab, but no less in fact than Ikbal-id-Doulah, the should be king of Oude, who some years ago was in England to obtain the assistance of government to obtain his own, but without effect. He is a fine old fellow, and lives like a prince, having an income of about £8000 a year. For the first time in my life I sat down to an Indian entertainment cross-legg'd on pillows. I cannot give a favourable report of the dishes, which chiefly consisted of curry and onions stuffed in various ways. By the bye I had almost forgotten to ask if you know of a little insect which destroys everything in the shape of animal production, cloth, clothes, brushes, combs, etc., etc. It is here in multitudes and we are obliged to expose all our stock to the open air every day. I do not know whether it is known in India. It is like a small worm, 1/8 inch long covered with long black hair and frequently casts its skin. I have half a dozen by me feeding in a pill box most voraciously on the tops of pens. Will you be good enough to tell Mr Blacklock that I received the vote of thanks at Mosul with a few lines from himself, for which beg him to accept my thanks. I should have written to him by this post, but I find I have not time. Remember me most kindly to Mr Alder, Mr Howse [?] and Dr Charlton and to all my Nat. Hist. friends in the "canny" town. I hope that now you have once broken the ice you will not suffer it to freeze again. Do not fail to write me a long letter and remember your promise that "when you hear from me you will do all you can to make a suitable return". Tell your brother John I was exceedingly disappointed at not seeing him before I left Newcastle. Nevertheless the case of instruments has been frequently called into requisition and I hope to send him home a good series of bird skins.

With many thanks for your kind wishes,

I remain, my dear Hancock,

Yours sincerely,

Wm Kennett Loftus.

Ps You will oblige me by telling Mr Radford that I have written to you.

CHAPTER FOUR

Letter 13, Baghdad, 23 May 1849

My dear Cousin,

Your acceptable letter of the 5th April reached me yesterday and I hasten to reply by the post which leaves for Stambul today. I have already written a long letter to Mr A. Hancock and asked him to let you see it so that I have little more to add except on business. I am glad to hear the day for the spring meeting proved fine, tho' I had expected rather larger receipts than you say were taken. I mentioned I think in one of my former letters that I thought the admission should have been 2/- & not 1/6. However, all has I am sure been done for the best. With regard to Brown's behaviour it is only in a piece with the whole of his former conduct and I am sorry that he had the refreshments. After this specimen you will not I think be inclined to let it to him another year. I am the more and more convinced that I was correct in my calculations and I really hope you will carry out the plan you propose of taking careful observations next race week.[46] I fear this will not reach you in time or I should strongly urge the necessity of this being done. Those parties too who were so kind as to bear evidence in my favour I wished to have free admission this year, but this I dare say you have thought of as I expressed my wish to this effect before I left Newcastle. I am truly sorry that there should have been any unpleasantness between Gray and Brown, but I am sure that the former will for my sake take no notice of his abuse. I am sorry that it was for me that he had to put up with it, but I am sure that Gray is a man of too good sense to be long annoyed by it. I am equally disgusted with you at Brown's conduct, as after all the kindness he has invariably received I did not expect this from him. However he will sooner or later meet with his reward. Other points in your last letter I have previously attended to. To answer your former one:- The Russians' fleet and Count Titon affair I had full knowledge of from the best authority but as it was not publicly known I did not consider myself at liberty to mention it: the Turkish Empire cannot long hold together. It is now in the last stage of decay unless some means are soon taken to bring matters round. I mentioned

---

46   Race Week at Newcastle Races was a major event in the Newcastle calendar.

in Hancock's letter the affairs that are taking place here. Last evening I learned that the Commander in Chief sent by the Pasha of Baghdad to punish the Arabs of Hillah will not act against them till he knows the justness of the quarrel. The Pasha of Mosul has been removed for his oppression, partly I believe on the representations of Col. W. These are moves in the right direction and it is to be hoped that they will continue. It is probable that this Pasha who was the cause of the massacre at Kerbala a few years back will have to go also. English influence is not wanting to effect so desirable an end! Under a good Government this country might again become one of the most favor'd spots on the surface of the globe. The dismissal of the P. of Mosul has given general satisfaction and gained another laurel for the caps of the English as it is pretty well understood that it is partly thro' our means. I am glad that my letters afford you any pleasure, tho' written off hurriedly as they are. I have no time to correct mistakes and must beg you will excuse all such, which I know are frequent. Major Rawlinson had not previously seen Layard's book till I lent him mine. The impressions brought by the Col. for the Major from Kouyunjik are quite new and will throw further light on the history of Assyria. Layard has at last got a paid attache'ship & is I hear expected to commence further excavations in September. The country is full of mounds and many valuable records lie buried within them as perfect as on the day of their erection. The Major is a first rate Eastern scholar and works hard the whole day long. We shall no doubt have the results of his researches shortly before the public. Read Ross's account of his journey to Al Hadhr [Hatra] in the London Geographical Journal[47] and also Major R's into Kurdistan[48] if you feel inclined to run thro' the country to which we are shortly going. I am delighted to hear so good an account of my brother Jack.[49] I was sure he would realize all our expectations.

---

47 J Ross, 'Notes on two journeys from Baghdad to the ruins of Al Hadhr in Mesopotamia in 1836 and 1837', *Journal of the Royal Geographical Society* vol 9 (1839), pp 443–70.
48 H C Rawlinson, 'Notes on a journey from Tabriz, through Persian Kurdistan, to the Ruins of Takhti-Soleiman, and from thence by Zenjan and Ṭarom, to Gílan, in October and November, 1838, with a memoir on the site of the Atropatenian Ecbatana', *Journal of the Royal Geographical Society* vol 10 (1840), pp 1–64.
49 Alfred John Loftus, born 1836. Known as Jack, he went to sea at the age of 13. His first voyage was to India.

CHAPTER FOUR

If you will send me his address in your next letter I shall feel obliged as I will write to him in case of his going to India again. We are now within 12 days steaming of Bombay. You ask if you should continue to address letters for me to Constantinople. I think so, as it keeps my name in remembrance at the Foreign Office, tho' I should get them a fortnight sooner if sent to the address of Col. W. at Cocks & Co's I believe. I find I must conclude as post time approaches and I must [?] be off to the Col with my letters or the Enclosure may be sealed.

Pray do not fail to give my best remembrance to Mrs R., Mr Ridley, Edward & Mrs M, Mrs Whitfield, Mrs Lough & my good friend Ben Green whose accident I am truly sorry to learn. He will I hope soon recover and write me a long epistle in answer to mine from Diarbekir [Diyarbakır]. I shall probably write my next to your namesake in London. I have long intended writing to him. I have no doubt you have now and then mentioned me in your letters to him. Do not forget me when you next write.

Now I must close.

Believe me, my dear cousin,

Yours ever sincerely,

Wm Kennett Loftus

I find I have omitted Mr Gray in my list of remembrances. Tho' last not least deserving.

Letter 14, Baghdad, 5 June 1849

Dear friends at Newcastle,

Stationed as we are in this place I have little to communicate in this letter. With the exception of the Queen's birthday all has gone on very quietly. Shortly after sunrise on May 24 that event was announced by the "Jacks" on board the E.S.C. vessel by three hearty British cheers. The vessel had taken up her station immediately in front of the windows of the Residency with

Major Rawlinson's yacht and a row of boats in [the] rear all trimmed out in full rig for the occasion. Immediately after breakfast, a Levee was held in the reception room, which is almost covered with glass ornaments on the walls & ceilings. The Major and Colonel attended by our party in full dress received the congratulations of all the respectable inhabitants of Baghdad. They entered the room in parties of the same religion together, kissed the Major's hand, paid some little compliment, eat sweetmeats, smoked pipes, drank coffee & retired. Little was said by any one of them, but their various picturesque costumes and different castes of countenance afforded great amusement to those of our party who had not previously seen such an exhibition. There were the Armenian priest in full canonicals, with his silver headed staff, accompanied by his Christian flock. The Greek priest, with his – Turks, Arabs, Persians, Indians and natives of Ceylon – the last with their dark skins, intelligent faces, large expressive eyes & white teeth, make it their no small boast that they are "subjects of Victoria" ! Some of [the] turbans of the Baghdadees were of large size, standing out a foot & more from the forehead. The Jewish turban was rather peculiar – a red fez, raised high above the head was bound with a rich drab cashmere shawl with elegant border. Shortly after 12 Capt. Jones & the officers of the vessel arrived in uniform and immediately a royal salute of 21 guns was fired from the vessel & returned from the major's yacht in first rate style. Standing at the door the effect of the whole must have been very fine:– in the elegant room sat the party assembled in rich uniforms & costumes, while thro' the open windows the gaily trimmed vessel could be seen sending forth the loud thunder of her guns which rolled thro' the date tree groves in the background. As if to add more enthusiasm if more were wanting to the enjoyment of the day the Indian post arrived with the news that [the] British arms had again been victorious and that 16,000 Sikhs had laid down their arms and given up 40 pieces of ordnance. Our dinner party consisted of all the English in Baghdad (among whom was one English lady, Mrs Vicars the missionary's wife), Aristarche the Pasha's dragoman and the Nawab – in all 22. After the Queen's health, the vessel fired another round of 21 guns in honour of the late victories. After dinner we proceeded to the terrace on the top of the house to join the ladies who began to arrive about 8.

CHAPTER FOUR

The terrace was carpeted, with sofas & chairs around the walls while the railings of the court was illuminated by coloured lamps. The Pasha sent his band who played really well for Turks, and enlivened the evening. At 10, rockets and fireworks were going on below in front of the house. This done, "the Jacks" gave three hearty British cheers for the Queen & victory which were answered by the English on the terrace. At 11 a smart fellow from the vessel appeared in his uniform on the "Deck" of the Terrace. The picture of an English sailor, with the union jack in one hand and hat in the other. All the English gathered round him and while he waved on high "the flag that's braved a thousand years" we joined to the chorus of the "Battle and the breeze". At 12 we sat down to supper, where every delicacy was served up. And now a word on the ladies of Baghdad. Few and far between are the beauties – two faces, which otherwise would have passed as pretty in England, were so pale & sickly from the too frequent use of the baths, that it was evident their beauty was soon doomed to suffer decay and they would become premature old women. It is "the thing" in Baghdad [for] the ladies to stain their hair with henna, so that they all appear red haired and at the same time they all paint [their hands?] more or less. The fillet or band of gold round their heads is pretty, while the dress is loose and decidedly elegant bound round the waist with a richly silver-ornamented belt. As for their manners I cannot say much. It is the custom for women to sit apart from the men.

Therefore, when anyone was introduced and ventured to sit down beside them, he suddenly found the lady's back turned to him, and not a word would she utter. Dr Hyslop presented a bouquet to one, which she accepted – but judge his horror & dismay, when he saw her lift up her leg and put it under her rump! He was once called in to see a lady, who was ill, but he could not prevail on her to show her tongue, least [sic] as he discovered afterwards, he should find out her age by her teeth as we do a horse's age! The only thing that appeared to excite any interest among these ladies was the lascivious dance –the national Turkish dance! For anything beyond this they have no mind. Tired and disgusted I laid down upon an empty sofa & fell asleep, to be only wakened by the Major's asking if I was going to sleep there all night! I found we were alone, all the rest having vanished, and so with them the Queen's birthday for 1849. I said in my last, that I thought of going with the vessel to Busrah, but was dissuaded, and am now glad that I did not. She got back yesterday with 5 fevers on board, and they all represent the heat as intense. The Russians arrived on the 28th May and we hear today that Dervish Pasha (the Turk) is at Mosul, where he intends staying for some time, as he has received no instructions from his government!!! Jafar Khan too has betaken himself to Kerbala [?], "to purify the soul", he says. The Col says D- on his soul, and with some justice if they intend to treat us in this manner. He is today giving them a stiffish letter. He told me yesterday that there was every prospect of our starting for Yushade [?] and the cool mountain shade, but this behaviour of the Turks will frustrate our plans, I fear. By the next post I hope to tell you more clearly of our movements. Heaven forbid we should stop here all the summer, as we are already nearly roasted. We now all sleep on the Terrace and it is delicious – a cool wind always blows at night. This almost compensates for the hot day. I am going ahead collecting, and have capital assistants, everyone taking an interest in my work, and sending grist to the mill. I have taught my servant to skin birds, and am much pleased with him generally. Dr Ross has this morning received as a present a Persian hunting leopard, which is now pacing about in the veranda outside my door, without any fastening. He gives a growl now and then but is I think pretty tame. If we cannot get away from here soon, I shall endeavour to visit some of the mountains myself with a proper escort, as I have much to do in geology & I consider I am wasting time & opportunity here.

I conclude with best remembrance to all friends & believe me

Sincerely yours

Wm Kennett Loftus

Letter 15, Baghdad, 6 June 1849

My dear Cousin,

By yesterday's post from Constantinople I received two letters from you, one dated April 25th and the other without date but with the N'castle postmark of Apr 15th. For these accept my very best thanks, more especially for the

CHAPTER FOUR

hints therein contained as to Book concocting and Paper writing. I keep a regular journal and on my return, should there be anything in it sufficiently interesting for publication we will then consider the matter. To make a little money by this means would be certainly desirable, and I intend to keep this in view. Our work will not be within 300 miles of Nineveh & Layard's researches, yet who knows what may yet be undiscovered in the yet unvisited mountains. With the exception of, perhaps, Wood, I do not think any of our party have any idea of publishing unless Glascott writes papers for the Geographical Soc. I have been considering whether, as I intend sending now and then as opportunity happens to the Geological Society, we should make a joint series, i.e. in the event of his writing. Sir Henry will of course read anything he considers worthy [of] the attention of our society and I have promised in my letters to him to send all the information I think worthy [of] his notice. I always intended keeping my name known in the Geological Society. Your plan of sending matter monthly to some of the journals is not I think feasible, first because my collections now begin to take much time & secondly because I do not know whether I should be justified in writing, as my instructions say "I am at liberty to do so on my return". As to geological matter that is different as I am requested to communicate with Sir H. De la Beche. Many thanks nevertheless to you for your kind suggestions. Your report of Glynn's interview with Sir H. is most pleasing to me. I am fully aware that I have an excellent friend, who has it in his power to push me forward. I am proud of his high opinion of me and depend upon it that I shall stir every nerve within me to prove myself worthy of it. Thru' his and Col. Williams' influence I hope all will be well, and that I shall have no cause to repent the step I have taken. It certainly is a severe trial to be separated so long from my wife and children, but we both believe it to be for our good. We must look forward with hope for the future. In a letter I received from a friend at the last meeting of the Palaeontographical Society, I find that Bowerbank in returning a vote of thanks to the Honorary Secretaries made especial mention of me, and my services. I do not at all regret the trouble I took in that matter as it may eventually be of service. The naval gentleman Glynn met in the Exeter mail must have been my old friend Capt. Russell of the Erin, who did lend me his maps of the Tendos [?] locality. He is a most gentlemanly nice fellow, and he was exceedingly attentive to me his only passenger.

THE LETTERS

You will be all glad to learn that Layard is again about to pursue his investigations at Nineveh etc. Many discoveries are yet to be made. I hope we shall see him in the Kurdish Mountains. So you have been reading Frazer? [sic].[50] His account of the plague & inundation of Baghdad in 1831 is I understand it not overstretched. The ruins still visible on the desert side of the city attest the havoc which was then made. In the course of a few years, and after a few more inundations as this last, the place must be forsaken or the water will destroy it, as each succeeding deposit is raising the level of the desert above that of the town. In fact, but for the dyke it would have been washed away. The walls in the interior of the city are melting away & falling in many places & part of one of the bazaars came down a day or two since. By this post I have written Gray & Mather, to the last intimating that Sir H. De la Beche will have some money to pay him on my behalf. The Russians are foolishly going off to Babylon and Dodson, who has been seriously ill of fever, is to accompany them. Our party declines going on account of the heat. The Birs,[51] or tower of Babel as it is supposed, will turn out to be no tower of Babel after all. Major Rawlinson has a brick from it, which has the name of 'Nebuchadnezzar' distinctly written on it in arrow headed characters! So much for somebody's forced hypothesis concerning it.

I am glad to hear that there is a likelihood of the road to the stand [grandstand] being put into a good state. It has long been most disgraceful. I hope Capt. Gilbert will like the place. The roof ought frequently to be looked at and the chimneys swept every quarter without fail. You will now be about preparing for the week – May it prove a fortunate one. Your account of the hospital arbitration is not pleasing news, yet as there is no help for it, it must be borne, but 146 £ is a large sum extra. I hope the Railway Company will settle matters now without fail, and let you have what now remains to be paid. I should like to have a statement of how I stand in this and other matters.

---

50   Presumably James Baillee Fraser (1783–1856), who wrote *Travels in Koordistan, Mesopotamia, etc, with sketches of the character and manners of the Koordish and Arab tribes* (London 1840) and *Mesopotamia and Assyria* (Edinburgh and London 1841).
51   Birs Nimrud (Borsippa).

CHAPTER FOUR

Your balance will I fear be heavy against me. I must now conclude. By the bye if you should see Albany Hancock, tell him that I have just seen a composition cast of his brother's figure of the "sleeping beauty".[52] It has come from Bombay for the Major, and is much admired.

Kind regards to Mrs R, Mistress Ridley, Mrs Whitfield, Mr Lough, Mr Green, Glynn and any enquirers. Many thanks for the papers. I see old Wolff[53] is to lecture. He is considered an infernal old rascal in the East [?].

Ever yours most truly,

Wm Kennett Loftus

Letter 16, Gherrara near Baghdad, 17 June 1849

My dear Hancock,

I flatter myself that you are glad to hear now and then of my proceedings and as I have a little in the natural history line to communicate my short letter will be more interesting. On Tuesday we paid a visit to the ancient ruins of Ctesiphon & Seleucia (of which I have given a short account in a letter to Mr Benj. Green which I doubt not you will see) and found among the walls and among the bushes surrounding a strange monster of a spider a sketch of which I enclose. I have an idea that it is new, at any rate I have not seen it elsewhere. Can you by any means ascertain if such is the case or not? The surface of the body is shining and appears like enamel or china. The thorax is exceedingly like a spalangus in the marking and covered there with minute hair. The eggs are deposited in a truncated cone inverted and suspended from the walls etc. by the web. As I have only this sketch perhaps you will be good

---

52   John Hancock (1808–90) was a well-known ornithologist, artist and taxidermist working out of Newcastle; he produced some famous taxidermy mounts, one of which was shown at the 1851 Great Exhibition. See also Ch. 1, n.8.

53   Possibly the missionary and traveller Joseph Wolff (1795–1862). For a recent article on Wolff, see H R Leach, *Asian Affairs*, vol 38, 2007, pp. 218–336.

enough to return it. I have put several specimens in spirits but their colour is quite changed. Can you tell me of any mode by which I can preserve spiders etc. not in spirits? If anything casts up which I think interesting I will with your leave send a sketch for your inspection, tho' I cannot expect to sketch like you [sic] delicate nudibranches. I hinted in my former letter of 23rd ult. that I hoped the Newcastle Museum would come in for a share of my spoils. I may now say that such will be the case as Col. Williams has left the disposal of the duplicates to myself after supplying the Br. Museum with a full series. I am therefore omitting no opportunities of procuring as many specimens as possible of each species. I have now collected 109 species of insects which for such an arid country is not amiss. Baghdad was becoming such a furnace that we have flitted to a country house built of bricks and where alas! we must remain till the end of October as it is impossible to be out at midday. Our rooms are infested with rats, geckos, snakes, fleas, 5 sp[ecies] of wasps, scorpions and flies [?], while in the garden at night we have jackals howling as if the last day were arrived. The wild boar lies hidden in the neighbouring marshes, and we shall in times, as the waters abate, have a little hunting. We have seen none of these or of the lion of the Tigris as yet. One third of the inhabitants of Baghdad are laid down with fever and at this instant only three are able to work out of twenty four of our servants who are lying in the doorway unable to move and glad to get the slightest breath of wind. I thought I had it myself on Friday as I felt exceedingly ill and am now very weak but the Doctor says it is not fever. All the rest of the party are healthy.

You will I am sure excuse a longer letter and all mistakes. Remember me most kindly to your brother John and all our mutual friends and believe me, my dear Hancock,

Yours most truly,

Wm Kennett Loftus.

P.S. Should you be writing to Charlesworth or Mr Wood of Richmond pray remember me. I have not yet had any time to write them.

1. Photograph of W.K. Loftus, courtesy of The Literary and Philosophical Society, Newcastle upon Tyne.

2. Engraving showing bust of W.K. Loftus (from Welford 1895: 69).

3. The notebooks with copies of the Loftus letters, courtesy Luke Tredinnick.

> Letters and Copies of letters written by
> Mr William Kenneth Loftus to friends at
> Newcastle-on-Tyne, between Jan.y 29th 1849
> and May 24th 1851. from
>   Southampton
>   Off Cape Trafalgar.
>   Off Island of Pantalaria
>   Constantinople
>   Diarbekir
>   Mosul
>   Baghdad. Vol. 2 - Pages 33 to 45.
>   Gherrara.
>   Mahommera - Persia
>   Bussora.
>   Dizful - Persia -
>   Mountains of Mungerrah.
>   Kirmanshah - Persia.
>   Summit of Mungerrah Range, Dizful, Persia
>   Susa.
>   Mungerrah.
>   Hamadan, - Persia.
>   Shiraz
>   Ispahan. ___ Vol. 3 - Pages 41 + 58
>   Kirrind - Persia.

4. List of contents inside notebook vol. 1, courtesy Luke Tredinnick.

Hamadan, Persia
Oct 25th 1850.

My Dear James.

I have only time to say that we arrived here all right on the 22nd after a most delightful journey from Kirmanshah. My hands are quite full enough of work without attempting to write duplicates. I have very little time to complete my notes on the road as our stages are long & at night taking latitudes fills up the time after dinner till tired out we tumble into bed. The Geology of the Kuh Elivend (Orontes) is highly interesting granite elevating Slate & Mica rocks but I am much disappointed in the height of the peaks but magnificent Mountain Scenery is not to be expected when the country rises by a succession of steps from the plain of Susiana. I cannot guess the height of Hamadan as our Barometers are most unfortunately broken and our spare ones at Busra. This is a sad loss to us & all we can now do is to guess heights. Tomorrow we start for Isfahan 300 miles ride! About the 15th we expect letters and you shall hear from me. You must now excuse me as I have much to do & write before I go to bed. With best regards to all friends I remain in haste

Faithfully Yours
Wm Kennett Loftus.

5. Copy of Letter 48 written to James Radford from Hamadan, 25 October 1850, courtesy Luke Tredinnick.

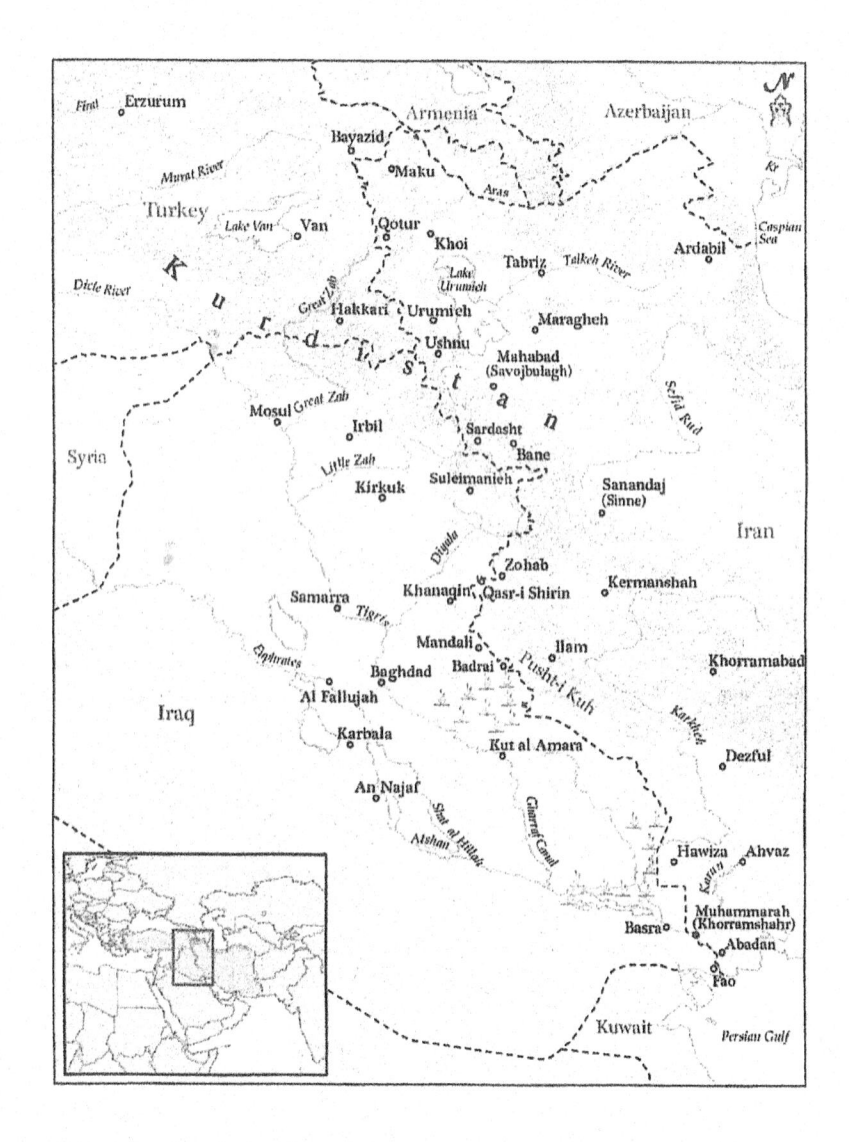

6. Map showing modern boundary between Iraq and Iran (from Ateş 2013: map 1 on p. xxi).

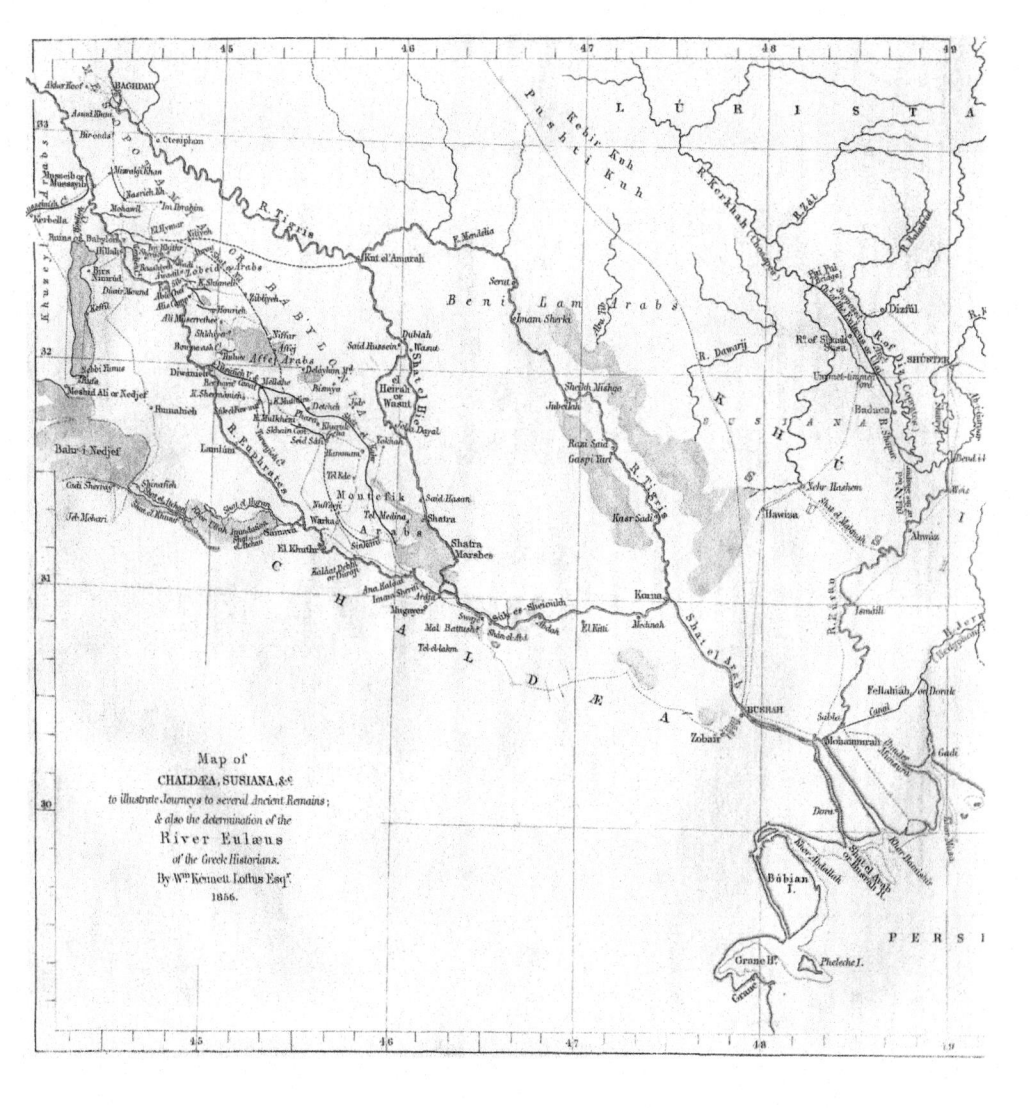

7. Map of Chaldaea and Susiana to illustrate journeys by W.K. Loftus (from Loftus 1857).

8. General Sir William Fenwick Williams (1800–1883) (engraving by D.J. Pound, from a photograph by J. Watkins). Private collection.

9. Henry Adrian Churchill (1828–1886) (engraving by D.J. Pound, from a photograph by J. Watkins). Private collection.

10. The 'Lion of Babylon', about 8th century BC. Photo by J.E. Curtis.

11. View of Tell Hammam. Drawing by H.A. Churchill, courtesy Trustees of the British Museum (*Drawings in Babylonia by W.K. Loftus and H.A. Churchill*, pl. I) (Photo ref. Archive_S22-022).

12. View of Tell Ede. Drawing by H.A. Churchill, courtesy Trustees of the British Museum (*Drawings in Babylonia*, pl. III) (Photo ref. Archive_S22-024).

13. The Buwariyya ruin (ziggurat) at Warka. Drawing by H.A. Churchill, courtesy Trustees of the British Museum (*Drawings in Babylonia*, pl. IV) (Photo ref. Archive_S22-025).

14. Façade of a temple building at Warka, *c.* 3000 BC. Drawing by H.A. Churchill, courtesy Trustees of the British Museum (*Drawings in Babylonia*, pl. XIV) (Photo ref. Archive_S22-035).

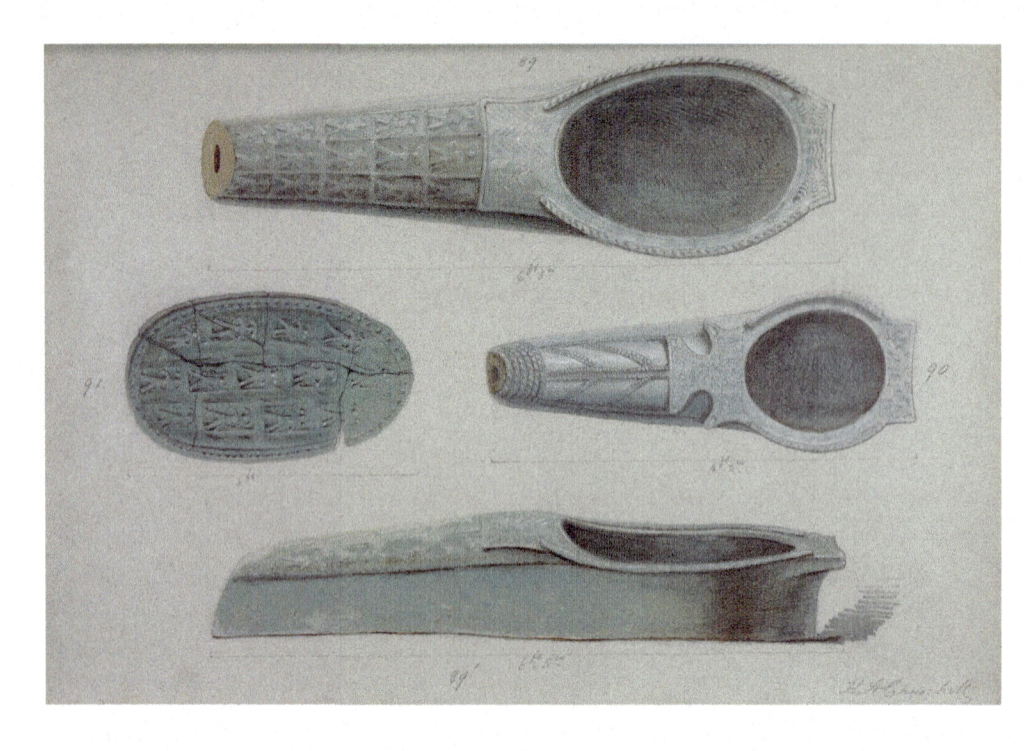

15. Parthian slipper coffins from Warka, 1st–3rd century AD. Drawing by H.A. Churchill, courtesy Trustees of the British Museum (*Drawings in Babylonia*, pl. XIII) (Photo ref. Archive_S22-034).

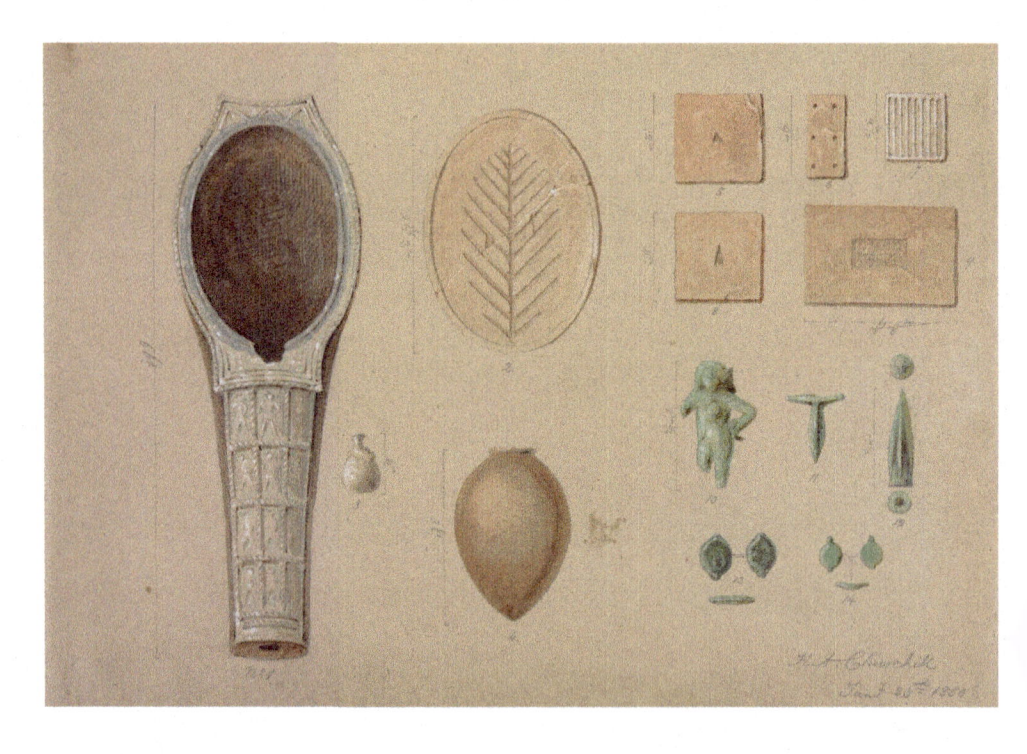

16. Parthian slipper coffin and various antiquities from Warka. Drawing by H.A. Churchill, courtesy Trustees of the British Museum (*Drawings in Babylonia*, pl. V) (Photo ref. Archive_S22-026).

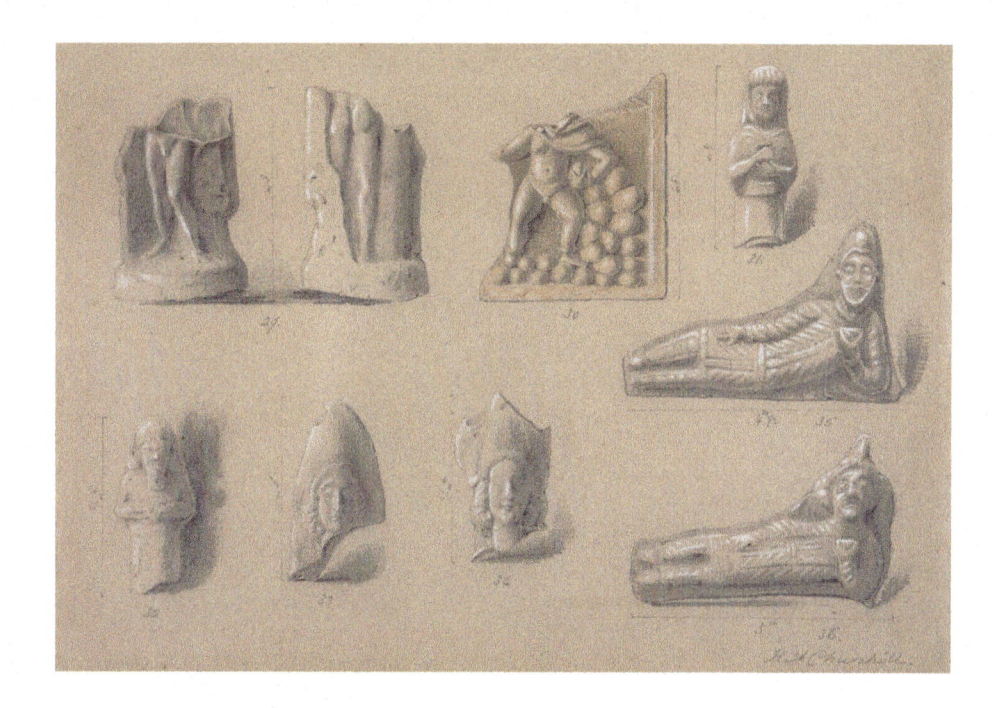

17. Hellenistic and Parthian terracotta figurines from Warka, 2nd century BC – 3rd century AD. Drawing by H.A. Churchill, courtesy Trustees of the British Museum (*Drawings in Babylonia*, pl. VIII) (Photo ref. Archive_S22-029).

18. Fragment of coffin and terracotta figurines from Warka. Drawing by H.A. Churchill, courtesy Trustees of the British Museum (*Drawings in Babylonia*, pl. IX) (Photo ref. Archive_S22-030).

19. Parthian pottery vessels from Warka, 1st–3rd century AD. Drawing by H.A. Churchill, courtesy Trustees of the British Museum (*Drawings in Babylonia*, pl. XI) (Photo ref. Archive_S22-032).

20. View of Tell Mugeyer (Ur). Drawing by H.A. Churchill, courtesy Trustees of the British Museum (*Drawings in Babylonia*, pl. XVII) (Photo ref. Archive_S22-039).

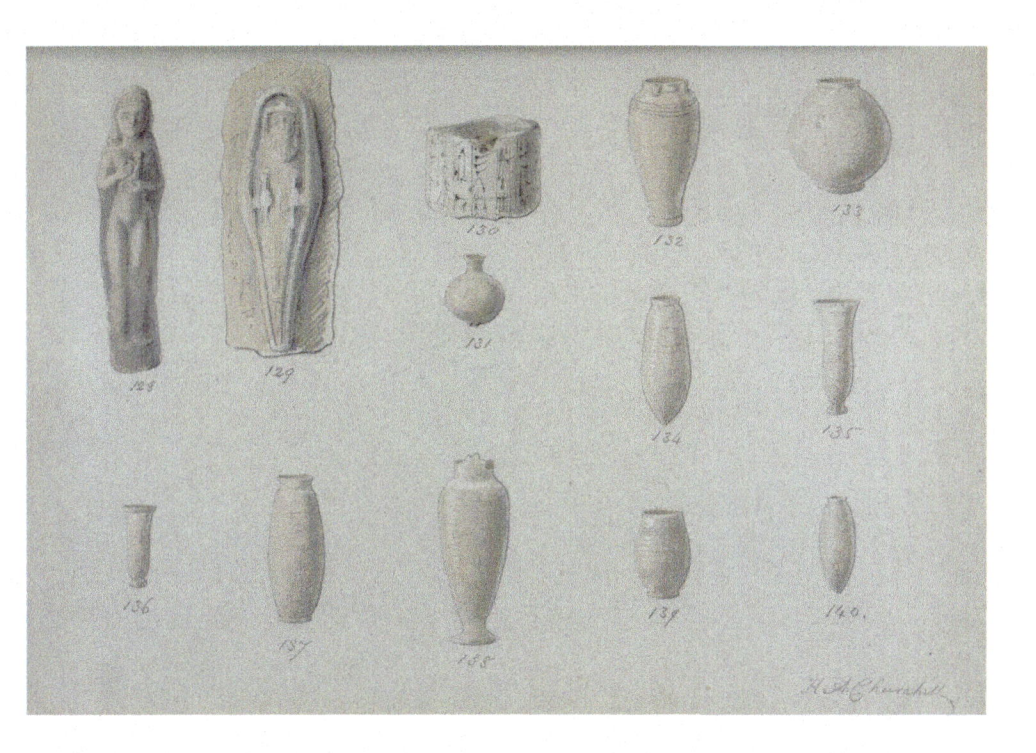

21. Babylonian antiquities from Sinkara (Larsa). Drawing by H.A. Churchill, courtesy Trustees of the British Museum (*Drawings in Babylonia*, pl. XVI) (Photo ref. Archive_S22-037).

22. Achaemenid column capital with bull protomes, side view, Susa, 5th–4th century BC. Drawing by H.A. Churchill, courtesy Trustees of the British Museum. (*Susa Drawings*, pl. 7) (Photo ref. Loftus_drawings-3).

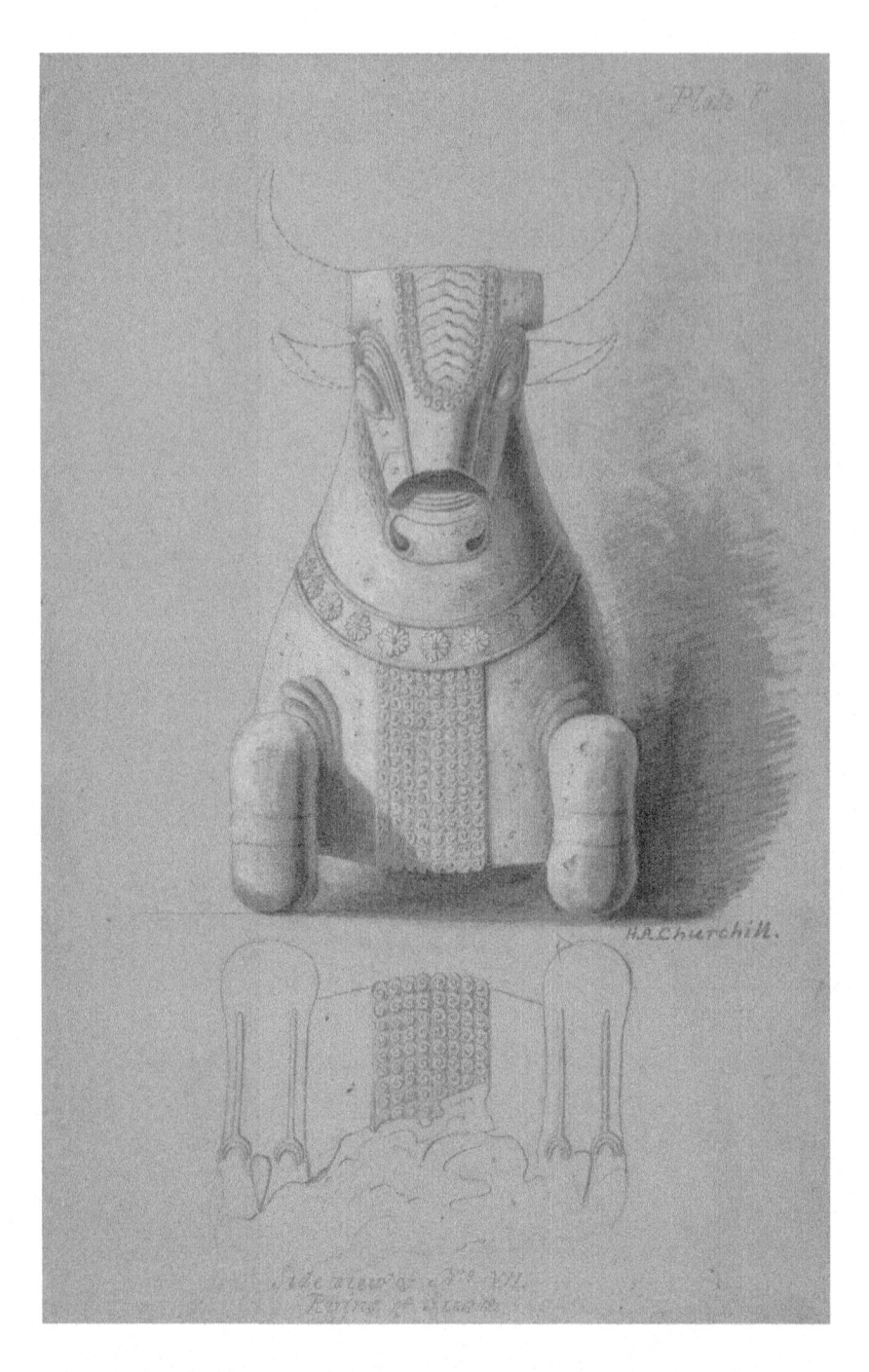

23. Achaemenid column capital with bull protomes, front view, Susa, 5th–4th century BC. Drawing by H.A. Churchill, courtesy Trustees of the British Museum. (*Susa Drawings*, pl. 8) (Photo ref. Loftus_drawings-4).

24. Achaemenid column base and column drum, Susa, 5th–4th century BC. Drawing by H.A. Churchill, courtesy Trustees of the British Museum. (*Susa Drawings*, pl. 1) (Photo ref. Loftus_drawings-2).

25. Achaemenid column bases, Susa, 5th–4th century BC. Drawing by H.A. Churchill, courtesy Trustees of the British Museum. (*Susa Drawings*, pl. 14) (Photo ref. Loftus_drawings-6).

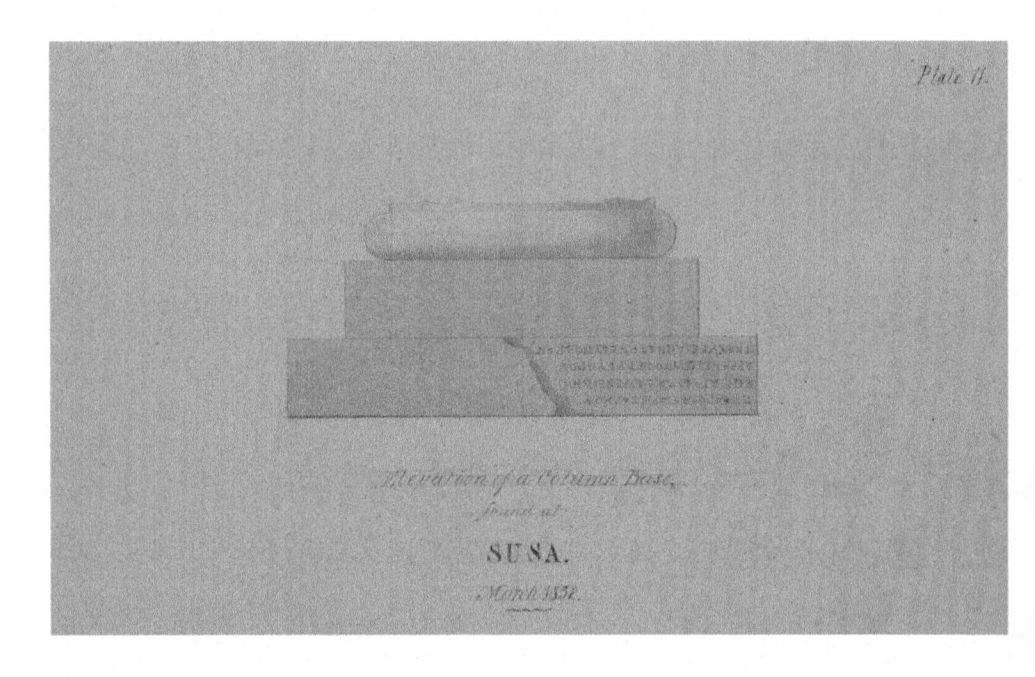

26. Achaemenid column base with added Greek inscription, Susa, 4th–3rd century AD. Drawing by H.A. Churchill, courtesy Trustees of the British Museum. (*Susa Drawings*, pl. 11) (Photo ref. Loftus_drawings-5).

27. Terracotta figurines from Susa, Elamite, about 1200 BC. Drawing by H.A. Churchill, courtesy Trustees of the British Museum (*Drawings in Babylonia*, pl. XXVI).

28. Grotto at Taq-e Bustan showing Sasanian king Khusro II (AD 591–628). Photo by J.E. Curtis.

29. Graffiti at Taq-e Bustan with names of Col. Williams R.A., 1850, J. Olquin FRCSE, H.A. Churchill, and W.K. Loftus. Photo by J.E. Curtis.

30. Letter from W.K. Loftus to James Radford about the publication of his book on *Travels and Researches in Chaldea and Susiana*, courtesy Frances Radford.

31. Letter from Sir Henry Layard to James Radford expressing condolences on the death of W.K. Loftus, courtesy Frances Radford.

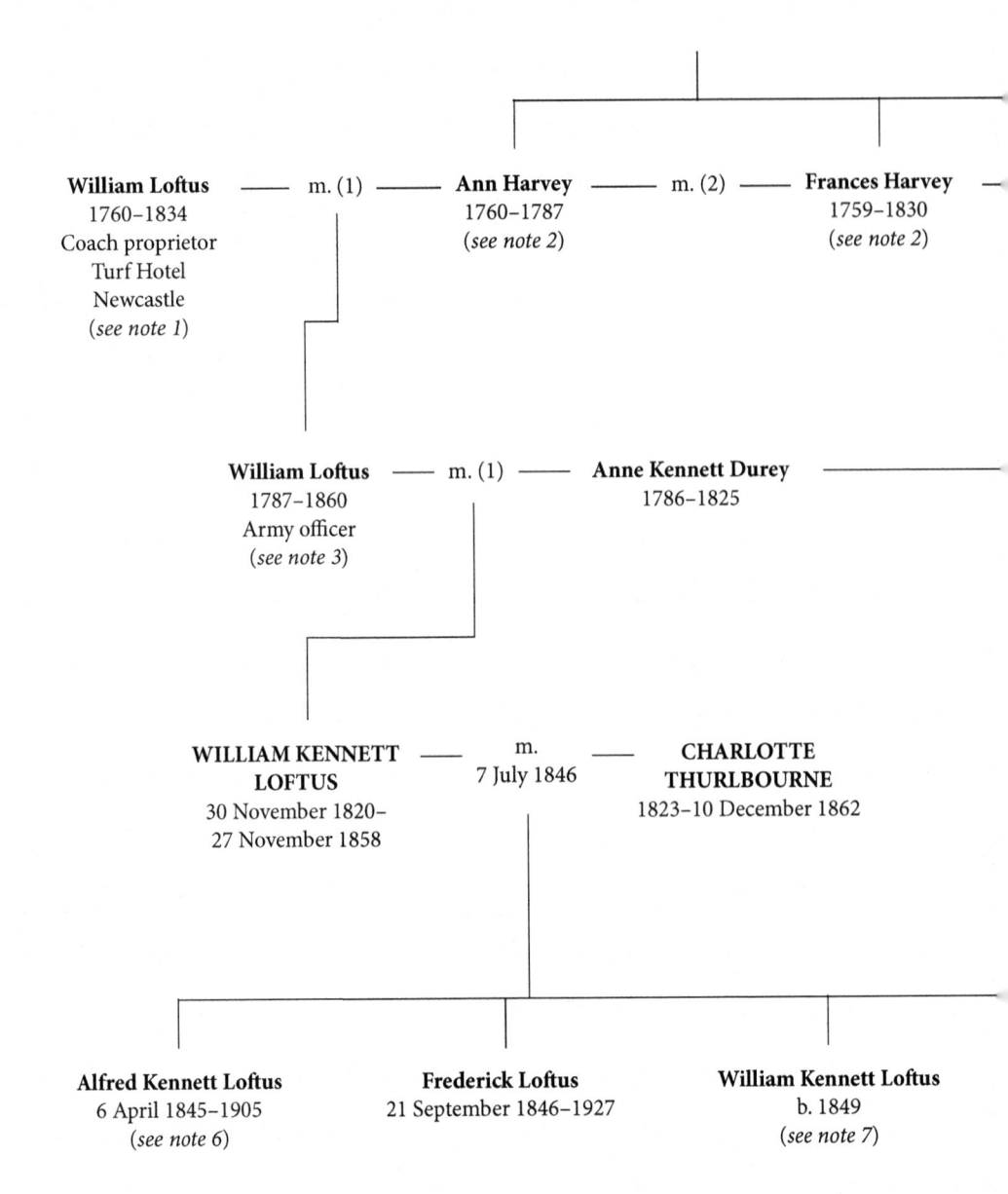

```
William Loftus ── m. (1) ── Ann Harvey ── m. (2) ── Frances Harvey
  1760–1834                  1760–1787                1759–1830
Coach proprietor           (see note 2)             (see note 2)
  Turf Hotel
  Newcastle
 (see note 1)
                │
                │
      William Loftus ── m. (1) ── Anne Kennett Durey
        1787–1860                    1786–1825
       Army officer
        (see note 3)
                │
                │
    WILLIAM KENNETT ──── m. ──── CHARLOTTE
        LOFTUS          7 July 1846   THURLBOURNE
   30 November 1820–                1823–10 December 1862
   27 November 1858
                │
      ┌─────────┼─────────┐
Alfred Kennett Loftus   Frederick Loftus   William Kennett Loftus
 6 April 1845–1905    21 September 1846–1927      b. 1849
   (see note 6)                                 (see note 7)
```

32. Concise genealogical tree showing children of W.K. Loftus and his relationship with James Radford (information from family papers and genealogical information on www). See also accompanying notes on pp. 242–3.

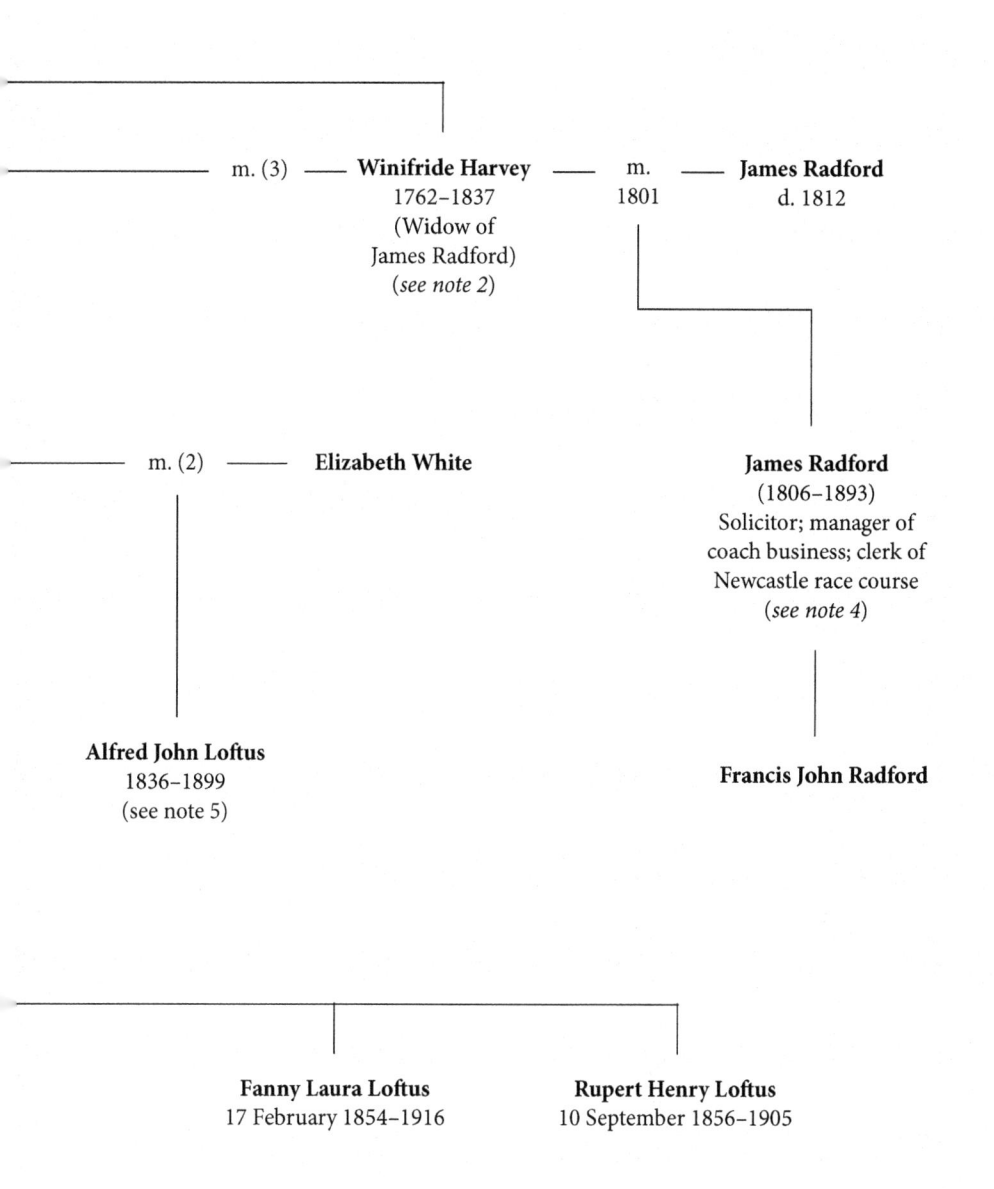

m. (3) —— **Winifride Harvey** —— m. —— **James Radford**
1762–1837 1801 d. 1812
(Widow of
James Radford)
(*see note 2*)

m. (2) —— **Elizabeth White**

James Radford
(1806–1893)
Solicitor; manager of
coach business; clerk of
Newcastle race course
(*see note 4*)

Alfred John Loftus
1836–1899
(see note 5)

Francis John Radford

Fanny Laura Loftus   **Rupert Henry Loftus**
17 February 1854–1916   10 September 1856–1905

CHAPTER FOUR

Letter 17, Gherrara near Baghdad, 18 June 1849

My dear Ben,

As by tomorrow's post I half expect to receive a letter from you in answer to mine from Diarbekir [Diyarbakır], I sit down to anticipate its arrival. Mr Radford or Mather would of course let you hear of our proceedings and I therefore need not repeat what I have written, but proceed at once to our doings since last post day. On Tuesday morning last at 11 o'clock, accompanied by the Russian Colonel, we went on board the EIC vessel the "Nitocris" (last queen of Babylon) and steamed down the Tigris to visit the ruins of Seleucia & Ctesiphon, the once magnificent cities of the Sassanian kings. Of their history I must say nothing, but refer you to History. From Baghdad nothing is to be seen on either side but a vast desert, as flat as a pancake, with here and there a black tent of an Arab family. At 2 p.m. we reached the ruins [of] Seleucia on the R & Ctesiphon on the L bank. Of the former only the remains of the outer wall are visible. Of the latter great city, all that remains from the devastation committed by one of the Pashas of Baghdad who pulled down every other ruin to procure bricks for building Baghdad, is the celebrated – and justly so – Arch of Ctesiphon. "Jack and all its men couldn't pull it down." The building consists of the front facing the east, consisting entirely of ornamental arches, built of brick, for the sake of giving strength. In the centre of this rises the most magnificent arch I ever beheld, 106 feet in height rising to the very summit of the brickwork and extending backwards to a distance I did not measure. Tho' it has existed for so many centuries, if fairly dealt with, it will exist yet for ages to come, a monument of architecture, the surprise of all beholders. The arch springs from enormous beams of wood which are as perfect as when placed there. Would that you could have been here with us! I know well what your state of feeling would have been – somewhat akin to what you experienced at first glimpse of those glorious Alps, whose valleys and snowy passes you and I enjoyed so much enjoyed together. My companions are all good fellows in their way but without that enthusiasm which one like you or I can feel. I cannot therefore give vent to the excess of my feelings, but bottle the same up in my own breast. Altho' I have now visited some of the most remarkable places in the world, Constantinople, Nineveh, Baghdad, yet I must say again that they have not half the charm for me that I experienced in the fresh mountain air and amidst the snows of the higher ranges. Nature for me has far more charms than art, however much I may enjoy the latter. What would I now give to be off to the mountains of Tohab! [?] Alas! It is impossible. Here we must remain till October or beginning of November on account of the heat which scorches everything and to be out at mid-day or after 9 a.m. would be utter madness. Dervish Pasha too has not yet arrived and Jafar Khan (the Persian) has not returned from Kerbala. To resume – we spent the day under the shade of the arch, [and] returned to the "Nitocris" at sunset when we dined off a most sumptuous spread, sang "the battle of the breeze", drank to "Little Vie and Big Nick" & kept the game alive till 12 p.m. when I took up my berth on the top of the paddle box, slept like a top & found myself by 4 next morning at this place which is a ride of about 4 miles from the walls of Baghdad which is now become a furnace. We have taken a country house consisting of three rooms & <u>in</u>conveniences, all built of brick and mud mortar. The centre room has an open arch on one side facing the garden which as well as the windows are filled up with a sort of lattice work of camel's thorn on which water is constantly thrown, which produces a delightful coolness in the air of the room. On the bank of the river our tents are erected surrounded by the same device so that we contrive to spin out the day some way or another. Our beds are placed on the terrace on the top of the house where under the bright canopy of the heavens & surrounded by a gauze curtain we pass the most delightful nights covered by a single sheet & fanned by a cooling breeze from the north which sets in about 9 p.m. No sleep after 5. The sun rises red hot and all at once, and turns us out, nolens, volens, unless you wish to be found burned to a cinder in a few minutes. Our costumes during the day are very various, some appear only in shirts and trousers like ostlers, others in long night gowns and drawers, some in Turkish bags [?] and slippers, anything in fact for comfort. We have plenty of things to amuse us, books, snakes, scorpions, fleas, mosquitoes, rats, wasps, lizards! all are to be found in our three rooms !!! Habit is everything as we think nothing of it. As soon as we got here, all our servants (about 24) except two were floored with fever, and it was a most wretched scene to walk thro' the entrance & see the poor devils all prostrate & unable to move. On Friday

I thought I had got it myself but the Dr says no. He gave me an opium pill and all Saturday & yesterday I lay on the sofa but am better today, tho' as weak as tho' I had been laid up for a month. A little bile I think. All the rest are as hearty as possible. At Baghdad the fever is very bad and about one third of the whole place is at this moment down with it. Major Rawlinson our excellent host had a severe attack before we left him, but this fever is not supposed to be dangerous & we live carefully. The post from Constantinople has this moment arrived, but by it not a single letter from England, tho' the government messenger had brought dispatches for the Embassy. It is supposed that matters being important they would not send private letters from the Foreign Office via Vienna, By the way, what a precious kick up the Hungarians are making. The Russians will be getting pegged into on all sides if the Georgians should rise. What will be the end of all this I wonder. We have nothing particular here. The Arabs are out and plundering in every direction as usual. 1 p.m. It is now getting very hot, so I shall conclude. At this time all my good friends will be busy preparing for the Race Week. Before the next post arrives all will have been finished yet I shall not hear the result till six weeks hence or more. By the bye at the beginning of Novr we expect [?] to proceed south to Mohammerah & probably take a trip to the ruins of Persepolis near Shiraz, thence run the boundary, reach Van or thereabouts in June & Ararat in the winter. The Col. also hopes to be able to return by Syria! In any case two years from my leaving England will not finish our work. This is my opinion contra the Col's who calculates on no disputes. I shall certainly have seen much in that time yet I feel as tho' banished for that time. However I will not say "die".

Give my best remembrances to all my kind friends around you & believe me when I say that I frequently think of the many acts of kindness I have received from you & them.

Salve, Adieu,

Yours most sincerely,

Wm Kennett Loftus

19th June, 2 o'clock

It is with great sorrow that I have just received notice of the death of my late excellent host Dr Ross. There was no room for me to sleep at Major Rawlinson's and I was quartered on his house. He has long been in a delicate state of health, and removed about a week ago to Capt Jones's of the "Nitocris" for change of air. He has been Surgeon to the residency for 17 years and had only tendered his resignation about a week [ago] on account of ill health. He is much respected and we all attend his funeral tomorrow morning at 6 o'clock. He was the author of several interesting papers in the Geographical Soc. Journal on the ruins of Al Hadhr [Hatra], Opis[54] & other ancient ruins. I used to go and sit in his room for hours hearing his descriptions.

You will oblige me by allowing my cousin and Mather to see my letter as well as any other mutual friends who may request so to do.

Letter 18, Gherrara near Baghdad, 3 July 1849

My dear James,

Your letters of May 13th & 20th reached me, with one from Mather, yesterday afternoon, for which I beg you both to accept my best thanks. You little know what pleasure is conveyed in a letter from England! We look forward to post days as boys at school do to the holidays! You would hear of me by last post from Green and Hancock. Little has occurred since then. We buried our poor friend Dr Ross in formal state as an officer in the EIC's service. Since then the fever has been raging in the city and throughout the whole country. Ride thro' the streets of Baghdad and you will see nine tenths of the population lying at their doors in a most pitiable state. They are dying at the rate of 100 a day even here. Every one of our servants (27) have been floored, 20 at a time. George is down a second time this morning. Garey our Commissariat is the only one of us who has caught it and he but slightly. The crew of the Nitocris

---

54   In the 19th century Seleucia-on-the-Tigris was thought to be on the site of ancient Opis.

CHAPTER FOUR

(66) were all on the deck at once and they had great difficulty in working the vessel down to Gherrara where she now lies about 300 yards below us. They lost a man last Saturday.

The Captain, the Dr & the Purser [?] are the only ones who have escaped. No doubt but the malaria arising from the inundation is the cause added to enormous amounts of water melons and cucumbers which the people live wholly [?] upon. You may see a fellow sitting down to have a dozen of the latter & a melon three or four times the size of his own head: this at a meal. We on the contrary live on wholesome food and take plenty of exercise, with our glass of sherry or port after dinner and very little fruit. We have brought our Arab steeds, rise at 3 1/2 every morning, have our gallop before the sun rises, return and pass the day as we best can in the house as it is dangerous to be exposed to the sun. In the shade when there is no breeze the therm[ometer] stands at 99° [and] in the sun at 115°. Rising so early we take our siesta during the day. I am about to learn Persian. The steamer being so near, our party is varied by the company of the officers who are all most excellent fellows. We give & return visits with the Ruskies and Orientals. By the bye Dervish Pasha and his suite arrived on Thursday. He speaks English and French very well indeed and it is not improbable that he will be Ambassador to England when the Boundary question is settled. His engineer was also educated at Woolwich [?], his Dr in France while his Naturalist or rather, botanist Mr Noé is a Russian. So you perceive that we have quite an European party. Mr Noé is pronounced to be in search of the fossil bones of his progenitor and the hinges of the Ark. Jafar Khan is taken ill of the fever this morning. By the bye he was Vizier when Col. W[illiams] was at Erzerum and he sent Mirza Taqi,[55] nolens volens, and at the latter's own expense as Commissioner. The tables are now turned and Mirza Taqi, now prime minister, sends Mirza Jafar Khan; I don't think the old man will live to see the question settled. He is in a very delicate state of health. It is decided that we are to remain here till the summer is over as we shall only be tempting our fate if we attempt to spend 6 days in crossing the desert to the

---

55 Mirza Taqi Khan, later known as Amir Kabir (1807–52), was appointed Chief Minister by Nasser al-Din Shah in 1848 but murdered on the orders of the shah in 1853 in Fin Garden near Kashan. See also Ateş 2013: *passim*.

mountains. Independently of the heat the whole country S of Hamrin Hills including all Mesopotamia to the Persian Gulf has been under water. Dodson is still with us tho' he went to see Babylon last week travelling by night & resting at the khans during the day. As I cannot work out of doors I have been reading all the papers on this country in Geog[raphical] Journal and Major Rawlinson's account of Khuzistan & Luristan[56] has made me quite anxious to get away to that region where he supposes the cradle of the human race to have been situated. The relics of antediluvian cities appear to be as abundant as blackberries. By the bye I am delighted to tell you that Major Rawlinson has received leave of absence for a year on account of ill health, and that he intends starting for England in October, so that the public will soon be put in possession of the results of his laborious studies at the cuneiform writings. This work will create as much if not more excitement even than Layard's. He has devoted the last 10 years entirely to the subject and he will announce much that will astonish and puzzle the learned. The bull we saw lying in the excavations at Khorsabad is now lying in front of the residency about to be transported to Busrah [Basra] for the British Museum direct. I am glad to hear that you got my letter from Mosul as well as the one I wrote Green from Diarbekir [Diyarbakır]. I shall run over yours and reply. I can only repeat that I may consider myself most fortunate in receiving this appointment, especially as we have so worthy and delightful a Commander. He treats us all as his equals and he denies not the slightest wish. His kindness is not therefore abused as we are as happy and comfortable as possible. I am convinced that I could not have met with any employment in England so suited to my tastes, or so likely to prove advantageous to me and mine hereafter. That I have done my duty in accepting this appointment I am quite convinced. Why do you persist in calling me a Commissioner? I am not one. You would do me far too much honour. I am glad you have seen Layard's work and are pleased with it. You are of course as well up in his subject as myself. Christian Rassam is our Consul & not Hormuzd whom I have not seen as he was absent from Mosul at the time of our visit. You will be surprised when I tell you that Layard cannot speak either Arabic or Persian and very little Turkish, tho' he certainly

---

56   Rawlinson 1839.

manages them well. Tho' all Orientals are most unqualified liars I believe from what I have seen that the Arabs are a grateful race and kindness will have more effect on his conduct than is generally supposed. For an Englishman they have great respect as they know that his dealings are just and that his word of honour is never broken. I speak of the Arab of the desert as here they have imbibed all the bad qualities of the Persian & Turk. Here they are a cringing set and a good hearty kick is the only means of making them do their duty. We have several in our employ. The Bedouin says you are like us you are free – and we love freedom! In your letter of the 13th you say that the extremes of the heat and cold are the causes of the strange salutations [?] and customs of the Asiatic Turks and of their slow advance towards civilization. No doubt these causes have a certain influence, but I conceive that bad government had much more – war & barrenness of soil are not the chief obstacles to population but insecurity implied in tyrannical government is the chief [reason for] depopulation [?]. Men will not labour where they cannot be certain of the fruits of their labour. They sink into lassitude, indolence and beggary. In the mountains of the Taurus I will grant that climate is the chief drawback to civilization, but not here – not at Mosul – not all along the banks of the Tigris where it is evident that labour is what is required to make this immense country as fertile as it was in those days when its surface was covered with the cities of its ancient inhabitants. What do the solid dams of brickwork in the rivers, the network of canal and water courses, seen throughout the whole country east and west, north and south imply? Why, that it was highly cultivated and that it supplied the wants of a dense population from the mountains of Luristan to far west of Kerbala [and it] was, I have no doubt, one vast field of cultivation. The soil is so rich that the grain thrown loosely on the surface without any cultivation produces an abundant crop. Depend upon it that climate is not the cause of misery in these countries. No one can possibly starve here tho' he does not work. It is nothing but the brutal rule of the Pasha who takes good care to enrich himself at the expense of the subject. I have forgotten where it is but in one Pashalic and I dare say in all that if a man cannot pay his tax they make his neighbour pay it – if a village cannot, the neighbouring village must! Under such government, I ask you, can a nation become civilised? There is not a single city or village throughout this country whose population is not decreasing and so it will continue until some other system of government is adopted. The Turkish Empire, as well as the Persian, is on its last legs. A few years more, perhaps before I return, one or both will cease to exist. I fear that our mission will have little effect on these matters. But I have dwelt for longer on this subject than I had intended. Many thanks again for your suggestions regarding matter for the magazines. I think I explained myself on that point. As soon as I have matter to communicate I shall of course send the Geological Society all I can thro' Sir Henry; and the Council will publish it or not, as they think best, in their journal. With regard to any other notes I may make I would prefer keeping them till my return, as I do not know how the Foreign Office might take my publishing anything during the progress of the Boundary Commission and it might be more valuable on my return. We are all glad to hear of Layard's appointment and that he is coming out again. He sent me by this post two sheets of the Manual publishing [sic] by the Admiralty of which I got the first part thro' Sir H. when in London. We hear all the news thro' Galignani [57] which we receive by every post and Major R. sends [us] his later ones received by way of Damascus. I am sorry to hear of Hudson's[58] downfall. I think he has been rather ill-used on the whole tho' he may have acted indiscreetly. I have been defending him all along here as I do consider him an honourable man. We can only speak of him as we find him. You have I hope got settled as you expected with the Railway Company and in a satisfactory way. I do not see how they can get over the compensation, but of that too I shall hear when you next write. My best thanks are due to Mather, Gray & yourself for the trouble you have taken in getting the road put in order to the Stand [grandstand]. It certainly much needed it. You will I am sure do what is proper and therefore I need not interfere in any way. You all do your best and I am certain I could not have left matters in better hands. The Races are now over but you will not yet have had an opportunity to send me the result. I hope all things went off well and that you had a good take. I saw in the papers that Nunnykirk[59] has won the £2000. Pray offer my congratulations to Mr Nichol and I hope he has netted the Northumberland Plate likewise. My

---

57 *Galignani's Messenger*, published in Paris, was a widely circulated newspaper at this time.
58 Probably George Hudson, Director of Newcastle and Berwick Railway Company.
59 Nunnykirk was a famous thoroughbred racehorse, born 1846.

kind remembrance likewise to his good lady. Tell Mather I am obliged by his hearty [?] letter and am glad to see him in such spirits. I trust all his wishes on my behalf may be gratified. I had intended writing him by this post but having spun you such a devil of a yarn I must leave him till next time. I promised to write James, but must treat him likewise. Do not fail to remember me to him & Mrs J. Junior as well as to Mr Harvey [and] your friends at Manchester. I must now go and have my nap as I was out [at] 3.30 am with the "Nitocris" fishing. We caught 30 lbs of fish [in] four hauls.

Fail not to remember me to Mrs R., Edward & Mrs Mather, Mr and Mrs Gray, Mr Whitfield, Mrs Lough, Green & all friends too numerous to name. I expect a letter by next post from Green.

Believe me, my dear James,

Yours always,

Wm Kennett Loftus

P.S. Olquin tells me that poor Dodson has got a roaring fever. His exertions to Hillah have been too much for him as he has never recovered [from] his former illness.

Thank God, I feel in excellent health and do not fear catching this same fever. It is not malignant.

Letter 19, Gherrara, near Baghdad, 17 July 1849

My dear Ben,

Your most acceptable and delightful letter of June 5th has just reached me, and I sit down at once to express my thanks and to give you what little news we have here to communicate. The fever has been playing sad havoc in the neighbourhood. In Baghdad it assumed a typhoid form and it is said that 6000 have died in the city; at the lowest computation 4500! It has carried off more than the cholera two years ago – only one European, a sailor has died of it, altho' nearly all have had it. Col Williams has had a most severe attack and is now very weak tho' recovering very quickly. Out of our party of 40, only 5 have escaped, viz. the Dr (of course), Wood, Glascott, an Arab servant of Dodson's and I am glad to add myself. Thank God, I never felt in better health than at present and when the fever was at its height I said in my last that I did not expect to catch it. It did not assume a dangerous form with us – Jafar Khan, the Persian lost 3 men and 5 more ran away from sheer funk back to Persia! My servant Georgio I have been obliged to dismiss as his Ionian intrigues kept up a constant commotion among the servants. I believe it was from no ill disposition but that the feeling was innate: I believe he was honest and he was not otherwise a bad servant. It is a nuisance to me as I had taught him to stuff birds & that not amiss [?]. I have now got a servant of the late Dr Ross', Mathus [Matthew] by name and an Armenian but not a blessed word of English can he speak. I am therefore picking up a few words of Persian. Major Rawlinson has promised me one of his servants when he leaves for England in October, but in the interim I have determined to keep Mathus. I yesterday engaged an Arab, a son of Saiyd Hindi mentioned in Dr Ross' journey to Al Hadhr [Hatra] in the Geog. Soc. Journal. He is my sportsman and will carry my geological bag, etc, etc. He speaks only Arabic, so that I have my work pretty well cut out. It is with great pleasure I announce that old Nedjib Pasha is kicked out and that the cannons are now firing for the appointment of the Mushir or Seraskier Pasha (General of the Pashalic) who behaved so well regarding the Hillah business. I believe him to be a good fellow and I sincerely hope he will govern with more justice than his predecessor who was a villain of the first class – see the account of his murdering the Shammar Arab chief Sofuk when under his safe conduct as detailed by Layard.[60] When at Mosul we saw the arrival of £25,000, a bribe to Government to retain him in his place! I have however a bad opinion of all Turks. Even Dervish Pasha our Commissioner received £2000 from him to report in his favour concerning the dispute between him and the Mushir! It is said that Dervish also received 7000 £ from the Pasha of Mosul. But what can you expect from the officers when the Government itself will receive a bribe. Behold another effect of

---

60   Layard 1849: I, p. 114.

CHAPTER FOUR

Nedjib's conduct – the Chief of the Beni Lam Arabs, between this [place] and Busrah, being in considerable arrears of his tribute was deprived of his sheikhship and the tribe, itself one of the most warlike of the Arabs was placed under their enemies the Montefic while the chief's sons are taken prisoners to Baghdad. The Montefic have revolted and are now stopping all caravans, shearing the camels' hair and detaining the goods and also blockading the river. All the goods however are carefully laid aside and restoration will be made when Nedjib puts the tribe in possession of its honors [?]. I have no doubt the new Pasha will do what is just. I admire the Arab, why, I scarcely know, but to prove to you that they are honourable and susceptible of kind treatment, I must mention the fact that Mr Lynch, a merchant of Baghdad and an Englishman, had two boats laden with goods on the way up the river. They passed untouched and without paying toll or bribe thro' the whole distance 500 miles from Busrah while every native boat is captive! The Englishmen in these parts have always acted straightforwardly and honourably and for this he is the pet of those Arabs with whom he has dealings. I do not say that this is the case with some of the tribes in the interior who hate all nations but their own. By the bye Busrah is to be separated from Baghdad and will form a new Pashalic. This will deduct materially from the revenue of this place, but things appear to be taking a turn for the better here: the Peninsular Company have an idea of starting vessels from Bombay up the Tigris and a small steamer actually came up nearly to Busrah. There is a great trade carried on with India and I can't conceive how they have hitherto managed. With the institution of steam communication let us hope that civilisation will progress. Layard leaves the Embassy next month for his new labors and we expect to have the pleasure of his company here for a short time. The 1st Conference was held here yesterday when it was decided to send notice to the various Governments of our detention here on account of the heat. And now I think I have given you all the news and therefore turn to your letter: – You say truly I am a most lucky fellow indeed at having the opportunity of beholding all these scenes, as interesting to us all as being the cradle of our race. It is yet I hope to be my lot to behold many more of them before I return and when that happy time does come, to recount to you all the scenes I have witnessed and the dangers passed. If then I can communicate half the pleasure I feel I shall be content. I cannot speak too highly of our party and especially of the Colonel. He is without exception a most splendid fellow. I heartily wish with you that you could be here to see and speak for yourself. What happy days we should spend together rambling over the relics of past ages and imparting to each other those feelings of admiration and wonder which we enjoy in, I believe, similar degree! Would that you were here to sketch but half what I see every day! Your devotion to antiquarian research might be gratified to the highest extent. Yesterday I rode along the bed of an old canal behind our house to an old tell or mound called Tell Mohammed.[61] For 3 miles the ground is covered with broken pottery and a sailor from the Nitocris found an urn and other antiquities soon after I left him there. We could distinctly trace the line of the Nahrawan[62] Canal in the distance while the space between is occupied with innumerable mounds and canals now all dry. You say you propose travelling with me in my course on the map. If such be the case I shall not fail to give you an account of our wanderings and if you derive as much delight and information from it as I do from your letters. I hope you will not fail to reply frequently. My cousin informed me of your accident: – need I say that the news afforded me true sorrow. I know how you would fret and be annoyed that you could not be working at your infinity of plans & business which would of course then be more urgent than ever! I am glad that you have recovered the use of your arm & are able to set too [sic] once more. The account of Hudson's downfall I read in the papers which we receive from Constantinople by every post. I think he has been shamefully abused and I hope the kicks will recoil on the kickers in twofold. He is not perhaps without blame, but I believe him to be an honourable man. I am extremely glad to hear that your opinion coincides so exactly with mine as to taking account of the consumption at the Stand. In my letter to Mather of 15th April I expressed a wish – a strong wish – that such should be done and I shall be much disappointed if it has not, as I am convinced we were right. If it should prove the contrary to our expectation I would forthwith write an abject letter of apology for my doubts respecting

---

61   Tell Mohammed is an important site of the Old Babylonian period. See Layard 1853: 477 and Curtis 2004.
62   The Nahrawan canal system, mostly dating from the Sasanian period and on the east side of the Tigris, was much praised by Arab geographers.

CHAPTER FOUR

Brown's truthfulness. I hope my letter and your entreaties have had an effect on my cousin, Mather and Gray. I know that my cousin does not like to quarrel with Brown but I think he will see the propriety of this step. I am most anxious to hear the result of the week which I shall not till a month more is past. By that post I hope too to hear of my dear wife's confinement as she was unable to write her letter out which I received today [?]. The children have both been ill of the hooping [sic] cough and she gives but a poor account of Fred. He cannot shake it off and she has been much harassed in attending to him. I am sorry you did not get these articles you mentioned. They must have been forgotten. I have now written you a long letter in little time and as the perspiration is running off me as if fresh from a bath (thermometer 100°) I find I must conclude. You may make your letters as long as you please provided there is no enclosure besides. Remember me most kindly to all my friends and believe me to remain

Yours faithfully & affectionately

Wm Kennett Loftus.

Letter 20, Gherrara near Baghdad, 31 July 1849

My dear Cousin,

Many a time and oft have I threatened to inflict you with a letter and as often as I have had this intention so often has it been thwarted. Tho' six months have now passed away since I left the shores of my own dear land, I have had little opportunity of writing as I wished. Each post brought [letters] from Newcastle and as only a day intervened between the arrival and departure of the Tatar I could not indulge my wish of writing to you. No doubt James has duly informed you of all my movements as he tells me that my letters go the round of my friends and I am sure he would not omit you. And here let me return you my sincere thanks for all the kindness and attention received from you during my short stay in London. Tho' my thanks are returned this late you will I am certain believe that I do not feel the less grateful. Having now sat down to write I scarce know with what to commence as having so much to say it would be impossible to communicate one quarter of that which you would desire to hear – Constantinople, my journey to Mosul on horseback, & by raft [to] Nineveh and its remains, the ruins of Al Hadhr [Hatra] in the desert of Sinjar, our trip down the River Tigris to this city of the renowned kalifs, the city itself, would all furnish me with sufficient matter for a letter apiece. Coming as I did straight from England everything was strange to me, and of the highest possible interest, but what shall I say were my sensations when I found myself first in these regions of thrilling interest, the lands first cultivated by the sons of Noah, the cities first formed by their descendants. Never shall I forget the sensations which first came over me when I viewed the wondrous works fresh brought to the light of day in the long buried habitations of Nimrud's mighty city. Would that you could have been with me to share my delight. Since that sight [how] can I enumerate all the ancient Assyrian and Sasanian remains I have beheld, of which little now remains but huge mounds of earth covered with great quantities of broken bricks and pottery and whose names have long since been lost to the world except when now and then some fragments [of] inscription dug from these ruins disclose [to] my learned friend Major Rawlinson the name and founder of some long lost city of ages past. The country on every side is covered with mounds and canals and much light will be thrown upon the history of remote antiquity now that the attention of the learned is directed to the subject. At Nineveh in especial I believe that sculptures yet to be disentombed will rival those already discovered. But a small portion of the mound of Kouyunjik has yet been excavated; what may not yet be discovered in the interior? Behind the little house we now occupy (which is actually built of bricks from the ancient ruins of Ctesiphon) are various mounds at one of which some very curious relics have been lately found, so interesting in fact that Major Rawlinson is about to make excavations in it. You no doubt wish to know what sketches I have made. I am sorry to say I have not done much. With the exception of the leaning tower or minaret at Mosul, a general sketch of Kouyunjik from Mosul, and a mosque at Baghdad, I have done nothing. The weather is so awfully hot that it is a labour even to move. In the shade at this moment the thermometer stands at 98 while in the sun it is 122. With almost no clothing on me the perspiration is running off me in streams. To go out after 9 am is quite out of the question, and except in Baghdad there is nothing to sketch in the desert.

CHAPTER FOUR

In Baghdad itself there is little or nothing left of the ancient buildings of the kalifs. War, inundation and gradual decay have done their work well. It is really after a short residence a most wretched place. On first arrival after travelling thro' wretched villages of filth & horrors it does appear cheerful from the presence of the light green branches of the date palms peeping over the flat tops of the houses, a sight we had not before seen. But only begin to examine the town and you find more than half the space within the walls covered with the ruins of houses destroyed during the inundation and plague of 1831.

From that visitation the place has never recovered. Upwards of 7000 persons have died since our arrival out of a population of 80,000 in consequence of the great inundation of this year. I am one of three who have not had the fever out of our party of 40. Fourteen out of 15 have been floored in the city. Never was known such an epidemic except the plague. Several of our people have had four attacks. At other times this is a most healthy place. I presume I need not say that the costumes (and in fact everything) are most picturesque. What in the East is not so? The crowds of Arabs in the most amusing dresses or rather undresses who pass this [house] on their way to and from the city afford us no small fun. One fellow in his brown shirt and sword of course is sitting on the stern of his white ass, another is driving his poor brute before him in evident fear of a heavy headed stick. Now we have a sheikh [?] in his clean white abba on his splendid steed carrying his long shining [?] lance and attended by some of his tribe. Then will come an Arab lady in her blue, what shall I call it, shift I suppose, for nothing else do they wear over their mahogany skins. In fact sitting on carpets cross legged after our early ride we have daily a living panorama before us. I intended to make a few sketches of costume tho' really anything you choose to put in your picture will not be amiss. All this is very amusing to hear and read of, but the reality is not quite so agreeable. The beautiful picturesque costume[s] are accompanied by the most squalid filth and misery, not misery from want since want is not really known in this country where food is almost to be had for nothing, but arising from the bad government of the Pasha. No one will of course labour [when] there is every probability that his productions will be seized for the use of the state. How different are our idea[s] of the last from what experience reveals.

The more I have travelled and the more I travel I am convinced that there is no country like my own, and although John Bull is continually grumbling, he would grumble ten thousand times more had he to submit to the impositions of an eastern rule. It would be a good plan if a few of the most discontented should be sent hither for a time. England is truly a happy country and happy is the man who can say I am an Englishman. Even the very Arabs admire us as a free people and from this feeling an Englishman will pass scot-free thro' them when a Turk, a Persian or even an Arab would be stripped of his all. My companion Dodson, aware of this, is about to start on Thursday for Damascus by way of Hit and Palmyra. I would have gone with him as far as Hit were it not for the heat and fear of fever in the desert. At Hit are naphtha springs supposed to have produced the pitch with which Noah's Ark was covered. It is on the Euphrates – we shall however in October visit Babylon and Hillah and hope to get [there] from thence. On Sunday morning I nearly had two serious accidents. Four of us went out to the desert in search of a hyaena which had been seen the day before. I was off my horse gathering some insects when a horse kicked at me and struck my right arm below [?] but fortunately the fleshy part; but for my arm he must have broken my ribs. As it was his hoof passed close to my chin and pulled my beard which is now by the bye a pretty considerable one. With my arm stunned I rode on toward the ancient mound where we found the hyaena had his abode, from the many large holes in it and the remains of the various animals. He had buried something, probably a dead Arab from a nearby grave which sent forth a most abominable stench. We were examining the various entrances when without any warning the ground gave in with my horse and me and down we went five feet into the hyaena's den. Whether the grinning monster was at home or not I had no time to ascertain, but if he was he must have grinned to a considerable extent at such an unexpected visit! My horse plunged dreadfully and at last got out from the hole but slipped and I lost my balance. He then sprung to the other side and I expected he would come over upon me. As it was I fell upon my sore arm, but as good luck would have it I was unhurt. You know that I am not a bad rider and it must have been something extraordinary to throw me. The idea of a naturalist on horseback paying a visit to a hyaena has caused considerable fun in the camp at my expense. With my two bruises my arm is still very stiff and I cannot therefore write you as long a letter as I would wish. We expect

CHAPTER FOUR

Layard from Constantinople this month as he is about again to commence excavations at Nineveh and he intends joining us for a short time. For my own part I am fretting at being kept bothering here in one of the hottest places under the sun instead of going to the mountains as we should have done on our arrival here. Babylon however is to be seen and this is my solace. I hope likewise to get to the ruins of Persepolis, before we depart from Mohammerah, the commencement of our Boundary Line which runs thence along the Pusht-i Kuh or western district of Luristan, thence over the mountains east of Tohab [?] and Soleimaniyeh [Sulaymaniyah] to the mountains of Van. This district abounds with ruins [not yet] visited, tho' Rawlinson has been over a great part of this country. You will all shortly be astonished at his researches and study [of] the cuneiform writings. He is about to proceed to England to publish them. He has been engaged at this subject for 10 years. We were his guests for six weeks and spent a most pleasant time as you may conceive. My collections are [in] fact increasing and I propose sending off a box from Mohammerah in October if possible. I believe I have a few things which will be acceptable to the British Museum. Of our Commander Col. Williams I have only to say that he is without exception the kindest and most considerate and agreeable fellow I ever had to deal with. The rest of my companions are also excellent fellows and we have only to be happy as the day is long barring the heat. My acceptance of this appointment has given me introductions to many "first rates" whom I could not otherwise have become acquainted with and I do not experience the least regret at my decision in the matter. With health I do not fear the work cut out for me in the mountains and I only heartily wish I could now be at it and enjoy the pure air of the higher [?] banks [?] instead of breathing the foul fever-bearing atmosphere of the surrounding marshes. Presuming that you have heard details of my former wanderings in the Taurus and snow with the thermometer at 2°, I have nothing more to add except that I congratulate you and yours at your return from "Eternal Rome" before it has [be]come infernal, and probably extinct. I expect you will honour me with a reply to this long expected tho' better late than never letter, as long and thick as you please as government pays the postage. Pray fail not to remember me to your good lady and tell her I frequently think of the two happy evenings spent at your house when camera [?] and the cubes [?] were discussed [?]. I hope the little one has recovered. My wife tells me that my little ones have had the hooping cough but are now better. When you write to Manchester pray give my best remembrance to all my friends and acquaintances. Tell Wm [?] the Persian has brought with him an engineer with two driving dicks [?] as his instruments.

Ever my dear James sincerely yours,

Wm Kennett Loftus

Kind regards to mine Uncle

Letter 21 [extract], Gherrara, 1 August 1849

My dear James,

The post bringing your letter of 14 June arrived so late yesterday that I have only time to reply shortly to yours. I was engaged in writing to your namesake when the post arrived. Accept my very best thanks for the interest you take in my proceedings. I can only repeat that I am satisfied if my communications afford my friends any pleasure. As to having my letters published, it was very far from my thoughts when I wrote them. There are personal remarks etc contained in them that would never do, and besides I really do not think them at all suitable for publication. However, I thank you for the offer you make of seeking further information regarding this matter; should it prove worth my while I might perhaps be induced to try my hand. I make [sic] no doubt but that our journey along the borders of Luristan and thro' Kurdistan will be most interesting passing as we shall do over Parthian and Assyrian ground. Yet I do not think I am at liberty to write till my return, and then I believe a work will take [?] as in the interim attention will be drawn to these countries by Major Rawlinson's intended book. He must of necessity refer to many of the ruins on the Boundary and I imagine that will be my time "to come out". But I shall probably hear further from you. The letters I have written you have been scribbled off in a few minutes as they come uppermost and were only intended to amuse my friends if they could be amused by them. Enough of this at present. Dodson leaves us tomorrow for Palmyra and Damascus. He is determined to visit the ruins at the former place, tho' [it is a] 16 days journey across the burning desert with the thermometer above 125°. We all consider him mad. I wished to have gone with him as far as Hit on the Euphrates, to visit the springs of naphtha from which Noah is supposed to have obtained the substance which covered the Ark. It is interesting in a geological point of view. The heat however forbids my venturing [there]. I have nothing to add in the way of news. The fever still sticks to our people and Wood and Glascott have both had it since I last wrote so that the Dr and myself with the servant are all that are left sound out of our party of 40. I never felt in better health tho' I am getting far too fat from want of proper exercise. The heat is intense, 100 in the shade and 122 in the sun. We are here in the midst of [xxxx] and cannot get a morsel of ripe fruit. The brutes [?] pull everything when it is green and hard, peaches, apricots, nectarines, grapes being in the greatest abundance on the trees, but as soon as they show the least colour off they go to market. Last evening the sailors caught a young shark in the Tigris which they sent to me. They have only found their way up this far within the last few years and several accidents have occurred. It is strange that they should come so far up the river 700 miles from the sea. [Now] we have [one] 5 feet long. But I must now conclude & remember me to all friends. I do not mention names as I should have to add too long a list and might offend some by an unintended omission.

Letter 22 [extract], Gherrara, 1 August 1849

My dear Edward,

You see by the date of this that we still remain stationary at this place and likely to continue for nearly 3 months to come. I have therefore no news for you and if I had I could not write much more today as I received a kick from a horse on my right arm below the elbow the day before last and it feels very stiff and sore after writing to James Radford and another letter. My chin had a very narrow escape from the heels of the horse. The same day my horse and I fell straight [?] thro' the solid ground into a hyaena's den and in the floundering to get out I lost my seat and fell on my injured arm. These two adventures were quite enough for one day. I think you will allow either might have proved serious.

I am dying to be off to work. This is far too lazy a life for me. By the bye, you say my letters have gone the round of almost every one of my friends [in the] Natural History [Society] & our Field Club; you don't mean to say that they have been read at their meetings? They certainly were fit for no such honour. If you should again see Howe [?] tell him I should like to hear from him as to his Natural History Proceedings and I promise to give him a share among the round of correspondents, for to be expected to keep up with all at once is impossible tho' I do my best not to neglect any. My collections are getting large and I hope to send off a large box to the British Museum in Oct from Busrah by a vessel of Mr Lynch. We have an accession to our Bagdad circle, Mr Taylor (a son of Col Taylor the late resident) & really a nice fellow he is. At least 7000 persons died of fever in the city. The bodies are constantly passing our house, stretched on a board and hung across a horse or donkey. You have not got such a thing about you, I suppose, as a donkey load of potatoes that you could send by post? We haven't seen a vegetable of any description but barmias[63] since we have been here, we are dying for them.

Letter 23, Baghdad, 15 August 1849

My dear Blacklock,

Having a few minutes to spare before the post is despatched I don't know that I can spend the time better than in giving you a short [xxxx]. I mentioned in one of my letters to Newcastle (I think to Mr A. Hancock) that Col. Williams my excellent chief has left to my disposal the distribution of the duplicate specimens of my collections after supplying the British Museum with a full series. Of course after the National Museum the Nat. Hist. Soc. of Newcastle stands first on my list and I hope to send my first contribution from Busrah in November by a ship direct for England belonging to a merchant of Baghdad.

---

63   Bamya or bamia is the Arabic word for okra, also known as ladies' fingers.

CHAPTER FOUR

I would prefer sending my first sample in this manner to carrying it with me till my return to Constantinople as carriage on the backs of horses and mules is not the best for insects and brittle specimens. I do not know what the expense of carriage by vessel may amount to but as the package will be but small I do not think it will be heavy. Perhaps I may be able to get it sent "free" in which case I dare say the Society will not object to this plan. Should you however prefer my retaining what I have for you till my return I shall have great pleasure in doing so. There is abundance of time for me to receive your instructions on this point if you write by return of post.

Address to me at Constantinople and enclose the letter to E. Hammond Esq, Foreign Office, Downing St and it will be forwarded in the Embassy Bag. I have so frequently written to Mr Radford or to some of my friends at Newcastle that I have little or no news to send you presuming that you have heard of my journey and proceedings thus far. By the bye my cousin tells me that Dr Charlton has taken a great interest in Layard's discoveries. I should have written to him but that I consider myself in your debt. Will you tell him that there is a report arrived this morning to the effect the late Pasha of Baghdad Nedjib Pasha has been attacked by the Shammar Arabs when on his way to Mosul, that his followers & guards 1000 in number fled & that he is killed.[64] I do not know how far this may be true but it is generally talked of in the city and it is not at all improbable that the Shammar hearing of his about to pass that way on his return to Constantinople have left their plundering expedition near Nisibin and laid wait to take vengeance on him for his foul murder of their favourite chief Sofuk as detailed in Layard's work. After stripping the country right and left he has gone off openly with 13 mules laden with bars of gold refusing to pay just debts to the amount it is said of £200,000. If he has not already received his deserts from the Shammar he certainly will do so when he presents himself at the Porte. I hope the penny admission has answered your expectations and that the Committee will have no reason to regret the change. When you write pray let me hear you are flourishing once more & that presents are pouring in. How goes on the

---

64 This must have been an incorrect report as Mehmet Nacib Pasha, Governor of Baghdad, did not die until 1851.

Field Club? I often think of those pleasant rambles [and] I wish I could join you for one day at the Wansbeck or on the banks of [the] Tyne. I had a list of our meeting places sent me [but] having no railway or steamboat I am sorry I could not accept the invitation. Our stay at this once famous city has been a protracted one and we are all tired of so inactive a life & anxious to reach our starting point on the Boundary. The heat will not however permit us to start before the middle of October as an hour's exposure to the sun floors one immediately. We scarcely go out from breakfast time till dinner at seven when "Jack" retires for the night as hot as he has been all day.

I find it now time to conclude. Will you present my best remembrances to Mr Alder, Mr Hayes [?], Dr Charlton, the Hancocks, Howse [?] & all my old friends too numerous to name separately and believe me,

My dear Blacklock,

Yours ever truly,

Wm Kennett Loftus.

Letter 24, Gherrara, 28 Aug 1849

My dear Edward,

Altho' today's post from Constantinople has brought no letters from "home" I write to let my friends know that all's well with me. Of news I have none. The report I mentioned in my letter to Blacklock last post is not authenticated that Nedjib Pasha had been attacked and killed. We have heard no news of him since and that report must therefore have been all humbug. On the 10th of next month I start with Captain Jones of the Nitocris for a week's survey of the Nahrawan Canal at its junction with the River Diyala. He has made a survey of the whole course of this ancient work from its commencement near Samarra to its junction with the Tigris near, I think, Koote [Kut] and this is the only part unfinished and is probably the most interesting. We take our horses & tents, and a yacht with a covered awning is to go up the river to the point of meeting. I shall not therefore write by next post. I intend

CHAPTER FOUR

taking with me my Chasseur as I propose making a collection of the fish of the Diyala. On the 16th we had a grand hunt after my friend the Hyaena. By means of smoke & sulphur we drove him out of his hole and he feigned lame. We surrounded him, tied him hand & foot and bagged him alive. He was mounted on horseback and was on the road to the camp when he bit his bonds asunder and made off followed by the whole party. Two got hold of the ropes and I held him down with the point of the spear which he bit slick [sic] in two and away he went again. But our sport was soon over for one of the servants of the Russians shot him dead, much to our disgust as guns are forbidden arms at field sports here. Only spears are allowed. My friend's skin is now hanging in the garden drying for the Newcastle Museum, but I fear it will not be worth the carriage. On the 6th, 7th and 8th the Turks celebrated their Festival of Beiram[65] with a grand [xxxx] match near the E. gate of Baghdad & within the walls. I went one day and sitting under shade of the Pasha's tent was much delighted with the novelty of the scene. The brother of the Sheikh of the Beni Lam was there and he divided his followers into two parties who performed most extraordinary feats in the management of their horses, swords and spears. The wild figures of the Arabs as they rushed to the attack and suddenly pulled up when at the top of their speed, producing such a dust as to as to render them scarcely visible, the gaudy colours of the holiday clothes of the assembled thousands, and the old mosque with its leaning tower and palm trees in the background, formed such a scene as the light of the fast-setting sun shone upon it [that] I shall never forget it. What a picture for a water-[colour artist] to have sketched; poor Churchill from the heat of that day is now lying in a raging fever. The Col. too has had another slight attack as well as Glascott while at new and full moon some of the servants are sure to be floored again. The Dr and I still stand out against [it] well. The heat has been perfectly awful for the last fortnight, 104° in the serdab kept cool with water on the [xxxx] at the sides, from 113° to 117° in the shade and 130° to 136° in the sun. The early morning is however much cooler than it has been and before we start for the Diyala I understand it will be much more pleasant. When the mercury rises to only 98° it is quite bearable, now that we have got

---

65 Bayram is a Turkish word for a festival or holiday. This was probably Eid al-Adha.

acclimatised, but our clothes are seldom dry as you may imagine. Tomorrow I intend to commence preparations for work by getting my maps ruled and marked off. I intend to make my geological map to the scale of ½ inch to the mile, leaving room for investigation [?] of miles on each side of the boundary line. Glascott's is to be one inch to the mile. In my letter a month hence I shall be able to give you an idea of when we are to leave this [place]; no one will be sorry I assure you.

Pray remember me to James & Mrs R., to Ellen, John & Mrs Gray, and to all enquiring friends.

Believe me my dear Ned,

Ever sincerely yours,

Wm Kennett Loftus.

Letter 25, Gherrara near Baghdad, 25 Sept 1849

My dear Charlton,

I promised you on my departure from Newcastle that my friends in the "canny town" should occasionally hear from me. In my last letter to Mather I said I should perform my promise to you by this post and I therefore proceed to inflict on you a short description of a journey which we have just performed, a journey which I am sure you would have much enjoyed. We have long planned a visit to the ruins of Babylon, and as soon as the weather became bearable we made arrangements accordingly. On the evening of September 13th our horses swam the river Tigris opposite our present abode and on the next morning we followed them in our boats of the E.S.C. vessel the Nitocris. Mounting our horses at 5.30 am we travelled for three hours to our first station Assad Khan,[66] where we found Dervish Pasha awaiting our arrival, attended by an escort of 40 mounted troops, a squad of Heiters [?] or irregulars and a posse of officers and domestics. Here we encamped and were

---

66   Marked on map in Loftus 1857, reproduced here as pl. 7.

shortly joined by the Russian party; thus our united force amounted to about 200 and this number was quite necessary as the Arabs are out plundering not as usual in fours and fives, but in parties of 2 or 300 at a time. On the 15th at 4.50 we broke up our camp and proceeded to Khan Mizrakji which we reached at 9.25 am – rested during the great heat, again set out at 4.20 pm for Khan Mohawil[67] which we reached at 9.20 performing a distance of about 30 miles this day. The Khan I have mentioned as well as various others we passed on our route are the only buildings on this [scale in] Mesopotamia. They are large square buildings with flanking towers at the corners to defend the inmates from the attacks of the Arabs; in fact, at the distance, each Khan has the appearance of a small fortified town. This being the great highway for pilgrims to the shrines at Kerbala and Meshed Ali, these khans are much larger, cleaner and in better condition than any others I have seen. The country we had thus far passed over is one vast plain of alluvium intersected by thousands of ruined canals forming a complete network for the supply of water. Not a single drop of that greatest luxury of the East is to be seen in one of them, and the khans are supplied only by artesian wells, affording bad water. Here and there too we passed a mound, the fragments of brick and pottery on which denoted that some town or village long ages now forgotten occupied the site. All that now remains is desolation and decay. On the 16th at 5 am we left Mohawil and in a few minutes we reached some huge ancient canals and mounds, and here the ruins of Babylon may be said to commence. At a little distance further on we first caught sight of the Mujelibè[68] which we reached about 7 am. It is not until you approach its base that its height and extent are appreciated – it there appears to be a vast pile of sun-dried bricks covered with remains of an edifice of bricks burned in the furnace which has been overturned as Mujelibè implies, and now covers its base and sides with fragments. Its height from the plain is about 135 feet on the E, side but lower

---

67 Mizrakji Khan and Mohawil are marked on map in Loftus 1857.
68 Tell Mujelibè (Arabic 'the overturned') also known as Tell Babil is the most northern part of ancient Babylon. It is often referred to as the Summer Palace of Nebuchadnezzar, but could also have been a residence of the Persian kings; see J E Curtis, 'Where did the Persian kings live in Babylon', in *Studies in Ancient Persian and the Achaemenid Period* (Cambridge 2020), pp 10–33.

on the W. side, thus affording a slight inclination towards the River Euphrates. The sides of the mound are irregular in measurement, the greatest according to Rich 219 yards, the least 136. Portions of the sun-dried brick wall are on the sides, and it is truly wonderful how these have withstood the effects of time, weather and the destroying hand of man. On being touched these bricks crumble[d] to pieces in my hand while the straw laid between each layer in many places remained entire. Strewed over the upper surface of the mound was to be seen here and there a piece of white mortar which had no doubt been employed in the construction of the kiln dried building. One of the party found a small onyx cylinder or bead. From the Mujelibè the view was much more extensive and picturesque than I had imagined. Rising from the flat plain around were the other vast ruins of [the] golden city stretching for the distance of 2 miles to the south. The pyramidal mound of El Heimar[69] was the only object which met the eye on the S.E. while on the S.W. the corresponding pyramid with its interesting tower on the summit, now called Birs Nimrud, occupied a similar position in the dreary desert. Between the latter and the mound we were on, the Euphrates winds her silent way, meandering among the date groves which conceal the town of Hillah. After visiting the other mounds to the E. of [the] high [?] road we made our way to our encampment which was pitched on the bank of the Euphrates about 3 miles above Hillah. Churchill and myself had separated from the [main] party and visited what I consider the most interesting part of the ruins, the Kasr or Palace, near which is the sculptured figure described by Rich as a lion and by the officers of the Euphrates expedition as an elephant with the tusk broken off (pl. 10). As we could not decide the dispute, in fact the animal looked to me quite as much like a poodle dog as a lion or elephant, we determined on returning and having a thorough examination, so we started from camp at mid-day under a broiling sun accompanied by four pickers and miners, servants and sketch-books. After setting our men to work we sat ourselves down and took various sketches of the building which still remains. There is but a little & that little not picturesque tho' truly interesting. It is constructed of furnace dried bricks of the finest quality &

---

69 Loftus 1857: 20.

cemented together with fine mortar. Each brick on the underside is inscribed with cuneiform characters, but so firmly did they adhere that I could not procure any. I was very anxious to obtain a few bricks for our Museum but after searching in vain among the ruins I gave up the attempt, as I would not desecrate the only remaining building by using the pickaxe with the chance of destroying many more than I could obtain. This mound is of great extent, being 700 yards square, but forming only a mass of rubbish (with the exception of the Kasr) owing to the excavations which have been carried on for bricks for building. When it is taken into consideration that all the cities or towns in the neighbourhood have been supplied with materials from hence – Baghdad, Busrah, Kerbala, Meshed Ali, Kufa, Ctesiphon, Seleucia – many of these now scarcely to be recognised – can it be wondered at that so little of Babylon remains. The only wonder is that there is yet so much existing. The house I now write from is built of bricks of Babylon taken from the ruins of Ctesiphon by Col Taylor. Babylon must have been a brick quarry for ages and is capable yet of furnishing material for ages to come. The mound of the Kasr has a most extraordinary appearance furrowed and overturned by the works which have been there carried on. It much more deserves the name of Mujelibè than the first mound. It is a mass of indescribable confusion & it is the opinion of our whole party that it is utterly impossible to recognise one single point in these ruins as described by the various early historians. Rich however correct he may be in his general account & measures of the mounds, has been misled and has misled others by his enthusiasm. I grant that it is most pleasing to speculate on these subjects but to attempt to trace out the plan of ancient Babylon is most absurd. Upwards of 2000 years ago the "mighty city" was a vast ruin – since that time what changes must have taken place in its remaining features – immense cities have been built of its ruins – the Euphrates has frequently overflowed its banks, probably changed its course and each succeeding overflow has left behind a deposit of thick mud or washed away a portion of the ruins. The heavy rains of winter, and the clouds of sand carried along by the winds of the desert, unchecked in their course, must all have lent their aid in changing the features of these ruins. Major Rennell's[70] idea [that] the Euphrates [might] have flowed between the Mujelibè and mound of Amran-ibn-Ali is I think outrageous. Notwithstanding this opinion that our writers have overstretched their mark, as I sat near the ancient tree, a tamarisk, the only tree existing on the mound, and watched the progress of the workmen, fancy, ever ready to impose on us, led my mind astray and pictured to me the astounding events which are recorded in our sacred volume as having occurred on this spot. Here was the "the beginning of Nimrud's kingdom", and here probably too was the tower whose top reached unto heaven built of brick which they had for stone & lime for mortar! The captivity of the Jews, Daniel and the lions [den], Belshazzar's feast and [the] writing on the wall, the siege by Cyrus, Alexander's visit, etc., etc. Here I sat undisturbed in pleasing forgetfulness of the present, when the Colonel and Dervish Pasha awoke me from my delightful dream, and I then found that my men had also been buried in oblivion tho' of a different kind; their work finished they had covered themselves up in their abbas and gone to sleep. There is no mistake about the sculpture. It is to all intents and purposes a lion, tho' still of the poodle dog breed. However it could have been mistaken for an elephant I can't conceive. He has a tail reaching to the ground, claws on his feet, short thick legs and a representation of his hairy breast, which roughness was taken for the trunk! After the party were gone, I cleared all the earth & rubbish from the various parts. The nose is broken off, but there can be no doubt about is being a lion standing over the prostrate body of a man with his hand raised to keep the lion off. It is the rudest style of art imaginable, yet the proportions are good. It appears to me to be occupying the same position as the bulls & lions at Nineveh, viz. the entrance. In the middle of the side is a hole into which I imagine iron or copper has been inserted to clamp it to the doorway. I took the dimensions of the figure which are length of body 8 ft 9", breadth 2 ft 10 ½", depth 9 ½ in, height of lion inclusive of the base 5 ft 4 ½ in. Churchill took a sketch, and the sun gradually sank in the horizon as we returned to the camp much pleased with our day's work. We gave a grand

---

70   Major James Rennell (1742–1830). See his *Geographical System of Herodotus* and C J Rich's two memoirs on Babylon (London 1815, 1818).

CHAPTER FOUR

dinner to the Pasha and the Russians. The governor of Hillah sent out a guard of honour and his military band. On the site of Babylon, we ate of soup, vegetables and cheese and salmon too preserved in London while at the anterior [?] we drank champagne and listened to the band playing, shall I say it, Strauss waltzes!! Any one of these things was enough to drive the thought of Babylon from the thoughts, and we gave ourselves up to the things that be, forgetting those that were. To amuse us, the governor had sent a dancing boy, who after dinner performed some of the most graceful dances I have seen in the East. There were none of those disgusting movements we had been in the habit of seeing. Seated around round a fire of date branches placed in a round grate & raised on a pole, our whole party & attendants gathered together formed a fantastic scene. One of the lad's dances was a most strange one – wheeling round & round he gradually undressed himself to his shirt! But his pace was so great that we could not perceive the slightest motions of his arms, or how he got rid of his clothes. He threw a blanket round himself and re-dressed himself in the same extraordinary manner. I should have mentioned that he was dressed as a girl in a sort of Spanish dress, decorated with silver ornaments etc. Instead of castanets he made the most dexterous use of silver rings attached to his fingers. The Turks were in ecstasies with his grace. He reminded me of "the Scarlet Lady of Babylon" and of the prophecy that "Satyrs shall dance there". After I crept into my little camp bed, surrounded by my mosquito net, I lay for a length of time thinking over what I had seen this day; that night I shall never forget as the delicious cooling breeze set in down the Euphrates, more delicious after the roasting we had experienced in the midday sun. I would gladly have gone to sleep, but the steady tread of the sentinel close to my bed kept me awake for upwards of an hour. The beautiful sky of this region appeared even more beautiful than usual this evening & the stars were bright. It might have been mere fancy, yet such seemed the case. It has often struck me & I believe I have mentioned it before that it is strange the British Association are erecting large observatories in various parts of the world, and yet Babylonia and Chaldea, the great region of astronomy, is forgotten or neglected. Surely [there are] no places so suited for astronomical investigation as this country, where stars of the fourth magnitude are distinctly visible to the naked eye. Since May not a cloud has appeared on the horizon & the number of falling stars, meteors, is almost incredible. More might be effected here in one year than in other places in 3 or 4. Baghdad would make a good position. At 5.45 am we left our camp, a grand parade, & I must say the scene was beautiful as we approached Hillah. Our guard of the previous night led the way followed by the band. The Governor and an extra guard met us halfway. Then followed the Pasha's 3 led [sic] horses, then the 2 incessant kettle-drums. The Pasha, the English and Russian colonel[s] followed & then ourselves & officers of the Pasha. Servants, baggage & escort brought up the rear. We rode thro' a grove of date trees, with their golden fruit, looking more golden as the sun fell on them. Hillah is essentially an Arab city and being far removed from the seat of government, the arrival of a Pasha and 2 European Commissioners was an event of a very uncommon occurrence. The whole population was therefore out to receive us, all bowing with the utmost reverence to the high dignity of our fat friend, who if he had not been so much like Punch we might have fancied to ourselves to have been Belus himself or Alexander, or any other great conqueror of old, entering conquered Babylon! But as there were a troop of soldiers before us, utterly unlike any Alexander led – in their European costume, the trousers over the baggy Turkish drawers, giving their sterns a truly Turkish aspect! Then there was the band, playing European marches & Strauss waltzes! The imagination could not be deceived so we rode on, taking the present moment as it appeared in reality. The dust was a great annoyance as it penetrated to every part of the body, & we were nearly choked by it – we crossed the wicker [?] bridge of boats in marching order, in momentary expectation of being precipitated into the Euphrates! But Allah was great & we all arrived safely on the opposite side, where Glascott's horse's head was nearly blown off by one of the cannon firing salutes! After taking coffee & sherbet at the Serai, we marched in the same order thro' the town which struck me as being rather more picturesque on the river than most Turkish towns. It is, however, like all others, in a most tumbledown condition & equally filthy with its neighbours. Near the West Gate the Hillah escort left us & conducted by Tahir Bey[71] the Military Governor, who continued with us for the rest of our

---

71 Mentioned Loftus 1857: 24.

journey, we proceeded across the plain to the celebrated Birs Nimrud, the supposed Tower of Babel, which at 6 miles distance rose in solitary grandeur before us. A mighty tomb to mark the burial place of "the mighty Babylon, the queen of kingdoms & the glory of the Chaldees' excellency".[72] The plain between it and Hillah is strewed with pottery & portions of bricks & [is] as usual intersected with canals. Whether or not it has formed a part of the city, it is I am quite certain impossible to say at the present day. The remains of pottery would induce me to the belief that it did, while the absence of mounds and its level with the surrounding desert would induce a contrary belief. As we approached the ground became covered with pieces of vitrified brick, having all the appearance of a glassworks slag, and just before reaching the large mound of Ibrahim al-Khalil we passed a small rise entirely covered with it. From the tomb on the former mound is obtained the best view of the Birs, the mound of which is circular and composed of sun dried bricks covered by an enormous quantity of debris from the upper building, and the ascent was by no means an easy one. Portions of the cuneiform inscriptions were visible on the bricks, none of which I saw perfect. I may here mention that Major Rawlinson has decided the building to be of the date of Nebuchadnezzar from the inscription [on] one brick in his possession.

Layers of brick are distinctly visible, but I will not enter into a longer description of the Birs, or attempt to speculate on its origin, as this has been done at length by others who had more time to devote to the examination of the mound than we had. From its top the view was most extensive and I took bearings [on] the Mujelibè, Keffil[73] and the Tomb of Ezekiel, Meshed Ali, Kerbala, etc. On the north-west like a vast sea extend the marshes of Babylon, constantly kept in existence by the annual inundations of the Euphrates. Of this I shall say more by next post, as I have exhausted both paper and postage allowance this time. But as I stood on this mound and viewed all the scene around, the prophecy struck me as being fulfilled to the letter: "I will also make it a possession for the bittern, and pools of water, and I will sweep it

---

72   Isaiah 13: 19.
73   Marked on map in Loftus 1857.

with the besom of destruction" [74] and "Babylon shall become heaps, a dwelling place for dragons (wild beasts), an astonishment and a wilderness, a land wherein no man dwelleth neither doth any son of man pass thereby",[75] but I must conclude. Pray remember me to all my Nat. Hist. friends and believe me that all communications are thankfully received.

Believe me truly yours,

W.K. Loftus

Pray excuse mistakes as I write in a hurry

Letter 26, Baghdad, 9 Oct 1849

My dear Charlton,

In my last letter I endeavoured to convey to you some idea, a vague one I fear, of my impressions on visiting the ruins of Ancient Babylon. In this I shall endeavour to conduct you back to our starting point [of] Gherrara. After our extended tour to the most revered of the shrines of Shia pilgrimage at Meshed Ali and Kerbala – places seldom visited by Europeans on account of the great difficulty of access to them thro' tribes of plundering Arabs. After resting during the heat of the day at the foot of the wonderful Birs Nimrud, we again started at 3.15 pm and arrived at Keffil at a little before six. The road lay along the E. shore of the great 'Paludes Babyloniae'[76] – "the possession of the bittern" – which extends from the Euphrates below Musseib[77] round the N & W of the Birs and thence southwards till they join the marshes. Of these I shall say more afterwards. Our ride was a rough one owing to the enormous quantity of ancient canals which crossed our path. Arriving at Keffil we encamped on the S.E. of the town under two date palms, which from their great scantiness

---

74   Isaiah 14: 23.
75   Jeremiah 51: 37.
76   The marshes. See Loftus 1857: 46.
77   Marked on map in Loftus 1857; see Loftus 1857: p. 69.

CHAPTER FOUR

of leaves, as the light of the rice straw torches fell on them, appeared like two overgrown Dutch brooms; these were the only signs of cultivation. The foul air from the marsh laid the seeds of fever once more in our camp, which made its appearance as we proceeded. Keffil is chiefly inhabited by Jews, as Ezekiel's tomb is here. We of course visited the tomb, which is under a dome with an after dinner sponge cake – formed spire, rising from the centre! The tomb is covered by a large oblong box, ornamented with English chintz drapery and surmounted with little flags of crimson and green. With the exception of the underside of the dome, which was really beautifully painted in Arabesque, there was nothing more remarkable about the building, if I except the filth which surrounded and covered it. The holy roof of the tomb of the prophet appeared to be the dunghill of the town! It was at this little town after the affair a few weeks ago between the Arabs and the Kadi, who farm [?] the revenue of the government, that the present Pasha of Baghdad (then Mushir or Military Governor of the province) placed a garrison of 40 men. The Arabs soon after attacked the place and took it, but upon the Mushir's return they made off and he found it completely deserted, while the garrison was strewed about with their throats all cut. There are now no traces of this sad affair, and one can scarcely conceive that such an occurrence had so lately taken place. Having sent our horses by land, we embarked in small sailing boats and much enjoyed our trip by water to a place called Nebbi Yunus[78] (no relation I believe to the tomb of the same name on the site of Nineveh) which we accomplished in 4 ½ hours. The current setting in from the Euphrates runs thro' these marshes at the rate of 4 or 5 miles an hour where the stream is narrow. On either side of us were enormous rice fields, protected from inundation by dykes of matting and tamarisk stakes. The chief wealth of the province of Baghdad is derived from these paddy fields. The Arabs are here in the most primitive state, much more resembling the descriptions we read of the wild Indians of America, than what we picture to ourselves as an Arab. Almost in a state of nudity, with their skins brown as mahogany and their figures like so many miniature Apollos, and with their long black hair streaming in the breeze, they frequently paddled past us in their long & narrow canoes of

---

78 Marked on map in Loftus 1857.

teak. Their dwellings are equally rude – plaited rice straw arched overhead forms their only shelter from the intense heat [of] the mid-day sun. They appear to be a hard-working race, and would no doubt prosper under a better government but ground down as they are by the ruinous exactions of their Turkish oppressors, is it to be wondered at that they now and then break bounds, and destroy all they lay hands upon? If the various tribes could forget their deadly blood feuds & unite, how easily could they repay with interest the injustice they have so long suffered, and drive the effeminate Turk into other regions. The Arab hates the Turk as heartily as the latter does the Persian. At Nebbi Yunus we found the horses had just swum the marsh. Here I remained behind collecting shells for an hour and at 1.30 I mounted my horse for Meshed Ali which I reached at 3.15. Never shall I forget that short ride. The sun shone burning hot which even a thick umbrella could not ward off. The road itself was truly a burning desert on which not a particle of vegetation grew. The sun above and the refraction from the sand below almost roasted me while my poor horse was almost overpowered and at every 200 paces made for the little shade afforded by the little round towers which form a line of defence [for] the town against the attacks of the Arabs. On the road I traversed the ruined heaps which mark the site of Mohammedan learning, Kufa, the [xxxx] of the then conquering Arabia [and] the origin I believe of Kufic characters. In the ruins stands a mosque where Ali the son-in-law & successor of the Prophet fell and whence his body was conveyed to Meshed Ali which sprang up around the tomb.

Our party it appears visited the mosque at Kufa and were shown several remarkable spots, where the angel Gabriel descended from Heaven [and] prayed, where Adam first breathed air [?], [and] where the deluge first broke out from a hole in the earth. Entering the gate of Meshed Ali I found our tents pitched in a large oblong place between the walls and houses. This was at the request of our excellent friend the Governor of Hillah who accompanied us as he did not deem it safe to encamp without the town. After washing and dressing ourselves we proceeded with a strong military guard to see the Mosque of Imam Ali. We went straight into the middle court and were all perfectly astounded at the magnificent scene before us. We had all heard that the mosques at Meshed Ali and Kerbala were beautiful buildings but we had formed no conception of the reality. Like all eastern places of worship this mosque stands in a square courtyard around which the wall, adorned with exquisite Persian painting, excited the greatest admiration. Birds, flowers and scrolls are mingled in close array while the extreme delicacy of the whole was such as to give us a most favourable opinion of Persian art. The walls of the mosque are adorned in a similar style. The two tall minarets and the beautifully proportioned dome are formed of gilded tiles each of which cost 2 tomans, equivalent [to] a pound sterling. In the interior of course [we] were not admitted but we understood that it contains treasure to an enormous value and that a portion is paved with golden flags. I do not believe this to be exaggerated judging from the value we saw expended on the exterior.

Ali is, as you know, the great saint of Persians and the bone of contention between the 2 sects of the Mohammedan religion. It is therefore not surprising that they should enrich this shrine as much as possible. I cannot undertake to convey to you any further idea of this most beautiful building and shall therefore proceed to detail our own adventures, but before doing so I must notice "the stalls of money-changers and those who sold doves".[79] They crowd the court and one could not fail to remember the doings of our Saviour in the court of the Temple at Jerusalem. You are perhaps surprised at our being permitted to enter the mosque at all, so were we ourselves. The governor of Hillah who commands this district was anxious we should see as much as possible and the guard accompanied us lest there might be any attempt at an outbreak. He told us afterwards that he was once getting rather alarmed at the looks of the people who I really believe were only restrained from violence by the sight of the fixed bayonets of the soldiers. Meshed Ali and Kerbala are nests of pirates and vagabonds and I shall not easily forget the fiendish expression of the surrounding crowds as they gave way with ill grace at our approach only that they might escape contamination by coming into contact with infidel dogs who dared to enter their holy sanctuary. The scowl or frown and the hand on dagger were seen at every step and many a deep curse was heaped on our souls as we accidentally brushed past the filthy

---

79   John 2: 14.

garments of some Persian devil (please excuse the term). At night our guard was doubled and a strong picket stationed within ten paces of our little beds. A sentinel kept the Colonel and myself awake nearly all night by his incessant pacing backwards and forwards between our beds. But for the careful attention of the Governor our friends in England might have heard of our throats being cut in the night. The number of Persian pilgrims who visit the shrines of Meshed Ali and Kerbala yearly is said to be 100,000, while from 8 to 10,000 are carried to each place for burial. The corpse is conveyed in a wooden case through which the stench penetrates [in] so deadly [a manner] that out of 100 mourners 15 or 20 are generally carried off. On arrival the relatives endeavour to make a good bargain with the authorities at the mosque for burial, while the latter endeavour to screw out as much [xxxx] as possible. 2 or 3 days are generally spent in this manner after which the body is brought into the square where the bargain is screwed still tighter by the people at the mosque and the corpse is frequently exposed until one party or the other gives in or until the stench infects the whole neighbourhood. The relatives who are obliged to live during all time close to the body are generally obliged to cash up in self-defence. From 10 to 200 tomans (£5 to £100) is the sum charged for burial. We were not aware till the following day that several bodies had been removed to make space for us only an hour or two before our arrival but about 3.30 the wind changed and with it came such a horrid putrid & foul stench that we cut our [xxxx] as fast as our horses could carry us with our hands to our noses till we were fairly into the desert. With this exception we were all delighted with Meshed Ali which is in much better preservation than any town I have yet seen in Turkey but this is entirely owing to the Persians who are enriching the place considerably. It is supplied with water from the Bahr al-Najaf,[80] a large inundation slightly salt but kept fresh by the influx of the Euphrates during its rise. It stretches out in a vast sea to an unknown distance into the great Arabian Desert on the skirts of which we now travelled. As we left the gates a salute of guns was fired from the walls and as each flash was reflected on the golden dome of the mosque the effect was truly beautiful. Starting at 5.10 am

---

80 See Loftus 1857: 50 (Bahr-i-Nedjef).

we took the shortest route to Kerbala across the desert, one seldom traversed. We met nothing [and] we saw nothing but here and there an Arab tomb with a few rushes at the head and foot and now and then a human skull arrested the attention and afforded ground for reflection, pleasing or otherwise as the thoughts led onwards. At 11.30 am we encamped on the west side of the marsh in sight of the Birs Nimrud and on Sept 20th we started at 3.20 am and arrived at Kerbala at 11.45, a very long and tedious march without a single point of interest. At the entrance to the gardens we were met as at Hillah by the grandees guard & band, but such a band it would have made you grin like grim death to have heard it – everyone played his own tune in his own time and with all his strength so that if there had been any old cows there at the time they must have died of it. The remembrance of the scene even now makes me almost fit to die of laughter. We were all of us as much disappointed with the mosque of the Imam Houssein as we were pleased with that of Ali. There is really nothing remarkable about it tho' it is considered the more aristocratic place of burial. Here they would not allow us to enter the outer court & tho' attended by a strong guard we must have created a great row if we had made the attempt. One or two dervishes stood at the doorway armed with big sticks and would easily have excited the crowd. It is said that the Yerrimasis[81] are again gathering together on the move. If so, Abdi Pasha will have his work cut out before he will be able to rid the town of them. The marks of the siege under Nedjib Pasha are still visible on the walls and the still ruinous houses within the Hillah Gate show the destruction that was dealt from the batteries of the Turkish army. Many are the tales of horrid massacre we have heard related and judging from the well-known hatred between Turk & Persian, the uncivilization and fanaticism of both, we could imagine that they were not much overstretched. One or two of our Mohammedan servants took some of our Christians into the court of the mosque when they were all seized, shrieked [?] [at] and stoned and [were] glad to cut and run like dogs with their tails between their legs. It is well they got off so easily. You are aware that the then resident at Baghdad Col Taylor lost his valuable appointment in consequence of not

---

81   See Loftus 1857: 64–5.

having protested against the proceedings of the Pasha. I had forgotten to mention our reception at the Serai where a Turkish breakfast was prepared for us, 16 or 18 hungry animals after a ride of 9 hours. Fancy 32 or 36 paws thrust into piles of pilaf and dishes of greasy vegetables and the many slips which took place between the dish and the lip. After fairly and literally pitching into messes which at another time I should have certainly declined I felt that a good piece of English beef & a glass of ale would have been even then most acceptable. However what with laughing and a determination to do our best we succeeded in making the dishes look exceedingly foolish [sic]. The oil that morning ran down our beards to the shirts of our clothing. On 21st Sept we left Kerbala at 3 pm and reached the W. bank of the Euphrates opposite Musseib at 8.30. We encamped here for the night, swam our horses over early next morning [and] crossed ourselves by means of kufahs, the round wicker boats described by Herodotus and which are of precisely similar construction as the present day and covered with the bitumen from Hit where Noah is supposed to have procured the same substance to daub over the ark. Sept 22nd – left Musseib (a miserable place) at 7.30 am and reached our old encamping ground at Mizrakji Khan at 10 from which we proceeded in two parties. As Churchill was very ill of fever I stayed behind to take charge of him and it was well I did or he would not have reached camp that night. I succeeded in bringing the poor fellow in by 10 o'clock. To avoid the sun we were off next morning at 3.30 and arrived at Gherrara Ferry at 7.30, thus concluding a most delightful and instructive journey of about 200 miles. We remained at Gherrara till the despatch of the last post & on the 29th we were all again in motion to the Taq-e Kisra at Ctesiphon where we remained in camp till yesterday enjoying ourselves very much in coursing, shooting francolins (the game of this country) and more especially spear-hunting the wild boar or lion. After 3 days of hard beating we gave up the attempt of finding any. As to the lion, I imagine many of my friends would have turned to the right about and left the lion to pass his time most agreeably to himself. The lion is well known to visit Ctesiphon and every night we heard him within 100 yards of the camp seeking what he might devour. His cry at night is much more like a child or a jackal than a lion. In fact, I was much disappointed when I when I first heard him. Major Rawlinson spent a couple of days with us and leaves for England on Monday.

Capt Kemball[82] at Bushire has arrived to supply his place and with him Capt Newbold.[83] The vice resident is at the Deccan for the benefit of his health. The latter is a well-known geologist and as I have long had in contemplation a trip to the Hamrin Hills I think I shall join him on his intended trip to Mosul [?] & to the burning fountains of Kirkuk.

I have now I think written you a pretty long letter and must conclude. Give my best remembrance to all our mutual [?] friends in the "Canny Town" and please tell Blacklock that I have received his long and interesting letter to which I shall reply shortly. I assure you that such letters are a Godsend.

Believe me, my dear C,

Yours most sincerely

Wm Kennett Loftus.

Letter 27, Gherrara, 25 Oct 1849

My dear Edward,

I sit down to redeem my promise of writing to you by this post tho' I have little to say but I will relate what has taken place since last post. On the 14th Major Rawlinson left Baghdad for Constantinople by the route I came and attended by my old servant George. In return for him I have received an Armenian servant of the Major's called 'Ohannes' who I hope will be of some advantage to me when in the mountains as he not only speaks English, Arabic and Turkish but also Kurdish. With him and my good lad Saleh I think I shall do. Last Friday we lunched with Capt Jones and afterwards started for Akker Koof as I mentioned in the hope of getting a little pig hunting. We followed the course of the Doandi [?] one of the canals which connect the Tigris and

---

82 Captain (later General) Arnold Burrowes Kemball (1820–1908) was at this time Assistant Resident at Bushire. See Layard 1853: 474.
83 Captain Thomas John Newbold (1807–50) of the East India Company was an authority on the geology of South India. See Layard 1853; 100, note.

the Euphrates and plunged fairly into the fens of Mesopotamia where we remained encamped among the Arabs until yesterday. We beat the jungle on every side with a line of 40 spears and horsemen but all to no purpose. The pigs either were not there or they were making hookey at us in the water. I believe that the inundation destroyed them in the spring.

We saw not a [trace] of the pigs till Monday night when Casolani (Priv Sec of Major Rawlinson) and I saw but one. Our camp was at some distance from the ruin but I was so pleased with it on my first visit on Saturday that I made up another party on Monday afternoon. In my opinion it is as interesting as the ruins of Hillah and from its primitive style of architecture (if one can make use of such a term for a pile of mud) I believe it to be older than any of the latter excepting perhaps the Mujelibè which is probably of about the same date. In the distance Akker Koof much resembles the Birs Nimrud being built on the top of a lofty mound, though not so lofty as that of the so-called Tower of Babel. The ruin is a solid mass of sun-dried brickwork about 120 ft high but much worn down by the action of the rain upon it for an unknown series of years. The bricks each about 12 in square are cemented together with simple mud while between every layer of seven bricks is placed a layer of reeds probably for the purpose of forming a fresh and level foundation for the next series. These reeds have in most instances been plaited but here I remarked it was in a much more irregular manner and at one place I observed a projecting portion which was twisted like a cable. From the rains having washed the mud off the exposed surface of the ruin these layers of reeds are seen like so many penthouses projecting over and consequently protecting the bricks beneath. On the eastern side about 40 feet from the base of the structure is a large hole penetrating some distance into the ruin and which appears to have been a passage but although we brought ropes and instruments for ascending we found it impossible to effect this and so gave up the attempt. The building on all sides is pierced with small square holes similar to those seen at the Birs and which could only have served to ventilate and dry the bricks. By some this is supposed to be the site of Sittace but I conceive the ruin is of much more ancient date. The very primitive materials used and its similarity to some of the ruins of Babylon which are acknowledged to be at least as old

CHAPTER FOUR

as Nebuchadnezzar would certainly authorise us to assign it as ancient a date. May it not have been one of those "high places" so often mentioned in Scripture upon which the priests of Baal used to offer their sacrifices? The mound itself on which the building stands offered me sufficient food for enquiry. It is a natural mound (not artificial as is represented) and composed of gravel from the primitive or I should more correctly call it volcanic and igneous rocks of Kurdistan and the Taurus. The pebbles are small and much rounded by attrition and I believe this mound is an outlier of the same bed which running down the centre of Mesopotamia crosses the road between Baghdad and Hillah at Bir-onus Khan[84] and ends near El Heimar (the red). From this point to the sea will be nothing but alluvium. Whether this gravel is the effect of the sculptural Deluge or not I cannot say but further investigation may disclose something. I am therefore about making [i.e. to make] an extended tour to the Hamrin Hills and propose starting this week for Delli Abbas[85] and crossing the junction of the Diyala and the Alhen [?] , seek out the reported bed of coal and so on to Senn [?] on the Tigris. I expect to do this in a fortnight so that you must not expect to hear from me by next post. It is possible that I may get stripped by the Anazzah [Aneiza?] who are out plundering [and] if so I shall have to walk back in my buff jerkin as Layard had once to do when coming from Busrah.

I have determined upon this excursion as we have no instructions about proceeding down the river and if the Turks & Russians actually go to war of course Tcherikoff and the Muscovites will be recalled and we [will be] left for further instructions. This certainly is a pretty state of uncertainty. The weather is now delightful and tho' I am now (10 am) writing without collar or waistcoat the nights are cold and we took [?] to our tents on the 20th tho' we dined last night on the terrace. The doctor however and his servants who did not go with us are lying however at the Russian camp with fever & that very severely. The doctor and one of the servants had it. [From] the first they thought they were going to escape but it proved a case of no go. Wood is now the only one left scot free but he has taken at least a cartload of medicine. I am

---

84 Marked on map in Loftus 1857.
85 For Delli Abbas see map in Layard 1853: 100, note.

quite delighted with my little tent. It is so snug and comfortable and having it to myself is a great comfort. I was at first afraid the colonel intended we should be two in each tent which would have been anything but agreeable. We have not received your letter of the 9th ult. by this post in consequence of the detention of the steamer at Malta and elsewhere. One of Her Majesty's vessels brought the information to Constantinople. Next post will bring letters of the 29th. Will you be kind enough to tell Blacklock I shall probably tip [?] him a yarn on the Hamrin Hills if I find anything which I think will be interesting to the numerously attended meetings of the Natural History Society of Newcastle upon Tyne.

Having nothing else worth communicating I now conclude.

Believe me my dear Edward,

Yours sincerely,

Wm Kennett Loftus.

Letter 28, Baghdad, 4 December 1849

My dear Cousin,

The Dutch map enclosed in yours of the 15th has just reached me. It is exceedingly curious and at the same time most interesting and I am truly obliged to you for it. It must have cost you some time and trouble. I have looked it over but not examined it very closely and I think it has been constructed from a careful reading of the ancient authors and a good deal of imagination combined. The lower part is I believe pretty correct as regards the Tigris flowing into the Gulf in former days, at least I have so understood from what I have read on the subject. That the waters of the Gulf spread much further to the north previous to historical knowledge is certain as marine shells most of the same species as those at present existing in the Gulf have been found near Wasut [Wasit] above the junction of the two rivers. The course of the Phrat [Euphrates] in the neighbourhood of Babylon is most interesting and as I have just returned from a careful examination

CHAPTER FOUR

of the locality it will perhaps be a guide for me to direct my attention more particularly to the points which I have or may have already casually noted.

Captain Newbold and myself had a most delightful trip together of eight days and here we are safely returned in spite of the Arabs who are certainly out in every direction. Halfway between Baghdad and Hillah we met a party of about 150 who were returning from a plundering expedition against the Montefic[86] but they did not in the least interfere with us or our baggage. They raised their war-cry at first sight of our little party but as we rode forward boldly they ceased their song and seemed to enjoy the joke at not being able to alarm us as they grinned and shewed their beautiful white teeth and gave us customary greeting as we passed. We encamped two nights on the W. bank near the river on probably the ancient wall close to the mound of the Kasr and we enjoyed our examination of the old ruins undisturbed. I think I know every hole and corner about the place. We visited the Birs alone [but with] our cavass to hold our horses and there we remained two hours in the heart of the country of the Khuzeyl[87] tribe who are in revolt against the Pasha. Their tents were at a very short distance but no one annoyed us. Had we taken an escort as our cavass wished it is probable we should have returned in the primitive dress. I rode to El Heimar with only my servant (11 miles distant from the Kasr) and from thence across country to join Capt Newbold at Musseib as I went into Hillah for the purpose of hunting after antiques and a perfect Babylonian brick with cuneiform inscription for the Newcastle Museum. I was however unsuccessful as there were none in the place. I tried hard to procure one myself at the Kasr but the mortar is so strong that it is impossible to procure one whole. El Heimar is a very interesting ruin of red brick whence the name "the red", a Birs on a small scale, but I could discover no trace of the gravel which was the more immediate cause of my visit. Near Iskenderun [?] between Baghdad and Hillah I found a large bed of pebbles resting on gypsum in situ, a fact which [had] not been previously ascertained. It is exceedingly extensive and probably underlies the whole of this part of the country. We also fell in with it on our road to Kerbala which we also visited. I have become much interested

---

86   For the Montefic Arabs see Loftus 1857: 9.
87   For the Khuzeyl Arabs see Loftus 1857: 10–11.

in this pebble bed and have most carefully examined its composition and tho' I cannot as yet decide on its origin from want of sufficient data, I am inclined to think it diluvial and probably connected with [the] scriptural deluge. Further examination along the flank of the Persian hills will most likely throw light on this interesting subject. I purpose sending a series of the pebbles I collected at random to Sir Henry De la Beche with a list of such as I have made out and he may probably direct my attention to some future researches. We are now all actively employed in preparations for our final departure for Mohammerah and I hope to be en route before 1850. At Mohammerah I believe we shall remain four or five months as the sheikhs of the various tribes will have to be brought together there. This will facilitate our future movement towards the mountains. Should our horses proceed by land I hope to be able to visit Wasut and satisfy myself further about the marine beds there. It is difficult of access however on account of the Arabs. We did not succeed in reaching El Kaddar [?][88] not from fear of these gentry but because we found a certain person not to be named had evidently set his mind on describing it himself and we did not think it right to encroach on his domains. I am inclined to believe it is a Roman station.

However, we shall in due time see. As we cannot any longer with a shadow of decency be the guests of our excellent friend the Resident, the Col has taken the house next door for our final operations here. Immediately after the post tomorrow I commence preparing my first despatch for the British Museum. It will be sent off by the same vessel with the batch of Nineveh sculptures now at Busrah [Basra] so that they will all go direct to the Museum. My time therefore will be fully taken up and I fear my correspondents in England must not expect to have their letters answered for a post or two. I am in excellent condition & my late trip has taken down the superfluous quantity of fat I had previously gathered and which I feared betokened another attack of fever. Thank God the weather is now English and it is a perfect pleasure to be on horseback all day long. I wish the Colonel were not so fearful of the Arabs eating some of us up tho' of course it is right to look after the safety of his

---

88 This is presumably a reference to Ukhaydir, the Islamic period (8th century AD) palace about 50 km south of Karbala. To judge from the context, the unnamed person who wants to describe it is probably Layard.

party. He is too careful & unless he thinks a little otherwise than at present my work I doubt will be too confined. To perform it to my own satisfaction I must expose myself to a certain degree of risk. Every one of my profession in such a country as this must of necessity do so but there is no need to resist 50 men with sword & pistol who are determined to strip you. I have fully made up my mind to pay this penalty a few times before my return. And so the Turco-Russian question is settled. It indeed reflects the highest credit on the conduct of my noble friend Sir Stratford Canning and has added another feather to the cap of our country. Long may she remain in the same proud position to dictate justice & humanity to the world. The winter with you appears to have set in early. Give my best remembrances, etc, etc.

Wm Kennett Loftus

Letter 29, Baghdad, 19 December 1849

My dear cousin,

I scribble you a hasty letter. Mather will inform you of my movements and I have nothing more to add except that Newbold and I in returning from a visit to Akker Koof met a large party of Arabs, evidently birds of the desert. They were the finest set of fellows I have seen here. They allowed us to pass unmolested tho' evidently inclined to have a row with our Mohammedan servants. In a few days afterwards judge the astonishment of us all when our old friend Suttum our guide to Al Hadhr made his appearance. His whole tribe with their sheikh Ferhan, the son of Layard's hero Sofuk are come down to winter a little above Akker Koof. He stayed two days with us and was as delighted as ourselves to meet again. We asked him how the Shammar allowed old Nedjib to escape them and he said "Aha! The old fellow was wide awake for he turned off the road to the right or we would have pinned him". The 150 Arabs we met on our road to Hillah and those between Akker Koof & Baghdad were Shammar. The only autograph I have of Layard's is in a private letter which I wish to keep but Mr Watson is quite welcome to the envelope which I presume will answer his purpose and you will oblige me by giving it to him with my best remembrance. I have received your kind letter of Nov 4th but as you say there is nothing which requires an answer.

Yours affectionately,

Wm Kennett Loftus.

P.S. I have not written to Mr Sopwith[89] since I left London not because I have forgotten his kindness but because I thought you would not fail to remember me to him. When I have matter of a kind sufficiently interesting to him as a geologist I shall certainly communicate with him. If possible however I shall communicate with him from Mohammerah after we have got settled. I am now in utter confusion and you must please excuse more.

I had forgotten to mention that an account of a journey performed by poor Dr Ross and Fraser from Baghdad to Suk-es-Sheioukh and back is to be found in Fraser's work on Koordistan and Mesopotamia in 2 vols (1840). He gives also a short account of the Chaldaean mounds in his little book. Their journey and geographical notes have never been published tho' I have seen a private map of their route. Wasut[90] they did not attempt. If it is to be reached I am determined to go tho' I fear the waters are out. I hope to bring back a fine series of fossils from there and near Tell Ede.[91]

Letter 30, Baghdad, December 19 1849

My dear Edward,

I have scarcely a moment to spare and you must therefore be contented with a hasty letter. The final order has gone forth and we are in a state of the utmost confusion attendant on preparations for our departure from the civilized world

---

89 Thomas Sopwith, geologist and mining engineer. See Ch. 1, n.11.
90 For the location of Wasut, see map in Loftus 1857.
91 For Tell Ede, see Loftus 1857: 118–19.

for an indefinite period. I have just finished the packing of the first collection for the British Museum. In my last I told you I had obtained the Colonel's permission to accompany the troops to Busrah and Mohammerah, a journey of 21 days or possibly a month through the land of Chaldea, a land not of honey but of ancient mounds and wild Arab hordes. I am most anxious to see Niffar,[92] the Babylon of Major Rawlinson, and if I succeed in reaching [the] Wasut ruins I shall achieve what, I believe, but one Englishman has yet attempted. But to do this I must quit our escort as I certainly will not run the chance of the ill feeling between the Nazim [?] and the Arabs and besides, both places are far from our direct route. The Colonel has permitted Churchill to accompany me. He speaks a little Arabic and his company is very desirable. This is Wednesday and we start on Friday morning so that our Christmas dinner of this year will possibly be eaten under the shelter of the hoary ruin of some unknown city of the earliest ages. I have ordered our plum pudding to be prepared and I hope a wild goose will find its way to the festive carpet of our tent. But of course we must adopt the recipe of Mrs Somebody who advised "first catch your goose and then cook him". I only hope ours may not be a wild goose chase after all. We are both in excellent health and spirits and longing to be off. I dare say during some of your Xmas festivities in your very modern ! [sic] town [?] you may remember your absent friend and wonder what he is about and where he is, fancy him muffled up in all the clothing he can collect, journeying over the bare desert with a freezing wind & pouring rain, or spying out some distant ruin, all excitement till it is gained, or possibly sitting on our carpets in our little snug tent working out the observations of the day and pitching into our longed for meal. If we have to undergo some little [?] danger & discomfort yet the after recollections and possible success are quite sufficient to bear me through anything. I shall think of you all around the warm coal fires & perhaps say I wish I could feel the warmth they impart but I know some of my friends would gladly put themselves in my place for a day or two to obtain a peep at the interesting ruins I hope to see. The Colonel and the rest of the party start a week hence by the Steamer and it is expected that they will be detained at Busrah for a fortnight. Dervish Pasha starts on Friday also in a little vessel he has built since he has been here. I don't

---

92 See map in Loftus 1857; now known as Nippur.

know how the Persian goes. The Russians also go in the steamer. Christians versus Mohammedans! The Persian troops have I understand left Dizful for Mohammerah so that I expect work will instantly commence tho' we may have to remain some time there. My chasseur has turned tail and won't go so that all my trouble in teaching him to stuff the bird-skins is lost. Mohammedan-like his palm [?] has itched after more wages and his demand was absurd so I have sent him off and I am about engaging a nephew of Rassam's in his place. I am much annoyed about Latch [?] as you may imagine and so is the Colonel. Pray excuse a longer letter and tho' late present my best wishes on the coming year (come ere this reaches you) to our friends in the canny town and believe me

my dear Edward,

Yours ever sincerely,

Wm Kennett Loftus.

P.S. Kind regards to Ellen & the young kin [?] whom I hope are well.

Letter 31, Mohammerah Persia, 23 January 1850

My dear James,

We arrived here safely on the 21st after a journey of 25 days from Baghdad. How to convey to you anything like a notion of the interest attached to our wanderings I know not for time will not permit me to say one hundredth part of what I have to communicate and to explain to you my future operations. The troops crossed at Hillah to the W. side of [the] Euphrates taking a different route to what we expected and almost frustrating my plans but you are aware that when I am determined nothing can move me from my intentions and I had made up my mind to traverse Chaldea. Our old friend Tahir Bey the governor finding we were resolved on taking the E. route sent with us a few irregular troops. We reached Niffar [Nippur] the Babylon of Major Rawlinson and only visited by him and a Mr Hector. It is in the centre of Mesopotamia but of it, tho' a most extraordinary ruin, I shall say no more as I have matter of much more

CHAPTER FOUR

interest. We delivered letters to the Pasha of Baghdad at Diwanieh where the troops had already arrived before us. The Pasha was encamped with 5000 men collecting arrears of tribute I believe. He was most unwilling that we should proceed on the W [sic][93] of the Euphrates and tried every argument to change our determination but we were not to be done although he represented the country as flooded with water, filled with hostile Arabs, etc, etc. We told him at last that nothing should prevent us carrying out our plans so he bit his lip [and] ordered 16 irregular troops to accompany us and at daybreak next morning we had carried our point & were once more en route. I may here remark that we were the first Europeans who have passed through this part of Mesopotamia and consequently all we observed is new to the world. On the fourth day, after crossing several wide pieces of water for we had the foresight to take skins with us to make a kellek when required (so determined were we to proceed) we began to reach a few ancient mounds and now our excitement & expectations were raised to the highest pitch for our Arab guides mentioned the existence of a statue with an inscription. The mound, or rather building near which it was said to lie, appeared in sight and our impatience knew no bounds. We trudged on at our usual pace and at last reached the spot where sure enough there lay the broken fragments of a human figure without the head but with an inscription in cuneiform on its right hip and also on the back of the right shoulder. We took a plan of the spot and have brought our statue on the backs of our mules safely to Busrah to be transported thereafter to England. Only fancy our delight at the discovery of this interesting relic of antiquity which had evidently been hurled from its high place. It is of black granite and the naked shoulders are carved in the most exquisite style not inferior to Grecian art. From this place Hammam another lofty ruin was visible in the distance, Tel Ede, a high mound of sand and as far as we could judge of nothing else. This we visited also and from it we first beheld the vast ruins of Warka, probably the Erech of Nimrud. The majestic appearance of these lofty piles first seen in the distance towering in the horizon is most exciting. Covered with a blue haze, they seem like spectres of the past having no actual existence, but they must be seen, for to describe them is impossible. Next day we reached Warka. From

---

93 Clearly a mistake for E.

miles distant we ascertained that it was the largest pile we had yet visited and that its outer wall remained but we had no idea of its actual extent until we stood upon the wall, then what a scene was before us, and it was evident we had reached a city which deserved to be carefully examined & that our perseverance and determination had obtained their reward. We rambled over its vast area & were lost in astonishment. Next day returned & took plans of the walls which occupied us six hours in pacing. We also took a rough plan of the buildings existing. The wild Arabs of the wildest description, little better in appearance than the natives of Australia dressed in a simple abba, their long hair floating in the wind, every man with his spear or club, stared upon the newcomers and could not conceive what we were about but we soon set them to work. We observed several excavations had been lately made by them for treasure, and quantities of glazed pottery was strewed about, apparently coffins. By promise of a present we set them to dig and judge my delight when we dug upon a perfect coffin of glazed pot with a large oval aperture to admit the dead which was covered with a lid of unglazed pot. I believe we have discovered the burial places of the Chaldeans. Churchill made a sketch. We got sufficient to probe the place is full of antiquarian riches & we have brought away as much as possible. You will I am sure heartily congratulate me on my success & still more when I tell you that I am commissioned by the Colonel to return immediately and to commence excavations. He writes by this post to Sir Stratford to inform him of our discovery and I am now in such a state of excitement that I can scarcely write a word. I do not envy Layard his works at Mosul as I conceive that my discovery will create as much sensation as even his. With the means, I could at Warka astonish even him. I hope to produce a most interesting paper on my return accompanied by plans and Churchill's exquisite drawings. I can say no more for I am too excited. In 10 days more I shall be at Warka.

Yours

W.K. Loftus

Please send my wife a copy of this as I have no time to write. Use the contents with <u>discretion</u>. You need not fear [for] me among the Arabs [as] by judicious presents when we were there we paved the way for a future visit and they invited us to live with them. I am going to take lots of little things with me for presents, spear-heads, slippers, needles, kerchiefs, etc. I wish you had seen me sitting over the coffin overlooking the Arabs digging with their nails and spears surrounded by 150 wild figures. I shall never forget it nor their first appearance as they took us for their enemies & rushed forward singing their war cry and dancing, throwing up their spears and catching them again. I think I have made out the form of the Chaldean temple. But you will hereafter have all details. We visited the Mugayer [Ur of the Chaldees] W. of [the] Euphrates and we have got new inscriptions on bricks to be sent to Major Rawlinson, bulls horns, edicts on tiles, pots, jugs, coins, etc., etc., etc., etc.

Letter 32, Busrah, 28 January 1850

My dear Edward,

I came here yesterday from Mohammerah and I have spent today in making preparations to excavate among the ruins of Warka. Tomorrow last year (Irish) I left my native land and as an omen of future success, I hope, [I leave] tomorrow for the Promised Land. I am heart and soul in my enterprise, and if I have half the luck of my friend Layard I shall afford more food for the wonder and astonishment of the antiquarian. If I fail in accomplishing my object, it will neither be for want of courage or perseverance, but I have many serious obstacles to encounter. I must first pass all over a desert infested by the plundering Aneiza,[94] before I reach the tent of the all-powerful Sheikh of the Montefic, near Suk-es-Sheioukh[95] who holds the country really as well as nominally from the Pasha. I must then travel thro' his tribe along the Euphrates two days to Kalaat Debbi,[96] to the sheikh of the various tribes about Warka, and then I have nine miles to proceed inland, where I must entrust myself entirely in the hands of the wildest of the Arabs. They received me kindly before as strangers, but how will they receive me in

---

94   For the Aneiza Arabs, see Loftus 1857: 127.
95   Marked on map in Loftus 1857.
96   Marked on map in Loftus 1857.

coming to dig and take their treasures from them? They fear neither Pasha nor Sheikh, but are their own rude masters, but if I once reach Warka, I think I can work upon their weak points, and conquer them by kind words, and a little flattery of their love of hospitality & freedom. Layard had even less difficulty to encounter than I may have. He was near a great centre of civilization (Mosul) while I shall be nearly 200 miles distant from the world. If I succeed, so much more credit will be due to me. In the end, patience and perseverance conquer all things, and so shall I the wild Arabs. The Colonel viewed my application to return in a proper light; he considered that no one had so much right [to] any discovery as myself and that I should have the full credit which is reflected on the Commission. He has most handsomely taken upon himself to defray the expenses in case Sir Stratford and Lord Palmerston decline. He has given me every facility, servants, mules, tents, in fact everything I can require, and at Suk [-es-Sheioukh] I purpose procuring a boat to transport my treasures down the Euphrates. What I say in these letters about Warka is not, you understand, for the eye of everyone, but for the satisfaction of those who take an interest in my proceedings, especially as our discoveries will have to come down in a thunder clap on the world. The great interest attached to Warka is the discovery of the sarcophaguses of the Babylonians. Layard has never been able to fall in with them, but here they are one on the other, like herring[s] in a basket. It appeared to me to have been the great Kerbala or Meshed Ali of Babylon, and why not?, since many of the manners and customs of antiquity have been handed down to the present generations, and more so in this country than in any other. I expect to procure a great many things of interest in my diggings, gold not excepted, and if I do not err, I have got an inkling of the mode of structure of the Babylonian and Chaldean Idols' temples. There is one at Warka, which almost asked me to pull down a heap of rubbish that prevented the sun from shining in at the doorway. Who has ever seen sufficient of Chaldea to give an opinion on the subject? And why should not I be the happy mortal destined to enlighten the benighted world? But let us cease joking. These coffins I so much value are most beautiful receptacles for (excuse the pun [?]) potted meat; potted meat the dead are, to all intents and purposes. They are made of pot, 2 inches thick, with a large oval opening to admit the dear dead, which is potted down with an oval lid of pot. On the outside are raised figures with

CHAPTER FOUR

strange headdresses. I have a bit of an earthen tablet, covered with almost invisible cuneiform which may have been an edict, but more probably a Chaldean almanac. Bricks with cuneiform are common, but I believe of a different character to the Assyrian and Babylonian hitherto discovered. It more resembles Egyptian hieroglyphics than anything I have yet seen, tho' certainly [not] Egyptian. It is probably as old as Layard's Assyrian, and older than the so-called Babylonian. I have by dispatch sent off the copies to Major Rawlinson as a little return for his great kindness and attention to us at Baghdad. I am, as you may conceive, most anxious that my labours may be well rewarded, as the Colonel has hinted to me that future diggings may be placed under my management, and this alone ought to spur me on to action, but I need no spur. Perhaps you say I am too sanguine of success, perhaps I am, but you know my temper, & make allowances. I am certain that you and all my friends at Newcastle heartily wish me every success in my endeavours, & I in return hope they will have no reason to be ashamed of me. You will be rather amused at my plan of proceedings. I do not wish to give the Arabs a high notion of the value of the antiquities and I intend therefore to give little trifles for articles brought me. I have spent today in purchasing a silk dress as a present to the Debbi Sheikh; 2 or 3 common ones for the lesser powers, keffiehs or headdresses, pipes and backie knives, coffee cups, spear heads, belts, etc., etc., etc., for the men, beads, needles, slippers for the ladies, caps, and little dresses for the bairns. In fact, I am going to commence as general merchant, but I must be careful how I distribute my wares, or I may get my throat cut, in expectation of something more. I don't think I told my cousin of the scene we had near Warka one night. Of course, we encamped near an Arab camp [?] and as usual the sheikh sent watchmen; about one o'clock we were suddenly roused from sleep by the retort of a gun close to our tent; in an instant the war song of the tribe was raised, and we were on the point of getting up when Ohannes put in his nose to say there was a thief about. When our tribe had exhausted their lungs we could hear on all sides the war songs of the various camps, gradually approaching our own, like bees swarming to their hive. Imagine what a din there was when they clustered round us, ready to attack their foes, or to defend their friend & guest. We were snug in our beds all the while. This I suppose is the last you will hear of me for six weeks, unless I send a messenger to Mohammerah.

I should like either you or my cousin to write a few lines to Sir Henry De la Beche in my name to announce my proceedings. I should have written him but my time has been so occupied in making plans the last week. Kind regards to all yours. There is a pretty good account of Suk-es-Sheioukh in Fraser's Mesopotamia, but he has made a precious mess of Warka which he never saw. Old Arrian, I believe, says something about Chaldean burials (or Assyrian). I wish you would hunt down [?] the passage for me.

W.K. Loftus

Letter 33, Clerk of the Works' Office, Meso-pot-am-i-(eh?) a, 7 Feb 1850

Pray excuse a bad pun, my dear Ben, but when a man is excessively well pleased he is often inclined to say and do things which at other times he would be ashamed of. My letters to my cousin & Mather would convey to you our discoveries in these regions and of my proposed second visit. Here I am again and as I am about to send a dispatch to my excellent Colonel, I do not know how I can shew a greater proof of my friendship to yourself, my dear Ben – to you who are so interested in the study of architecture and of antiquities – than in scribbling a few hasty lines to you from this most interesting ruin of Warka, not Walker surnamed Hookey, but Warka with a deuce of a rattling r. Our little party left Busrah on the 30 ult. and arrived here on the 4th. No Aneiza disturbed our passage over the desert to Suk-es-Sheioukh, nor did we experience any difficulty from Fahed the great Sheikh of the Montefic and king of the Arabs. I had a great desire to see him & sent a message to the effect that an officer of the Sultan's desired a conference. Mounting my cap & gold band, I proceeded to the reception tent, and shortly afterwards he rode up in state, attended by about 40 attendants. All the inmates of the tent of course arose to receive him. After the usual compliments, I proceeded to touch him on the weak point of the Arabs, and in the hearing of the 200 desert lords around, I thanked him for his great attention & kindness to us as we passed thro' his domains on a previous occasion adding that such attention was a compliment to the sultan whose subject I am. His vanity was touched. He was thenceforward my friend, my

CHAPTER FOUR

servant, my slave – all that he had was mine. What did I desire? Two of his nobility were instantly summoned to take me where I pleased, with liberty to do what I pleased. One of the 200 by [sic] sitters then stepped forward and swore by Allah and all that was holy, that on my former visit I had given nine shammies [?] for something which was worth nothing! The lie told, and I was more and more in his good graces. The secretary was ordered to write a letter to Sheikh al Debbie [?] requiring him to see that no harm nor loss attended me, or my property, or woe betide him. Debbie and the nobles are in attendance on me and I am now encamped at the junction of the Grayim [?] and Euphrates among my wild friends, about 6 miles from the ruins. My little band of workmen was soon organized and on the morning of the 5th I found myself marching in procession to the ruins to accomplish my utmost wishes. Three days I have been in the trenches and many are the coffins we have found, but I have not yet been successful in procuring a perfect one. All we have yet met with are broken and unfit for carriage. I have opened several and have with sacrilegious hands disturbed the mouldering relics which have there lain undisturbed for centuries past. Portions of the fine linen which shrouded the dead yet remain, tho' it crumbles to dust on being touched. As yet I have found nothing in the coffins, but several interesting objects have turned up in the trench – glazed and unglazed pottery, lamps, penates[97] shewing costumes, portions of alabaster vases with cuneiform inscriptions, broken swords and pieces of iron, cuneiforms on bricks & tablets, a square stand of scoria, which I think must have been used as a fire altar, an exquisite little enamelled glass bottle, baked and glazed clay vases and urns, costumes [?] in clay and at this moment an Arab has brought me two more, one a woman with a high head-dress with two conical points like horns, the other with the sacred basket. Of these Arabs I have purchased two gold ear rings, 2 rings & an armlet of silver and I hope to procure many valuable articles to illustrate the domestic life of the Babylonians or Chaldeans. Layard has looked in vain for such, and here it has been my luck to find them in 3 days. I have obtained 66 articles – not bad, I think you'll say. I am now quite at

---

97 As Penates are Roman household gods, Loftus is possibly referring here to terracotta figurines.

home with my Arabs and am daily acquiring more influence among them. I ride home with them and with a kind word to one and a little expostulation with another it is wonderful how gentle the wild animal becomes, for wild these certainly are, tho' kind-hearted they are too. They are capital shots with a stick and knock down the frankolin right and left. Some of them came up with three on the second evening on our return from work and presented them to me:- "Beg, you have spent much money among us and have found nothing (!) and we have nothing to give in return, but pray accept these". Another, who has but one cow brings milk, another two eggs, always with a similar sentiment. It would do you good to see what a set of light-hearted happy fellows they are. When they find anything, their monstrous song is raised and they all dance with joy as they drag me to see it, perhaps nothing after all. Tho' slightly made, they are like so many living models, while their features are full of intelligence and expression. The water is beginning to flow into the channels from the Euphrates and in 20 days our tribe depart to their spring quarters near the ruins of Sinkara a day's journey inland. If I am not recalled I propose going with them. Sinkara has never been described. I have just got another silver bracelet and a little sacred Egyptian beetle (!). Today is wet and windy and I have spent it well in camp purchasing articles of the Arabs. I am working out the details of the ruins, the more I see of which, the more I am lost in astonishment. Standing on the top of the large and centre [sic] sun-dried brick tower, all around me is one vast sea of mounds from amidst which four rise conspicuous with their centre [sic] mounds surrounded by their elevated court [sic] walls.

These are most probably the high places of the most celebrated of their gods, tho' fire altars have evidently existed in every direction. I don't exaggerate in the least when I say that at every step within the walls, glazed coffins and sepulchral vases are to be found! What a mass of human beings have been buried in this vast cemetery! I cannot conceive how it has this long escaped observation (Sinkara is another great burial ground I hear). Has the eastern clime [sic] destroyed the energy of certain of my friends who have been 10 years at Baghdad? I have heard of another large statue with an inscription on the other side of the Euphrates. As I purpose penetrating beyond the Mugayer (which I have already visited) to a mound called Abu Sheher I hope to see him and if possible pocket him. I heartily wish you were here, just to join in my excitement and that I might see tears of joy and delight flow into your eyes. Kind regards to all. I must conclude.

Ever yours

Wm Kennett Loftus,

Clark of the Works!

Letter 34, The Camp, Mohammerah, 9 April 1850

Here I am once more, safe, sound and successful from my late expedition. I dare say, my dear Edward, you have been anxiously expecting a letter from me. I unfortunately reached Busrah too late for the last post, as the "Nitocris" was then on her way up the river (and I had only time to scribble two hasty lines to my dear wife to announce my safe arrival). This letter too must be a short one (!) as the steamer again starts tomorrow (and I am hard at work preparing a paper to flabbergaster [sic] the good folks of the talking societies at home). My second visit to Warka has been most eminently successful and I have fully redeemed my pledge to the Colonel that I would secure two of the glazed coffins. I have brought back three, which are now packed, and in three days more, will be shipped for England on board the good ship Apprentice which has arrived just in the nick of time to convey Layard's big bulls to the Br[itish] Museum. You can have little idea of the trouble, labour and anxiety I experienced before I secured my prizes. During my first 10 days at Warka I must have uncovered 100 coffins and I tried every means to move them without success, and I almost despaired of getting one at all. They were so fragile that they shivered into pieces when touched, but as I had adopted "patience and perseverance" as my motto I was determined not to be beaten and sent to Samava[98] for paper. We carried flour, and made paste on the mound, and when a coffin in pretty good state was discovered, I papered it

---

98   For location of Samava, see map in Loftus 1857.

inside and out with several layers, left it exposed all night and next day the plan was found to answer. We carefully placed it on a rude bier formed of my tent poles, and fasces [?] of my workmen's spears, and thus mounted on the shoulders of six men relieved by 12 others, it was safely conveyed to my tent at the mouth of the Grayim [?]. I wish you could have seen our processions, such yelling and shouting, and sham battles, such congratulations and compliments, such wailing and weeping [?] among the women when the strange coffin arrived. My workmen became as much interested as myself in the excavations and became quite attached to me. I had them perfectly under control. I have said, they belong to the wildest of the Arab tribes, and are called "Madan" from their strange habits.[99] A plundering Bedouin is a gentleman in comparison, according to all accounts, but I can only say I found them much more honest and trustworthy than their less savage neighbours. With the coffins are various forms of pottery and terracotta figures, gold and silver ornaments, but positively nothing which can definitely fix their date has yet been discovered. I am still of opinion that they are Babylonian, yet there are many things which are in favour of a Sassanian origin. Let the literati of England decide the question if they can. Layard has written, and is as fairly bamboozled as myself. Not to spend more time than necessary over their origin, I may just say that I have dug twenty feet down into a mound entirely composed of them! Generation after generation must have been here buried, most probably around the altars of their faith. But perhaps one of the most interesting discoveries made was a terrace outside a sun-dried wall of 40 feet long which was covered with rows of beautiful tablets of clay inscribed in delicate cuneiform characters. Being unbaked clay they were so fragile that it required my most careful management with a pen knife to extract them. Many were quite spoiled with wet, but I secured a good series of about 40 (!) of all sizes varying in length from 4 ½ to 1 inch. A piece of shell was found with them, having an exquisite engraving of horses in the act of drawing a chariot; the trappings much resemble those on the slabs from Kouyunjik while a wealth of lotus flowers and a basket filled with the same would denote a similar date and Egyptian origin. Near it lay a curious alabaster article (use unknown) with a true Assyrian

---

99   For Madan Arabs, see Loftus 1857: 102.

CHAPTER FOUR

inscription, and a much damaged fragment of ivory carving! Two large cylinders with inscriptions, a sword and various other articles were here also discovered. The whole were deposited over the sepulchral vases buried below the terrace! But I cannot attempt to enumerate here all the interesting relics I have secured. Suffice it to say that 300 and odd are now packed up for England: – silver and gold articles; copper; iron; pot, pot, pot, pot !!! etc., etc., etc. The bricks with cuneiform inscriptions are very interesting and I have discovered a perfectly new feature in Babylonian bricks, an inscription in relief in hammer-headed characters. The Egyptians I believe inscribed in relief but neither the Assyrians nor Babylonians. The greater part of the others are in the in the single line character and therefore probably of very early origin. I do not in the least doubt that Warka is the site of Nimrud's Erech, tho' probably none of the hunter's marks are existing. I traced the river which supplied the city for miles into the desert, and as it is called Nil, I believe it is no other than a continuation of the Nil which left the Euphrates at Babel and flowed past El Heimar, Jiblieh, Niffar, or Nuffar. My paper will be ready for next post, and of course you will soon hear of it. So no more about Warka. I followed the Nil to the ruins of Sinkara inland, and procured several things also from that interesting mound. No coffins here like those at Warka but vaults, terracotta figures, pottery etc. and baked clay dish-covers which were placed over the dead. The body was doubled up on the side and then covered down. In one I found an enormous quantity of hair in powder confined in a netted head dress! but which was dispersed by the wind. The bands contained the fragment[s] of a box which had no doubt held the cylinder, beads, and shells which I secured. A brass ring was on the little toe of the right foot. The skull tho' fragile I have saved. Hardened villain that I am thus to profane the sepulchres of the dead. I did not venture further than the Shat el Kahr, tho' I saw the mounds of Ablah, Tel Tefr, etc., etc., on the opposite sides. The tribes were here in revolt and I did not judge it prudent to risk the loss of my treasures, besides my Arab friends would not permit me. I arrived at Mohammerah on the 7th ult. and received the hearty congratulations of my friends. The Colonel is beyond measure delighted with my success, and so I hear is Sir Stratford. If the heat does not become too great, Col W. purposes sending me to dig at Susa as soon as I can finish my paper. At any rate I shall have to work there! Am I not a lucky fellow! I was almost knocked up by my hard work at the ruins. On account of the waters rising the Toweback tribe left the banks of the Euphrates and I was obliged to move my camp to Debbi. Up at daybreak I rode nine miles every day to the ruins, worked at my plan and in the trenches, taking notes all day, and my breakfast when I could find time. After my ride home, often in the dark, I took a hasty dinner and then had to fill up my journal, lay down my work on my plan and label my specimens. It was frequently 2 o'clock before I could tumble into bed, tired and worn out. Anxiety and excitement often kept me awake and I was not sorry when I could get a few days rest here. Churchill at the Colonel's request went with me to Busrah, where he has most beautifully sketched all the interesting articles to accompany my paper. All are packed as I have said before and we returned to camp the day before yesterday to finish the maps and plans. Our work on the road has come out well, and the map will be valuable to the geographer. Warka and the other ruins will make a good show on paper. I shall never forget the delightful days I spent among those wonderful mounds of coffins; they are such as a man seldom enjoys. I don't think I ever spent a more pleasing hour than on my last visit, when I took my station on the summit of the centre mound and looked round upon the sea of mounds below. My labours were over and I viewed the scene with a feeling of satisfaction and delight as I lingered over my breakfast of a cold fowl, maize, bread and dates. Every mound, every ravine was known to me, and the interest attached to them was as great as ever for obscurity still hangs over the origin of the majestic piles of building which rise in solemn grandeur from the mass of surrounding mounds. Unfortunately I had an end put [to] my reverie by a small wasp (name unknown) which I put into my mouth with a date and which stung me on the tongue as if to remind me that pain should always accompany pleasure, and also that natural history as well as antiquity was to be studied. I am a most fortunate fellow. Capt Jones of the Nitocris made an attempt to reach Niffar and Warka and the Arabs would not permit him. The Aneiza have crossed the Phrat [sic] and are plundering again. The whole of the Madan tribes are in revolt and no one can now and perhaps for many many months venture over the ground. They have been deserted [sic] at Baghdad and plundered the bazaar, while the Pasha's troops have also revolted at Suleimaneah, and are there playing the devil. Another matter of discussion has risen here and our movements are completely stopped for the present. The Commissioners have been hard at work tearing each other's hair out and it is expected we shall [only] get away

CHAPTER FOUR

from here when nothing of the worthy Commissioners is left but their tails! God forbid we should have to spend a summer on these hot plains. All the camps are healthy at present, but I believe it only requires a little sickness in some of the camps to set us all off scampering to the mountains of Dizful to spend the summer in the cool oak groves. What with geology and antiquity I shall have plenty there to employ me. Layard is off to the Khabur to visit some ruins there said to contain sculptures.[100] Rawlinson is playing the devil among the people of London we hear. He is a first rate fellow and will meet with all the credit his learning and researches deserve. No doubt he will be knighted. A few words on Mohammerah. The town situated on the Haffar[101] is a miserable place of reed huts within a mud wall. It is under the government of an independent sheikh, Jabba by name who boasts that he has paid taxes to no one Turk or Persian for 9 years. He will be handed over to the tender mercies of the latter nation. The Shat-el-Arab is a magnificent river about half a mile wide. Our camp is stationed nearly at the junction of it and the Haffar. Interminable date groves follow the course of each river and beyond them [there is] nothing but desert. The Commodore of our Persian Gulf squadron with two vessels is watching over the safety of our party, more for show than use. Col Tcherikoff is going off to Persepolis. I shall therefore hasten over my work to [visit] Susa where there must be sculptures in marble from its near proximity to the mountains. In the lower part of Mesopotamia I do not think sculptures are to be found, the ancient cities having been built of mud for want of stone. Best regard to all friends.

Faithfully yours,

Wm Kennett Loftus.

(PS) The English posts of January have been plundered and lost, the messengers not heard of.

---

100 A pair of winged human-headed bulls in the Assyrian style had been uncovered after the spring floods at Tell Arban. For Layard's excavations there, see Layard 1853: 275–84.
101 In the 19th century the estuary at the mouth of the River Karun was known as the Haffar.

THE LETTERS

Letter 35, Mohammerah, Persia, 4 May 1850

A few hasty lines, my dear James, are I fear all I can afford to bestow upon you by this post. I have been employed until the last minute with my paper. Thank God it is off hand, as the flies, dust and heat have almost done me up. I have written 101 well-filled pages of foolscap, and I have concluded by boldly pronouncing the coffins to be Chaldean. All circumstances taken carefully into consideration, I have been obliged to come to this conclusion. From my inexperience I had some hesitation in pronouncing an opinion at first, but I begin to think that, from actual observation, mine must be just as good as anybody's. The Colonel and all our party are very much pleased with the paper, and although I cannot write with the eloquence of some of my friends, I believe from its truthful account that it will create some little interest in the learned world. Col. W. has written a most flattering despatch to Sir Stratford Canning, representing my perseverance and conduct among the Arabs in very high terms of approval. Certainly I laboured zealously, but I had no idea of my work being so applauded. Churchill's sketches accompany the paper, with the map of Warka, and plan of our route. You will, I am sure, be surprised when I tell you that Warka and your humble servant were the subjects of conversation at the Queen's dinner table! It is a fact! Major Rawlinson received a letter from Capt Jones (who met me returning from Warka with my treasures) just as he was going to the palace to dinner! He was, as his letter expresses it, thus enabled to give Her Majesty the last news from Chaldea! She and the Prince were very much interested in his account. I have by this post sent the Major copies of 17 inscriptions from Warka, Sinkara, Mugayer, etc. in addition to some I previously forwarded from Busrah. All my treasures are on their voyage to England, having left this port on the 26th ult. with Layard's big bulls – you will be sorry to hear that one of the lions on its way by kellek has been lost between Baghdad and Busrah by being sucked thro' a broken sud, or bank, where the river had forced its way and is now overspreading the country. Jones is going to attempt its recovery with the

CHAPTER FOUR

Nitocris.[102] Baghdad is again an island with more water around it than last year. Our residence at Gherara is washed away. As a matter of course 10 or 15,000 more of its inhabitants will be carried off by fever when the waters subside. All Mesopotamia is under the inundation; the Arabs have taken to the mounds. A regular deluge on a small scale, and shews how all mankind may have been drowned in these low countries in the days of Noah! We are high and dry here, but the heat is going to be terrific. It is now up to 108° in the shade, and this [is] only May! We do not know how long we may have to remain here, probably all the summer! However I hope to escape some of the heat as Churchill and I start on our trip to Susa on Wednesday. I have planned a very interesting route which has met with the Colonel's perfect approval. Take the Journal of the Geographical Society, and you will find long papers of Layard's and Rawlinson's on Luristan. I purpose first of all proceeding to Shuster [Shushtar], to obtain the Governor Suleiman Khan's permission, and escort to dig at Sus [?] or Susa. The inhabitants are awful bigots, and we must proceed cautiously. If I meet with Daniel's autograph I shall secure it for you! I shall also examine the ruins called Iwan Kerkh on the left bank of the Kerkah. From Susa, we shall travel through Dizful to the maiden fort of Dix [?], in the Baktiari country. I wish to go this far in order to examine the structure of the Persian mountains. If we hear of ruins of course we shall visit them. Returning to the Karun, we shall follow up the stream to Susan "the palace" of Scripture according to Major Rawlinson. Layard says there are only Sassanian [?] ruins, but he has not examined the mound on which these stand. I am inclined to think the Major will prove correct. Are there sculptures beneath? We shall then, unless we hear of something beyond, return to the Jerrahi, cross the Harvisa, near which there are ruins, and so to Mohammerah. Possibly, however, we may remain some considerable time in these regions, if we have luck. Alas! we shall find no more coffins! but I hope, nay I am almost certain, we shall be successful in procuring something of interest. I do not despair of another trip to Mesopotamia! I have my eye fixed between Wasut and Warka, and the banks of the Hie. In the autumn I hope to pay that region another visit.

---

102 This attempt was successful; see Gadd 1936: 64.

We must be here again at that time and I don't see how in this barren desert I can be better employed than among those old Chaldean ruins, for which I now have as you may conceive the greatest affection. I have in this letter made some observations which are not intended for the sight of all. Pray therefore be circumspect in shewing it, and above all things don't let such stupid communications as Capt Rolland's [103] on Nineveh find their way into the paper. Will you oblige me be sending all the chit-chat etc about the coffins and Warka. I am very anxious to hear about them. Your letter of Feb 24th has reached me, for which my best thanks are due. Pray, inform Mr Sopwith that my next letter shall be addressed to him, on my return from Susa, and that without fail. I am exceedingly obliged by his kindness. Can I get a copy of the Field Club? Have the goodness to give the enclosed bill of lading to Charlton or Blacklock, with my best remembrance. I shall not forget the sword and coins. I hope Gray and Mrs R. are better. Kind regards to them and to all friends; many thanks for your attention about Fred.[104]

Yours ever,

Wm Kennett Loftus.

Letter 36, Susa, 31 May 1850

Dear James,

Aware of your love for reminiscences from celebrated localities I cannot resist the opportunity of writing these few lines from the ruins of Susa (now Shush). What site is possessed of more historical interest? It was the spring residence of the ancient kings of Persia, the city from whence Cyrus published

---

103 Stewart Erskine Rolland was an army officer who with his wife Charlotte helped Layard at Nimrud and also accompanied him on his expedition to the Khabur. He was thought to be the author of an unauthorised report about the discoveries at Nimrud that appeared in The Times for 6 March 1850 and which greatly angered Layard.
104 Presumably Loftus' son Frederick, born 21 September 1846, who in Letter 19 is referred to as having whooping cough.

CHAPTER FOUR

his celebrated edict, "Shushan the palace" of Esther and Daniel, the scene of the exploits of the great Alexander and of the early Christian bishoprics and a place of renown in the Kufic age.

Wm Kennett Loftus.

James Radford Esq.

Letter 37, Dizful, Persia, 14 June 1850

My dear Sir,

I have frequently intended writing you a letter, but not having any matter of geological interest to communicate, I did not think it worth troubling you with a bare recital of wanderings in the desert of Babylonian alluvium. As, however, in a letter written by you to my cousin Mr Radford, you appear desirous hearing of my "wanderings", I take the earliest opportunity of gratifying that wish, the more especially as it is to yourself that I am mainly indebted for the pleasure I now experience in visiting these truly interesting countries. I only fear that you may feel offended at my past silence. I hope however that the above explanation will prove satisfactory, and I promise that my correspondence with you shall atone in future for my apparent neglect. You have, I doubt not, heard from my cousin of our visits to Nineveh, Al Hadhr, and Babylon, and of my successful journey through Chaldaea, and of my discoveries at the ruins of Warka, the Erech of Nimrud. I need not, therefore, enter into a detailed description of these remarkable places. In my present letter I purpose giving you a short account of my journey from Mohammerah to Susa, the "Shushan" of our scripture. My excellent commander Col Williams, having been satisfied with my labours at Warka, was pleased to despatch me on this journey for the purpose of making excavations on a small scale at the celebrated ruin. Need I say that the commission was a delightful one, and that I lost no time in proceeding on my road! You will be sorry to hear that owing to the bigotry and misconduct of the Seyyids and Arab sheikhs, I have this time at least been unsuccessful.

Every impediment was thrown in the way of my proceedings, spies were sent to watch me and to create ill feeling toward me in the neighbourhood, and, on order to give some credence to the report which they raised on their return to Dizful, they fired the brushwood around the supposed tomb of Daniel and accused my companion Mr Churchill and myself of being the originator of it. A conclave of the seyyids and priests was held at Dizful, and but for the fear they had of the Governor of the province, we should have been "got rid of". Notwithstanding this behaviour, we stood our ground for ten days and encamped upon the summit of the great mound we succeeded in taking a careful plan of the ruins. An unfortunate fall of my horse upon my right side rendered it necessary that I should remain quiet for a few days and I therefore came hither. As however we were prevented in carrying out our intentions with regard to excavations, we are quite as well here as at Shush, where we every night ran the chance of an attack from the Beni Lam – I have sent a report of all that has taken place to Col Williams who is now at Shuster with the Persian Commissioner on their way hither to spend the heat of summer in the magnificent range of the Luristan mountains. Both the Col and Jafar Khan are highly indignant at the treatment we have received, and are determined on taking the matter up. I am glad of this, as it will teach the rascals to conduct themselves more respectfully towards those of our nation whom chance may bring into these regions. The Colonel writes "I shall not be disappointed in my purposed excavations". The ruins of Susa are of vey great extent and consist of three very large platforms of earth and sun-dried bricks. The highest and most important is about 80 feet high, and not 165 feet as Major Rawlinson (in his learned paper in the Geographical Society's Journal) has pronounced it;[105] it is not, however, of any great extent compared with the two lower platforms. For a description I shall refer you to the Major's paper. Large capitals and broken portions of columns in blue and white marble lie around in various directions and give promise to a rich harvest beneath. I am very sanguine in the hope of finding sculptures of great value buried under the surface. My friend Layard, I know, has his eye fixed toward Susa but you know the old saying "There is many a slip between the cup and the lip" and

---

105   Rawlinson 1839: 68.

therefore the present opportunity of our being on the spot is not to be neglected. Layard has his hands full for many years to come among the Assyrian palaces. The obelisk mentioned by Major R. still exists on the slope of the mound, and I was highly interested to trace identically the same cuneiform characters upon it as upon the bricks & other relics from Warka.[106] I hope and believe that the latter will throw additional light upon the early age to which they belong. The River Shaour (most probably the Eulaeus of antiquity) flows at the foot of the great mound, while the Kerkah (the Choaspes)[107] is seen about a mile or a little more to the south-west. The jungle on its banks is infested by lions. Among other wild rumours we are represented as having beaten a retreat in consequence of the Seven Lions which guard the tomb having given us notice to quit with an intimation that if we refused it we should be "chawed up"! The popular feeling is very bitter against Europeans and Christians. The Arabs have imbibed so much Persian blood and bigotry that they lost their national character. The Arab, the true Bedouin, is a gentleman, and the wild Madan of Mesopotamia is kind and hospitable in comparison with the Cha'ab and Al Kethir of Arabistan. In our journey from Mohammerah we followed the course of the Karoon (the ancient Pasitigris) as far as Shuster. At Ahvaz we visited the bend or bund, supposed to be that over which Nearchus conveyed the fleet of Alexander on its sail to Susa. It is a natural dam improved by art. A low range of sandstone hills here crosses the river, and a strong wall having been erected upon one of the ledges a large reservoir was formed above, from which extensive canals (the beds of which are yet visible) supplied abundance of water for the irrigation of the country on either side. The height of the water was regulated by sluices, but they have long since been destroyed. Along the Ahvaz range are extensive ruins, chiefly of the Kufic era, among which tombs, cut out of the solid rock and columns (now fallen) similar to those at Al Hadhr would appear to belong to a much earlier age. These ruins are said to extend an

---

106 On this obelisk see Loftus 1857: 343–4 and Curtis 1993: 13. This inscription is published in Loftus 1859b: pl. 13 and dates to the reign of the Elamite king Shilhak-Inshushinak I (*c.* 1150–1120 BC).

107 For Loftus's identification of these rivers see Loftus 1857a: 423–31 and Loftus 1857b.

enormous distance to the S. along the range. From Ahvaz we followed the course of the Karoon by Weis to the junction of the two streams of the Karoon and of the Diz river at Bender-ghil; thence to Shuster where we were most hospitably received by Mirza Sultan Ali Khan the governor of the town. Suleiman Khan the governor of Khuzistan was absent at the time of our visit and this I much regret, as he is an Armenian Christian. Bigots though the people are, they submit to his rule without murmur, and acknowledge that he is the only man who is able to keep the state in order. If they do not love him, they at least fear him, and fear is decidedly the more powerful passion in this country. He takes good care, however, not to trust himself to the tender mercies of the Mohammedans. His immediate servants are Christians, otherwise he would be poisoned in a week. Several attempts have been made on his life. His administration of the law, and the punishments he inflicts are strictly Mohammedan. How he has attained his present position I have not been able to learn, but certainly he is a great man. The ancient city of Shuster ("better than Shush") is sadly dwindled from its high estate. Altho' several noble families reside there, it is almost a heap of ruins, and it is melancholy to ride through the ranges of streets unoccupied. The industry of Shuster has been transferred to Dizful. It is however a place of great interest as probably representing the Sele [?] of Ptolemy, and from the existence of portions of these gigantic hydraulic works of the second Sassanian king Shapur or of his prisoner Valerian. The vast "bends" or dams across the river, the bridges, tunnels, etc., have been so very carefully described by Rawlinson & Layard in the G.S.J. that I must refer you to it. I may however observe that from personal inspection I am convinced that the E. branch of the river is the canal cut by Shapur. Several authors suppose the W. branch to be the work of that king. The canal has been excavated in the gravel rock on which the town stands to the depth of about 120 feet! The castle is a perfectly modern building, Arabic. The whole town is, tho' filthy in the extreme, exceedingly picturesque and we took several sketches. From Shuster to Dizful the road passes over the great gravel beds which flank the Persian Apennines. It is composed chiefly of blue limestone, white marble, cherts, agates, and serpentine. These gravel beds cover enormous tracts of country, and I have passed over them on both sides of the Taurus. They extend thro' the centre of Mesopotamia to near Babylon and are again met with further south in the

CHAPTER FOUR

great plain in the Montefik Arab country to the W of the Euphrates between Suk-es-Sheioukh and Zobair [Zubayr], the site of ancient Busrah. It must have been a mighty and continued action which produced such gravel beds. Between Shuster and Dizful is Shah-abad, the Jundi Shapur of Rawlinson, which succeeded Susa in its greatness and was in turn surpassed by Shuster. The tide has again turned and the stream again flows back towards its former source. Dizful is thriving, and is now by far the most important town in Khuzistan. Industry has received considerable impulse through Suleiman Khan, who some years since introduced the indigo plant which is now extremely [extensively?] cultivated, and rows of dye-stoves line the riverside. It would indeed appear a fact that civilization only springs from Christianity! Dizful is, I may remark, the only town which I have seen in the East which shows any kind of prosperity. Elsewhere, the population is evidently decreasing. So much for bad government and oppression. How strange it must appear to the inhabitants that the Englishman insists on paying down cash for everything he requires, while their rulers take it by force! You would perhaps ask me how I bear the climate; it is intensely hot. My thermometer has been unfortunately broken on the journey, but the Colonel tells me in his letter from Ahvaz that it was 120° under his double roofed tent and with lattices [?] and water at the sides! I believe however that I bear extremes of heat and cold better than any of my companions, and tho' the heat makes me, like others, listless and fatigued, yet I have escaped hitherto with less fever than the rest. True I have been more constantly in exercise and I believe this to be the best doctor. One year and a half has nearly elapsed of the time for which I was engaged, and yet nothing has been done towards the settlement of the disputed boundary and I fear it will be a long, protracted affair. In these hot regions it is impossible to work in the summer and constant delays and questions arise. However, I must, as they say, "bide my time" and perform those duties for which I came hither, when opportunity arrives; in the interim my time will be well spent in the alluvial plains in examining the various ruins which stud the surface and relieve the tedium of travel. The Col appears to have committed this office to me, & he could not have chosen for me a more interesting and delightful task. Of Col Williams I cannot speak in too high terms, and our whole party, as well as the Russian Commissioner, are agreeable fellows. In conclusion, allow me to thank you sincerely for your kind wishes on my behalf contained in your letter to my cousin. And for the offer of your services should I require them in London. I have several times written to Sir Henry De la Beche but as I have never heard from him in reply I fear he has never received my letters. Will you present my remembrance to him and my respectful compliments to Mrs Sopwith?

Faithfully yours

Wm Kennett Loftus

Thomas Sopwith Esq

Letter 38, Dizful, Persia, 18 June 1850

My dear Blacklock,

A deep blush of crimson shame spreads over my brown cheeks, tinges the tip of my long beard, and is even seen to colour the soles of my naked feet, when I remember that 3, if not 4, letters from you lie unanswered in my writing case. As if to kill me outright, the last post adds another to the list! However, under the plea that I have been of late actively employed for the benefit of science, I trust that I shall this time at least escape your just condemnation. Your last of March 23rd was forwarded to me by Col Williams from Ahvaz, and for the last 2 or 3 days I have been ransacking my brains to think on what I should write a reply, for I find that I am without writing paper. Three sheets of the stuff I write on has, however, fortunately cast up in my companion Churchill's portfolio. Under [the] circumstances you must pray excuse it. Before proceeding to say anything else, allow me to thank you sincerely for your amusing and news-telling letters. I truly appreciate your kindness in thus writing me so fully. A letter in the desert is a great blessing. I beg to congratulate you and the Nat. Hist. Soc. on the state of the society's finances, and on your fortune in obtaining such excellent servants, may you go on swimmingly together. You say that anything forwarded by me will be acceptable. I have now, lying at Maghil [?], near Busrah, a package of inscribed bricks from the various localities I have been so fortunate as to visit. I will not at present offer them to

CHAPTER FOUR

the Society, because I may yet require them, but if you think the exhibition of them will add to your funds, and you will pay the expense of carriage, probably £2, I will gladly send them. In case an opportunity occurs for me to forward them gratis, I shall do so. A few old bricks and broken pots are all I have retained for myself from my lately discovered ruins [?]. And now, I suppose, you will expect to hear somewhat of my last doings. In one of my letters last month from Mohammerah I think I mentioned that I was about starting for the ruin[s] of Susa and Susan. The latter place I have at present given up the idea of visiting in consequence of the Colonel having at length determined on starting from the hot plain of the Haffer to spend the summer in the cool regions of the mountain[s] of Mungerrah. We await the arrival of our party at this place. I shall not rewrite the account I have already scribbled to Mr Sopwith as that would be wasting time as well as paper. You may however imagine how much I have been disgusted and disappointed at the bigotry and bad conduct of the seyyids and sheikhs. I fully expected difficulties, but I fully expected to overcome them, and (if the Colonel supports me as he gives me to understand he will) I shall yet overcome them and dig in spite of spite of man or lion. I am disappointed with Susa. In its present appearance, it is not to be compared with Warka but we must wait till we make an incision as the doctors say. It much resembles the mound of Kouyunjik tho' not so large, while the fragments, broken capitals, and the inscribed obelisk mentioned in Rawlinson's paper in the R.G.S. journal give me hopes of great things beneath. I must now curb my impatience and wait till the heat is over. It is impossible to go out (with the) thermometer (at) 120° in the shade. You will be sorry to hear that I have had a severe fall which very near[ly]put my pipe out. I yet suffer slightly from the effects. On the evening of the 29th ult. we went out for a quiet ride at Susa, and when returning we fell in with such a posse of pigs as would have astonished a Mohammedan's capacity, eight papas and mamas and a tribe of about 40 squealers. We could not resist the impulse of seeing them scud, so away we went after them, tho' without our spears. Mine is a clumsy brute of a horse, and we had not gone far before he turned a complete somersault with me, over a ridge of earth. I fortunately cleared my stirrups, but he fell upon my right side with his haunches, and as I have said, he nearly made a pancake of me. I do not know whether any of my ribs have been broken, but I believe I received a slight internal injury from the pain I have since experienced. I had of course no doctor, so as we could do nothing in the way of digging, I thought it best to get out of the heat and remain quietly here underground, and cool; I have [kept] all fever and inflammation down by living on tea and air, and I now only suffer pain in turning over in bed at night, in fact I am all right again and in good spirits, tho' I regret the time lost and to be lost. I presume by this time you have heard all about Warka etc. I see a notice of it in the "Home News" of the 8th April. It is no doubt Rawlinson's, the information obtained from Capt Jones who saw the articles I brought back. The account is correct, tho' I cannot with due deference to the learned opinion of the Major agree in claiming the honour for Warka of being the Ur of the Chaldees whence Abraham set forth to go into Canaan. If it can be proved, why so much the better. Ur of the Chaldees is Urfah or Edessa. Harran is a town (still so called) to the S. of it, and the Patriarch would "journey" going still to the south in going to Canaan, but I have no doubt of Warka being Erech, as well as the latter Chaldean city Urchoe or Orchoe. It will agree quite as well with Urchoe as the Muguyer is supposed to do, but whatever it turns out to be, I claim the undisputed honour of having first visited it. Dr Charlton's letter, lost in the deserts and date[d] January, has cast up, and he requests me to send a long and detailed account. Tell him I have already done so, and my paper notes on a journey from Baghdad to Busrah, with a description of Warka and other Chaldean remains, is by this time in the hands of Sir Stratford Canning, and ere this reaches you I hope it has been forwarded to Lord Palmerston. I have given the literati plenty to puzzle their brains for a month or two. I should not wish to write another paper on the subject for any money, tho' I hope I shall have occasion to employ my pen on similar subjects up the boundary. I have my eye upon many spots, unexplored, and I shall certainly strain every nerve to reach them. "Faint hearts, etc.", you know. The whole country abounds in antiquarian treasures, and between Hawisah and Holwan, I hope to stumble on something. By hook or by crook I must reach Wasut, also in Chaldea, and the country between it and Warka, that is the land of Shinar, properly so called, and the name is preserved in the ruins of Sinkara, Shinar, Singar, Sinjar, Singara, or Sinkara! By the bye, why is it called the land of Shinar? There's a riddle for you to answer next post. I don't think I ever mentioned the fact of our having visited the great Chaldean ruin called the Mugayer, on the W. of the Euphrates, where we found a broken statue, and an altar with an inscription. I see it is noticed in the papers. I don't intend giving you an account of this huge pile, as it has been pretty correctly described by Frazer, but our visit caused a most comical adventure. The troops and caravan which we left at Hillah passed the Mugayer at some distance and some of Dervish Pasha's officers wished to ride to examine it. They got half way when they were alarmed by suddenly seeing the summit covered with men, and they went back for a few soldiers. On approaching it they found the ruin apparently deserted, but being afraid of an ambuscade, they held a conference and came to the conclusion that discretion was the better part of valour. The troops formed (a) square and waited for quarter of an hour, while the caravan was hurried forward under the charge of a few lancers. Will you believe it that Churchill, myself, two servants and 3 irregulars were the cause of all the commotion; [we were] ignorant too of the fact or I think we should have been induced to drive down full charge upon them. We had a most hearty laugh afterwards at the bravery of the troops. We spent 3 hours on the ruin, and I much regret not having had more time to penetrate to another unvisited site called also Shehrine[108] [sic], visible about 8 miles to the S.W. Much is yet to be discovered in the Montefik desert, and I strongly suspect that the great canal Pallacopas is to be yet traced past Abu-Shehrine and not at the Mugayer as is supposed. I must visit Jebel Sinam [?] on my return to Mohammerah July 2nd. Your letter of April 6th has just arrived. There is no need whatever to thank me for the few almost valueless articles I sent you. I am ashamed that they are not worth the carriage, to wit nothing. I shall give your vote of thanks to the Colonel today, but shall retain that for Messrs Lynch till I hear of their safe arrival in England and that there has been no mistake. You appear to think I shall forsake fossil for city hunting. Not so, but how could I better employ myself in these barren alluvial plains of sand than in hunting for human fossils (!) and their works, where it is not always possible for a European to penetrate. Altho' Forbes city hunted in Lycia, he did not altogether neglect his former love. The sight of the Persian mountains has again kindled the dormant flame of geological love within me, and I hope to ramble yet as I list, among the untrodden paths of the Bakhtiari Mountains. On the 22nd ult. Churchill and I took a short trip to the E. of Dizful

---

108 Abu Shahrain (Eridu).

and spent two days in the beautiful valley of Gilalahon [?], where I beheld one of the most interesting specimens of a valley of elevation, afterwards denuded by the powerful action of water, that can be conceived. The rugged edges of the anticlinal ridges were here stretched out for miles and miles, and resembled the ridges of a well ploughed field. The beds of [were] of unfossiliferous sandstone. We are off to the mountains of Mungerrah tomorrow night. In haste with kind regards to all mutual friends.

I remain

Faithfully yours

Wm Kennett Loftus

Letter 39, Dizful, Persia, 2 July, 1850

My dear cousin,

The lost letters of January have cast up; the Colonel sent mine to me from Ahvaz. They had been stopped by the Arabs in the hope of a "backsheesh" but, finding that not forthcoming, they restored the packet unopened. It brought yours of the 15th January (and the joint receipt for the money I sent in December). Yours also of March 23rd, April 15th and 25th reached me yesterday, for all of which pray accept my very best thanks. Your attention in writing so frequently is duly estimated by me. I was sure my letters of January would contain acceptable news. I am much obliged by your kind congratulations, and for the great trouble you have taken in sending me the various translations of Arrian etc. They are exceedingly interesting from the fact of my having so lately visited the classic ground alluded to. We have been highly amused at seeing me flourishing off in all the papers, foreign & domestic! I suppose some kind soul will be giving another article ere long. I have in my letter to Blacklock expressed my opinion as to the author. It may however possibly have been the production of a Mr Sterling of Sheffield, who, I have lately heard, has frequently urged on Rawlinson a visit to Warka where he supposes the Chaldean kings were buried! They are however quite mistaken about its being the birthplace and exodus of Abraham. That was at Urfah, below the Singar [sic] Hills. Had he started from

CHAPTER FOUR

Warka, journeying still on to the south, he would have walked into the Persian Gulf instead of into the Land of Canaan. I dare say long ere this you will have become sick of hearing so frequently of Warka. You must excuse this, but the fact is I am disposed to consider these ruins as entitled to even more attention & examination than I had funds or leisure to bestow on them. They may possibly tend to alter the supposed ancient sites of cities in Chaldea, but I wish to hear more on this subject before I venture even in a private letter to express an opinion on it. Strange ideas are floating in my brain which will require some reading and study to bring to maturity. (I must if possible have a trip across by way of Wasut. This you will please not to mention, as I believe parties are preparing likewise to take that track, and I wish to be the first). I have not received the paper sent by Gray but I have seen the article you mention. Thank him however for his kindness. I have written as promised to Mr Sopwith who will give you an account of our ill success at Susa.

The Colonel and Jafar Khan have taken the matter up, and the party who caused the ill feeling will not escape. The Colonel found Mohammerah too hot for him, and we are off this evening for the mountains of Mungerrah to eke out the summer as we best can. The heat is awful. Baghdad [is] nothing to this. We are melting in our very shoes and I have been living in a hole underground for a month, ever since we quitted Susa. We had very few books and no paper to write letters, so ours was not an existence to be envied. I am quite recovered from my accident tho' I still feel a little pain when I raise my arm quickly. You wonder how I should manage when not well and engaged on Special Service? Why, I should manage in this manner, I should pitch the Special Service overboard, and get well as I best could. The Colonel would say "Well done, that's right". I am about to ask you to perform a commission. If you will oblige me by doing so, it may prove of great value to me hereafter. The Colonel gets the Westminster Review and in it is a critique upon some papers of Major Rawlinson's on the cuneiform character published by him in the Royal Asiatic Society's Journal. There may be others on the same subject. These papers would be exceedingly valuable to me in my ramblings, and I am most anxious (and so is the Colonel) to procure them. You would much oblige me if you would hunt them up for me, and any expense you may incur I will remit in November. Mr Hammond at the Foreign Office would I dare say forward them, if you wrote him on the subject. By sending one or two at a time (if there are many) they would reach me by the usual channel of the Turkish Post from Constantinople without difficulty. If there are many they might be delayed some time. There is a Mr Norris at the Foreign Office interested in the study of the cuneiform and a great man at the Asiatic Society. He might probably assist in forwarding your labour of obtaining them. I had a letter of introduction to him when in London, but I could not find him in tho' I called on him thrice and left my card. He is the Asiatic Interpreter I believe. If you can get this matter arranged for me it will be of great value to me in my subsequent labours, and probably direct my attention to subjects worthy of investigation. I am sure you have by this time pronounced me antiquity-mad and have agreed with Blackstock that geology is totally forgotten, but my proper pursuit will have all due attention when the time comes. At present I don't know how I can better employ myself than in turning over the old ruins of antiquity. I may get [the] chance to stumble on something which may throw light on the lost records of early Persian history. I certainly have become deeply interested in this strange land, and who would not be so likewise, visiting as I have done some of the classic spots of our Scriptures, and of the early history of mankind. The more I think upon it, the more strange it appears, that within a year and a half since I left home, I have slept on the summits of the ruins of Nineveh, Babylon and Susa, the capitals of three vast empires, ages ago faded into comparative oblivion. I have drunk of all the classic streams, the Euphrates, the Tigris, Pasitigris, Eulaeus, Koprates and Choaspes,[109] famed for the passage of Alexander. I have certainly acquired more knowledge of ancient history and geography than books can possibly give. With luck as you say I shall yet do much, and with the twofold subjects, antiquity and geology. I hope to return to England with some store of eastern knowledge, or rather knowledge of the East! While we suffer from heat, insects, and other disagreeables, you good folks at home are I suppose going on in the usual sameness of everyday life! At any rate, you have a temperate climate: no torments in the shape of insects and clean homes, beef steaks & Porter! By the bye, I should like just now to taste an English dish, for our native cooks will deluge us with gee! When at Shuster, we had to do

---

109 The rivers are also mentioned in Letter 37. See n. 93, this Ch.

as others did, tuck up our sleeves & hunt for the meat in piles of greasy rice. (By this time all the bustle & excitement of the race week are passed, I hope favourably for us all. The result I shall in due time hear). I had intended writing a few lines to Mather but I have nothing further to add. I shall be glad to hear of the arrival of my clothes, as I am reduced to Persian big trousers. In a few months more, I shall have to adopt the high cap! You must make this letter do for both. I fear my letters from Warka have been lost, as the packet has not been heard of. I wrote B. Green. Kind regards to all friends.

Yours ever

Wm Kennett Loftus

(PS) A few sheets of black carbonic paper would be invaluable as mine are worn out. A letter would carry them. I shall write Dr Charlton soon.

Letter 40, Mountains of Mungerrah, near Dizful Persia, 2 Aug 1850

My dear Hancock,

I have some indistinct notion that one, if not two letters of yours remain unanswered. They are unfortunately left behind, with my writing case, at Mohammerah, but I think the last bears [a] date of October 8 and reached me at the end of November. I ought to have replied immediately but preparations for departure from Baghdad, and constant journeys and duties since that time have kept me fully employed. You, like others of my correspondents, have suffered neglect, not wilful tis true, but I am now endeavouring to pay all dues with the utmost despatch. You must not therefore be hard with me. I have little of novelty to communicate in this letter for we have just rushed out of the kitchen fire of Mohammerah and the Plains of Susa, and laid ourselves snugly on the cooler shelf in the garret of this Loorish [?] retreat. <u>Cooler</u>, I say, for the thermometer tells [?] 107° when old blazes get up. Though 5000 feet above the sea we are glad to remain under the shade of little cherdaks, viz. four oak poles supporting cross beams and covered with oak leaves.

Never were 7 mortal Europeans more delighted with a cold climate! We have left malaria and fever below and are all with one exception in the best of health; poor Wood is lying dangerously ill with ulcerated sore throat, caused by imprudently bathing when heated. Our present camp is 3 days distance from Dizful over one of the most rugged roads I ever traversed and in the midst of oak tree groves, orchards of pomegranates, figs and mulberries, with vines trained from tree to tree. Yet the country is barren, the people miserable, and lie, thieve [and] distort [?] to the utmost. I am much disappointed with the Loors. In geology and natural history I have indeed been on a barren field; i.e. hitherto. True, I have discovered a few of the medals [?] of creation in the rocks below our camp, but the stone is so highly crystalline that it is utterly impossible to extract them. One bed is entirely composed of nummulites. I shall however next month, I hope, have an opportunity of investigating the structure of these mountains when the heat of summer is over. As far as I can learn from the general character of the country as far as Suleimanea [Sulaymaniyah], it is a succession of limestone and sandstone beds of nummulite age (chalk or tertiary) with various beds of gravel conglomerate. The Colonel proposes, I believe, taking a ramble to Khorramabad and Busrah just before our return to Mohammerah. If so, I shall cross the beds of the great chain of Zagros. I wish that time were arrived. Before we left the plain, all vegetation was dead here, and with it insect life. A few crickets, scorpions and cicadas are all that remain. A few serpents are now and then brought and bottled. Of birds I have only seen one eagle, one falcon, one woodpecker, the red legged partridge, and a little reed warbler. Never was such a barren country. We have eaten frequently of the ibex aegaricus [?], I believe, though it does not quite agree with the descriptions I have in my books. The country is much more bountiful in antiquarian treasures & I am impatient to resume my researches in the curiosity-shop line. My work is assuredly cut out for me in this respect and I hope shortly to combine geology with antiquity in a trip I have in prospect. You no doubt heard of my ill success at Susa. I don't however despair yet, for I am going to have another trial and to make sure I have presided the Colonel to write to our ambassador at the Court of Persia for a firman[110] so that all responsibility may be taken

---

110   A firman (Persian) is a royal order or decree.

CHAPTER FOUR

off the shoulders of Suleiman Khan the Christian governor of Khuzistan. He would otherwise perhaps not feel justified in enforcing his power on my behalf. The Seyyids are a very ticklish set to deal with. I am in great hopes of finding buried there sculptures of great interest especially as I know that [it] is one of Layard's spots for investigation and Rawlinson is also in great expectation. From Susa I shall follow up the Karoon to Shishan, & excavate there, returning to Mohammerah by way of the ruins of Eidij [?], Tul, Munjanik [?], the naphtha pits of Ram Hormuz & the river Jerrahi [?]. Though I believe all the places have been visited by Layard or Rawlinson yet neither have made excavations and it is impossible to conceive the results if such are made. If I hear of anything further eastward in the Bakhtiyari I shall certainly attempt to penetrate to it, but all my proceedings must of course depend on the character and feelings of the natives. With the Arabs it is not difficult to gain one's point by setting about it in a proper way, but the Persians are such infernal bigots it requires some scheming and management. When we [will] leave Mohammerah I have no notion but I would certainly prefer travelling about to remaining there for a few months. I think I have now given you an idea of my future operations. I hope you think I am in a fair way of employment for some time to come. I am now about to ask you to hunt up for me a little information though I fear I shall be imposing too much on your kindness. I want to know what Herodotus Book VI ch 119 says about Ardericca, who founded it and where he places it? I think Major Rawlinson in R.G.S. vol 9 p. 194 has incorrectly identified the ruins on the Baladrud, or Ghil on Kir Ab. As far as I could judge they are Persian and of comparatively modern date! Another point I wish to learn is the character and description of the plants which produce the gums ammoniacum & asafoetida. I have instructions from the B.M. to pay attention to the cultivation etc. of these plants when met with [and] I have no books from which to ascertain their nature. A slight sketch of them would be valuable to me. You see I am disposed to make my friends at home assist me in my researches. Some information as to what is going on in the natural history world, of the proceedings of the Field Club, and in fact any kind of chit-chat you may please to communicate. What is Howse doing? And King? What discoveries have you and Mr Alder been making in conchology etc.? By the by, have you ever met with the mention of Warka in your classic reading days, or of any city of Chaldaean, Babylonian or Persian notoriety which will throw any light on the probable age of my pet ruin!

It cannot be possible that a city of such importance should be without some record of its existence. I am anxiously awaiting for Rawlinson's interpretation of the cuneiform on the copies of the bricks I sent him. I fear I shall not fall in again with another such interesting ruin. I presume about the time this reaches you my treasure [will] have arrived in London. My paper is now filled. I must therefore conclude. Pray give my best remembrance to your brothers, Mrs Alder, Fryer, Charlton, Blacklock, Howse, and all other mutual friends, and I remain,

Faithfully yours,

Wm Kennett Loftus

Do you know anything of the oaks and galls of the East?

Letter 41, Dizful, Persia, 3 August 1850

The Secretary of
The Farmers Club,
Newcastle upon Tyne.

Sir,

While making some investigations at the seldom visited Chaldean ruins of Sinkara in the interior of Southern Mesopotamia, I ascertained a fact that may not prove uninteresting to the Farmers Club.

As lately a member of the Newcastle upon Tyne Farmers Club I beg to submit [something] to your judgment if it be worthy to be mentioned at one of your meetings. There is an old saying that "nothing is new under the sun" and such would indeed appear to be the case! Will it be credited that the learned nation of the Chaldeans used draining tiles of precisely the same form and material as the farmers in our own enlightened land of Britain have only a few years ago adopted for the more complete drainage and consequent improvement of their land! Observing several brick built square holes of about four inches diameter on the surface of these curious ruins, I carefully examined one of them & discovered that it formed the entrance to a drain of considerable depth. On removing the bricks, I found a cylindrical & well baked pipe or tile of reddish clay, a yard in length & five inches in diameter at the centre & opening slightly towards the extremities. It rested nearly horizontally, well on end over the aperture of a large well-shaped clay pot exactly resembling those used in English gardens and known by the name of "rail pots". The other end of the pipe was met by a spout formed tile of similar material bent in this shape [diagram]. The "rail pot" was about a yard deep and a foot and a half wide at the base. The shaft of the drain was lined with large cylinders of baked clay, four inches in thickness & about three or four feet high. They were piled one upon another, & [thus] formed a continuous pipe from the bottom to the top of the drain. They were in most instances as perfect as when they were deposited many centuries ago! Around the interior of the drain was a wall of brick which retained the cylinders in their position & preserved them from external pressure and injury. How effectually the Chaldeans must have kept the rats from their drains. I observed similar cylinders here and also at the neighbouring ruins of Warka. Are cylinders of this description made use of at home for the purpose of lining drains and walls? If not, [could] they be so advantageously employed?

I am, Sir,

Yours obediently.

W.K. Loftus

Letter 42, Summit of the Mungerrah Range, Dizful, Persia, 3 September 1850

My dear Cousin,
On this elevated rookery [?] I cannot spare you much time for gossip so pray for this once rest contented with a few very hasty lines & the assurance that I am well and hearty. Your 3 letters of May and June 5th reached me on the 21st ult. having been delayed in the progress from Baghdad to Busrah by the new French Consul who took his time over the journey. In

consequence of the alarming illness of poor Wood there has been no return messenger despatched but I believe one will leave in a few days. Wood has had a relapse & is reduced to a perfect skeleton & I fear that all hope of his ultimate recovery is at an end. The Dr I know has given him up for several days. Should strength of constitution yet bear him thro', his recovery will be a miracle. Let us however hope that such may yet be the case. Glascott and I have for the last fortnight taken up our quarters on the summit of Mungerrah & have been engaged in making a panoramic view of the surrounding mountains. Altho' our labours are in a different fields yet we can unite them with advantage. I assist him & he gives me the benefit of his work for my geological sections. We are now no less than 8245 feet above Mohammerah and 3140 above the camp. Perched on a narrow ridge we have a most extensive view on either side. Dizful & the flat plains of Susiana to the south, the great range of the Kebir Kuh on the S.W. at the west foot of which runs the disputed line of boundary. To the N. are the great ranges which compose the Zagros visible as far as Khorramabad, extending in parallel line out of the power of vision to the N.W. and S.E. One of the highest [peaks], probably 10,000 feet, is called Koos! Can this be derived from the Kossoeans of antiquity? It is sometimes said "What is in a name"? Perhaps much more than is thought of in these countries. I fear our purposed trip over these ranges is knocked on the head in consequence of Wood's illness, but as soon as this panorama making is finished I purpose asking the Colonel to permit me to take a ramble of a few days to investigate the structure of these regions. I should propose going to Khorramabad, and Borujerd, & returning by the unexplored road by Deh-Liz or the Kashghan [?] river to Abi Garm & Perli Tang [Pol-e Tang?]. From what I can pick up from the Loors, Deh Liz may be one of the forts built by Alexander [to] keep the Kossoeans under subjection. This is also probably the route pursued by Antigonus after his defeat. I wish I had an English copy of Diodorus Siculus & one two other works on these regions. I am not one to be idle when there is anything to do & as there is no difficulty in the way I don't think the Colonel will object. The journey would not occupy more than 10 days or a fortnight. We cannot go into the plains yet as there are roasting hot temperatures in serdaubs at Dizful – 120°! Here altho' so high we sleep under an open tent & go without coats or stockings in the day time. I am much obliged for your 3 letters & the enclosed scraps. Mr

Colquohon or some such name is the author of the article. He is a friend of Layard's & appears to have seen a letter of the Colonel's to L – there is a great mixture of truth & falsehood in it combined as you know from my letters. Have you heard if my treasures have arrived? Give my best regards to Mrs Radford & all mutual friends & believe me

Ever yours sincerely

Wm Kennett Loftus

I am short of letter paper so pray excuse the half sheet.

Letter 43, Mungerrah, 17 Sept 1850

My dear Cousin,

Your letters of June 15th & 22nd and of July 5th reached me last evening and you may be assured that the good news contained in the last gives me no small pleasure. My letters to you of the 3rd inst. would announce the very dangerous illness of Wood. This letter I am sorry to say announces his death. The Colonel sent a messenger for Glascott and myself to come down on the 12th from the summit of Chaouni. We found him gradually sinking and for three days he was in a dying state. Every particle of food he contrived to swallow was the cause of intense pain & a sensation of suffocation from the closing of his throat & affection of the lungs. On the morning of the 15th he breathed his last and we buried him at mid-day. At the Colonel's request I read the funeral service over his grave. Tho' we were all fully prepared for this melancholy event yet is a great shock to us all and we shall be heartily glad of a change of scene. Of course, as long as Wood lay ill it was impossible to move or think of moving. Now however the case is very different & yesterday evening the Colonel sent off all our superfluous luggage to Dizful and as soon as the mules return we start[ed] off for Isfahan by way of Khorramabad and Borujerd! I believe it is the Colonel's intention to proceed thence to Persepolis & to return either by Bushire or (I hope) Bebehan. This will be a journey of very great interest and as the first portion has seldom been traversed. Glascott and I are going to put our heads together and hope to produce a good paper for the Geographical. I am now in a fair way to indulge in geological passion to the utmost. The geology of these great ranges is utterly unknown and as we proceed slowly we shall have abundance of opportunities for careful investigation. I need only say that Dizful is incorrectly placed on the maps by more than 20 miles to prove that much is to be done in these regions. In another week we shall be off. In the meantime Glascott and I must go up again aloft to finish our work, and this must account for my short letter. I believe Churchill will be appointed to succeed poor Wood & I must say that the Ambassador could not fix on a person more adapted to the post. He is an excellent linguist, an artist, and a good mathematician, & I sincerely hope that the Colonel's recommendation will succeed. Glascott will then have to get an assistant from the Gulf squadron. I shall not forget Charlton when I have anything to interest him. Excuse this scrawl and with kind remembrance to all friends, in haste, I am

Ever yours truly

Wm Kennett Loftus

Letter 44, Mungerrah, 20 Sept, 1850

My dear Edward,

I wrote a hasty letter to my cousin on the 17th inst. expecting that the post would have been despatched the same evening. [As] this arrangement was altered I have time to write a few lines in answer to yours dated July 3rd from Glasgow. The sign of your handwriting is a great pleasure. You ask if I have received the clothes etc. & if I am pleased! Alas! There are no railways in these outlandish countries. If after passing over mountains of snow sweeping streams from the higher regions & deserts of sand & Arabs, if, after all these casualities, I receive them six months hence I shall consider myself fortunate. We leave this [place] in three days' time, all heartily glad to escape from the scene of the late painful occurrence. The Colonel purposes proceeding across the Zagros to Khorramabad and thence to Hamadan (Ecbatana) and Bisitoon [Bisitun] to

CHAPTER FOUR

Kermanshah. From thence to Borujerd & Isfahan, Persepolis and Shiraz across the Bakhtiyari [country] to Babahan [Behbahan] & I trust we shall make a detour to Shushan & Masjid-i Soleiman. By that time I trust my firman will have arrived and I shall then proceed to excavate Susa. I may here mention that another post reached us yesterday by which I got two very satisfactory letters from Major Rawlinson. I was not mistaken as to the value and importance I attached to the inscriptions from Warka etc. I make a few extracts from these letters. "All the inscriptions are valuable, some of them invaluable. Several new kings are mentioned of whom no other traces are known to exist. The brick in relief in particular commemorates a son of Cambyses regarding whom Greek history is altogether silent xxx. Your copies have furnished some most important hints regarding the royal line of Chaldaea previous to the time of Nebuchadnezzar. I do not suppose the earliest specimens to be before B.C. 747 nor later than B.C. 500. I am all anxiety to know what you have been doing at Susa. If you can recover the fragments of the black stone[111] you will have done more for cuneiform than Belzoni did for hieroglyphics xxx. At any rate you are in a fine country for research and will I trust exhaust it." Inshallah! I'll do my best & endeavour to leave no hole or corner unexplored. If the Colonel only bears me out I'll astonish you yet. The Major promises me success at Susa, sculptures without end. This journey we are about to undertake will give us an opportunity of seeing all the most remarkable antiquities of Persia and I trust I shall not only pick up cuneiform but geological information. The whole country is unexplored & I shall have a fine dive into the bowels of the earth. Pardon me, I am indelicate, I should say the bosom. We shall be wandering for about 3 months [but] as [a] question has turned up on the Mohammerah affair. Why, we are better on the move than stewing in a stinking Persian or Turkish

---

111 This 'black stone ' was first noted at Susa in 1809 and a sketch of it was published in R Walpole, *Travels in Various Countries of the East* (London 1820), vol. II, p. 426. It was evidently a Babylonian kudurru (boundary-stone), perhaps brought to Susa as booty from Babylonia by the Elamite king Shutruk-Nahhunte. Loftus describes the history of the black stone and republishes the sketch of it in his book (1857: 416–23). He says it was blown up some years previously and the fragments built into a pillar in the Tomb of Daniel. He was not able to inspect this. See also *Encyclopaedia Iranica* 'Susa i: Excavations'. The 'black stone' is also referred to in Letter 48. For a recent study on "the Black Stone of Susa" see Potts and Basello 2022.

town. The difficulty regarding the Mohammerah question is this. By the Treaty of Erzurum the Turks were to give up Mohammerah to the Persians but now they decline giving any portion of territory adjoining and want to shut out the town from the Shatt al Arab which would in fact do away with the intention of the Commissioners when the treaty was made. This matter has been referred to London and Petersburg and we may whistle for at least 3 months for any reply. I begin to despair of ever seeing the end of the boundary settlement. Question after question is sure to arise & I have heard that the Ambassador has expressed an opinion that it is likely to continue for 10 years. If so, I don't think any of the present party will see the finish. Certainly I have no idea of being banished from my family for that length of time. The papers report the deaths of numerous great folks. This appears to be quite a season of death. A letter I wrote on arrival here to my companion on my second trip to Babylon Capt Newbold has been returned unopened with the intelligence of his death on his way to the residency in the Deccan. I shall send the letter to Charlton instead of tearing it up. Will you tell my Cousin that I shall endeavour to comply with Mr Sopwith's request on behalf of Mr Gould, tho' I fear I have not shot small enough for the purpose, nor can I get any. Oblige me by giving my cousin the enclosed and by excusing this hasty scribble as Glascott and I are busy with our observations taken up aloft. Remember me most kindly to all enquiring. I shall be heard of en route.

Faithfully yours

Wm Kennett Loftus.

Letter 45, Kermanshah, Persia, 11 October 1850

My dear artist Coz,

Perpetual motion & constant employment will I am persuaded prove a sufficient excuse for my negligence in replying to your letters dated ages ago. I have many correspondents and little time to bestow upon them. I have not your letter at hand but I remember that it contained many kind wishes for my health and success. For such I beg you will accept my best thanks. We are now thanks to a question which has arisen in the boundary matter taking a tour of 3 months thro' the Alps of Persia to visit the celebrated antiquarian lions [sic] of Bisutun [Bisitun], Hamadan, Isfahan, Shiraz, Persepolis, Bebehan etc. etc., in fact we are regular Hadji Babas.[112] We only arrived here yesterday afternoon after a long but interesting journey across the Zagros by way of Khorramabad and for the most part along the line of Antigonus' march after his defeat at Baduca. For 6 days we never saw a blessed soul, passing over barren gypsum deserts & marly soils, the latter beautifully wooded with the beliel [?] or oak but almost destitute of water. When we did fall in with a Lurish camp we found the poor devils most hospitable & our good name the 3 months residence in the heart of their mountains at Mungerrah had procured for us rendered it less difficult for us to obtain grub than Antigonus [had] found it. At Khorramabad we were lodged in a [?] palace [?] of Mohammad Ali Mirza, a late Governor of Khuzestan. Rawlinson describes it as well as the beautiful situation of the town in his paper in the Geog Society. We were politely received by Ardeshir[?] Mirza the son of Fath Ali Shah who inflicted a terrible bastinado on the officer of his troops for impertinence to the Colonel. I procured with Churchill's assistance a copy of the Cufic inscription which has never been copied & which I believe records the deeds & death of somebody "the father of Jafar Codger".[113] Whoever it was from Khorramabad crossed the great plains of Alister[114] & Khawa [?] which according to Rawlinson were the great horse breeding Nisaean plains. They may be so but now only donkeys and cattle are bred there. Where water exists cotton and wheat are largely cultivated and more pains are evidently taken with the ground than I have seen anywhere in the East. Descending from Khawa, we came into the very lovely plains of Harsin and Bisutun. The extensive valleys are all green with cultivation and bounded by lofty and picturesque ranges of peaks. It can indeed be no wonder that the monarchs of Persia in the days of her chivalry, inspired by the majestic beauty of these mountains and the smiling verdure of these wide plains, should have achieved the performance

---

112   This is a reference to the well-known book *Hajji Baba of Ispahan* by J J Morier, first published in 1824.
113   Qajar?
114   Aleshtar.

the wonderful monuments of Bisitun and Hamadan and indeed of the whole of these countries. We have not seen [the] Bisutuni Sculpture but we passed within in an hour's march of it and followed the course of the great mountains upon which it exits. On our route from hence we [will] spen[d] a day there so as to enable me to visit Takht-i-Shirin about an hour distant for the purpose of digging out the big white slab which is said to contain an inscription. My friends at the "Canny Town" charge me with the crime of love for antiquities. I plead guilty at once to the charge and always did so and I am now in high delight at the prospect before me. Of course you are aware that I am blushing under the honours and being the first Kafir who ever ventured to penetrate the Chaldaean deserts to the birthplace of Abraham. My learned friend Rawlinson (now no longer Major but Lieut. Col. and Consul General at Baghdad) tells me that the inscriptions I there procured are invaluable. The whole of that region abounds in the ruins of cities every one of which will afford cuneiform annals. I hope to be able to visit it again but much fear that other spots will require attention previously. In that case others must do what I have begun. On our return from our tour I commence excavations at Susa with a firman from the Shah which the Colonel has received from Tehran. The great slab which I saw there attests [to] the existence of inscriptions and sculptures and "inshallah" I shall meet with objects not unworthy of the residence of the Persian kings of old. You perhaps ask if I [have] altogether neglected the duties more immediately connected with my office. I will not plead guilty to this. During our route Glascott and I have been carefully laying down the road we have traversed and I have not been idle in the geological department [but] the rapidity of our march has not afforded me the opportunities I could have wished. The best maps are out 30 miles in 90 so that we shall be able to add considerably to the geographical knowledge of these countries. What with geology and antiquity therefore you will perceive that I am fully employed and have much before me. The Bakhtiari country is almost wholly unexplored and I have suggested to the Colonel that in case the complicated Mohammerah question is not settled this coming spring we should spend next summer in these regions. The Colonel quite agrees with the plan and is always anxious to comply with any reasonable suggestion. Possibly if the Commissioners again assemble in January I shall take a trip along to the Bakhtiari [country] but at any rate on our return from

CHAPTER FOUR

Persepolis we shall visit Shusha [Susan?] in the mountains. The weather is now truly delightful and wherever we go piles of the most exquisite fruit are sent as presents. Just fancy a large tea tray piled with grapes, another with melons [and] a third with pears and apples, peaches, plums, water melons [and] guanoes[115] [sic]. Lurs and Persians endeavour to surpass each other in doing honour to our party. We are now located in the magnificent ruins of a summer palace of Mohammad Ali Mirza, the walls most elaborately painted in colours and gilt. The windows, i.e. such as remain [are] of coloured glass [and] the garden is laid out in extensive terraces with reservoirs for water, but all in the most wretched state of decay and ruin. How can it be otherwise in a country where might is right, the Shahanshah plunders the princes, the princes the khans, the khans the people. "Poor Persia, ah! poor Persia" often sighs our friend Mirza Jafar Khan and at the same time he gives an order for the Lurish Fushmal [?] at Mungerrah to bring in a supply of every description of grub "free gratis, for nothing", of course to feed his 290 hungry attendants. The more the natives see of the European Commission the more they must be [dis]satisfied with the injustice and oppression of their own government. I believe we have left a good name behind us wherever we have been and that European travellers will hereafter receive kindness and attention wherever chance may lead them in these regions. You would perhaps hear from my cousin that we have lost one of our party. Poor Wood, our secretary, after a tedious illness we buried on the 15th ult. at Mungerrah. All the rest of our little circle are well tho' our servants have been terribly afflicted with fever. I have no time for using the camera lucida, and as Churchill sketches so beautifully it would be useless my making scratches. The scenery here is certainly very beautiful and would suit your taste to a T. I often thought of you as we rode thro' the magnificent oak groves and of the pleasant days we spent together around the ruins of Rievaulx and Bigland, etc., etc.

Faithfully Yours,

Wm Kennett Loftus

---

115   Possibly guavas.

Letter 46, Kermanshah, Persia, 12 Oct 1850
[The original letter from Loftus is pasted into the third notebook].

My dear Cousin,

On arrival here on the 10th we found a post awaiting us, in which were your letters of July 16th and 26th, for which my best thanks are due. I am not quite sure about my artist cousin's address and therefore enclose a letter through you. I have not sealed it, that you might take a peep before posting it. I have been long in replying to his letter of last year, but I hope he will pardon my negligence. So! Charlton is astonished at the heat! He would truly be so if he passed a summer at Baghdad or Shuster, and be devilish glad to bear 101° and 120° in the underground holes which are called sirdabs. Why, at our mountain abode of Mungerrah we had the thermometer seldom below 90° all night, and we'll say nothing about the day time! I had a slight touch of the sun from 12 hours exposure on the 9th even on these high regions and at this late season of the year. We have had desperately long journeys, too long for Glascott and myself to do our work so well as we could wish. The Colonel is fond of making long stages. Rawlinson, now no longer Major and Resident at Baghdad, but Lieut. Col. & Consul-General, has kindly sent me a copy of his "Commentary on the Cuneiform" in which he makes mention of my excavations at Warka, with an intimation that I intend shortly laying the result before the public. That is now done. He seems quite decided as to Warka being the birth place of Abraham, and I should not be in the least surprised if it also turns out to be Taha Dunis[116] of the Nimrud Obelisk. Sinkara may be Rawlinson's Sarrakam, the Soracte of Pliny. We have much to learn yet from Chaldea. Layard is expected at Baghdad but what his intentions are I am not aware. It would almost appear that he is coming to investigate the ruins S. of Baghdad as this is about the season for work; yet one can scarcely imagine that he would leave a certainty at Nineveh for an uncertainty elsewhere. If he purposes going to Susa, I don't think he will receive the Colonel's benediction, for he has received the firman from the Shah. Rawlinson says that the slab on the side of the great mound attests the existence

---

116 See H C Rawlinson, *JRAS* vol.12 (1850), p. 429.

of sculptures. I have myself little doubt of this, and Layard is of the same opinion. For this reason I think Layard's journey is for Susa, and for Susa alone. The Takhti-Bostan [Taq-e Bustan] is visible from our present residence, & we visit it on our way to Bisutun. Our house has been a magnificent place in its day with its lofty iwan, stained glass windows & ornamented walls, but it will soon be a heap of ruins. I said windows! i.e. such as exist, for one would suppose there had been a street row, and that the navies had been having a turn at the aristocracy. We breakfasted with the Governor this morning on our haunches. The court was elegant, and the scene exceedingly picturesque & odd with a row of high pointed caps ranged round the room in attendance.

Ever yours faithfully,

Wm Kennett Loftus

Letter 47, Hamadan, Persia, 25 October 1850

My dear James,

I have only time to say that we arrived here all right on the 22nd after a most delightful journey from Kermanshah. My hands are quite full enough of work without attempting to write duplicates. I have very little time to complete my notes on the road as our stages are long & at night taking latitudes fills up the time after dinner till tired out we tumble into bed. The geology of the Kuh Elivend (Orontes) is highly interesting granite elevating slate & mica rocks but I am much disappointed in the height of the peaks, but magnificent mountain scenery is not to be expected when the country rises by a succession of steps from the plain of Susiana. I cannot guess the height of Hamadan as our barometers are most unfortunately broken and our spare ones at Busrah. This is a sad loss to us & all we can now do is to guess heights. Tomorrow we start for Isfahan, 300 miles ride! About the 15th we expect letters and you shall hear from me. You must now excuse me as I have much to do & write before I go to bed. With best regards to all friends, I remain, in haste,

Faithfully Yours,

Wm Kennett Loftus.

THE LETTERS

Letter 48, Hamadan, Persia, 25 October 1850

I have not written to you since 11th of June because I have had a great many correspondents and also because Mr Radford informed me that he let you know my whereabouts. From him therefore you will have heard that after the death of our poor friend Wood at Mungerrah we started on a tour into Persia. I wrote last to Mr R from Kermanshah on the 12th since which we have visited 3 celebrated localities, the Taq-e Bustan, Behistun and the site of ancient Ecbatana. Independently of the high interest attached to the antiquities at these places the country is really beautiful not so much so from the altitude of the mountains as from the vast plains which lie at their feet, richly cultivated and sprinkled with villages [and] gardens. A more fertile and beautiful series of plains do not perhaps exist in the world than in the high table lands between the two great ranges known in antiquity as the Zagros & Orontes. It was here that the Median and Persian kings spent their summers & Persian poets composed their lays. It would be useless to give you a geological sketch of these ranges because you are not interested in such dry subjects. I shall therefore endeavour to amuse you with a description of the antiquities I have mentioned. The Taq-e Bustan (arch of the garden) consists of two arches cut out of the solid rock which bounds the plains of Kermanshah to the N.N.E. These arches have evidently been excavated in different periods. The smaller is the older. The figures sculptured at the back are exceedingly rude, representing two kings in short tunics, big wigs and skin trousers with bows in their hands. A Pehlevi inscription on either side announces that the gentlemen are the Sasanian kings Shapur Dhu-l-aktaf [?] and Shapur III. The larger arch contains many subjects and is supposed to be of the age of Khosraw Parviz tho' it contains no inscription. At the back on the level of the ground is sculptured an enormous figure on horseback in chain mail with a spear over his right shoulder. The curious streamers which always accompany the sculptures of a king of the Sasanian dynasty are seen floating from his helmet. A compartment above this warrior contains three figures, a king in the centre refusing the offered emblem of royalty from another king on his left and a female on his right. These three figures are adorned with an in infinity of ornament & jewels. On the sides of the arch are two angels springing for a cornucopia and holding the royal emblem over

CHAPTER FOUR

a crescent and a ball. A very elaborate ornament on each side of the arch as well as two columns and a wreath of acanthus (?) leaves under the three figures is generally supposed to be of Grecian workmanship but I see no reason to come to this conclusion. Neither the angels nor the scrolls are in the Grecian taste & the sculptures generally rude. To my eye the scroll much rather resembles one figure in Layard's work from Nineveh & it is now quite a matter of dispute whether Greek art was not rather borrowed from these regions of the East, than Eastern art from Greece. This is a very intricate question & one which will probably never be decided. I am disposed to be of the former opinion. From hence we followed the line of Alexander's march to this place and I might add the march of Semiramis also. At Behistun we of course were much interested in the rock sculptures. One almost defaced probably the original one engraved by Semiramis and above it the Greek inscription of the "Satrap Gotarzes" concerning whom Major Rawlinson enters into a very long argument in his paper in the journal in the Geographical Society. The most interesting object at this place however is the sculpture and long trilingual cuneiform inscription of Darius Hystaspes in celebration of his expedition to Babylon to quell the insurrection of its governor Nebuchadnezzar. The inscription which is carved high upon the rock quite out of reach has been copied by the Major and it is remarkable as by means of it he was enabled to make out these three written languages of the ancient inhabitants. There are upwards of 1000 lines. The sculpture represents the king trampling on his fallen enemy while nine captives are being brought before him tied by the neck. The size of the figure is smaller than I had expected. At Takht-e Shirin (the throne of the fair Shereen) we examined the great slab of white marble but found it without any inscription or sculpture. The district still bears the name of Chambatan [?] the Cambadence [?] of Alexander's march! Our route lay through Kangavar ancient Concobar where there are the magnificent remains of the columns and basement of the temple of Anaitis, said to be [a] portion of the palace of Semiramis. From a pretty little town called Essad-a-bad,[117] we crossed Kuh Elwen (the ancient Orontes) & reached this town on the 22nd. Yesterday

---

117   Asadabad.

we visited the rock tablets in the mountains 5 miles distant & there saw another of these celebrated trilingual inscriptions cut in the granite and as perfect as when first sculptured. The site of Ecbatana is a heap of mounds and rubbish to the E. of the town. From it a view is obtained over the vast plains of Hamadan with its 45 large villages and gardens. Hamadan is the coolest place in Persia during the summer and here probably if the boundary business is not begun before that time we shall spend the hot months of next year. There is no fever, the weather is delightful and wherever we have been the authorities of the towns as well as the inhabitants have paid us the utmost attention. They deluge us with presents of the most delicious fruits & sweetmeats. The princes and governors will not even permit us to pay for the ordinary necessaries of ourselves, servants and animals. No small number of living creatures I can assure you, we are always lodged in the best abodes & are much pleased with the interiors of the Persian houses, always clean and well carpeted and ornamented in various ways with painted glass and flowers. In fact we are living on the fat of the land of Persia, a land of milk and honey. Having rested three days we start tomorrow for Isfahan, a journey of about 300 miles. But what is that to us so accustomed are we now to riding our 10 hours a day. By the time we have seen Isfahan, Persepolis, Shiraz, Bebeghan [sic] and returned to Dizful we shall have traversed a distance of 1100 miles and seen all that is most worth visiting in Persia! On reaching Dizful we shall all go to Susa if the Commissioners do not meet at Mohammerah. If they do I shall go there alone to excavate for sculptures as we have received a firman from the Shah. I have obtained such intelligence yesterday as leads me to believe that the black stone[118] with the trilingual inscription said to have been blown up by Firingi Sey'id is still existing buried secretly by the Arabs to prevent its being carried off. The obtaining of this stone or a copy of the inscription will be of inestimable value to the future investigations of the cuneiform character of Susa which differs from the other and is yet almost entirely unintelligible. You may therefore conceive that the information I have obtained as to its actual burial place renders one exceedingly anxious to commence operations.

---

118   See Letter 44 and footnote.

As to there being sculptures and inscriptions in the mound itself I believe there is not the slightest doubt. However interesting the sculptures and antiquities we are now visiting they do not to my taste equal those of the deserts of Chaldaea and Susiana. The doubt and uncertainty which hangs over the huge mounds of those regions renders them doubly interesting, and I would much rather prosecute researches among the wild tribes of the Mesopotamian desert than in any other part of the world. Here we must look for the earliest historical records. From Sinkara I could see mound upon mound as far as the eye could reach, and in each of these we may expect to find new inscriptions. From the Tigris up to the base of the mounds near Susa are innumerable mounds of the same description. Time will not permit me to continue in this mad strain and I must therefore cease. I am glad my letters amuse you but pray do not make them too public "in London and elsewhere" as they were not written for such purpose. To amuse my more intimate relations and friends is their object. I am in first rate health and spirits and highly enjoy our journey tho' I am occupied incessantly in laying down our route and making geological notes. In fact I have not a spare moment on the road. This labour however relieves the tedium of the daily travel considerably. I must now conclude and hope you who have more spare time than I will be more bountiful in your correspondence.

Wm Kennett Loftus

Letter 49, Isfahan, 12 Nov 1850

From the far famed city of Isfahan, Hadji Loftus sends his salaam to his Cousin in England. Peace and health to him. May his shadow never be less! But mashallah my head is swimming and I am perfectly lost in amaze. Allah akbar! But who ever expected to behold such scenes as I have witnessed! I must be in a dream and my ideas are wandering among the palaces of Aladdin and the Arabian Nights. I write to you from the Chehel Sitoon, "the palace of the 40 columns", the great reception room of Shah Abbas the first. The magnificence of its vast open hall, with its lofty columns supporting an immense veranda is utterly beyond the power of description. The columns are of glass. The walls also of glass, huge mirrors and arabesque designs of glass set in scrolls of gold. The ceiling of the veranda is most elaborately painted in the first style of Persian art. That of the hall itself is of glass with similar painted ornaments. Slabs of white marble painted with flowers form the lower parts of the walls, the floor paved with tiles gilded and designed with flowers and Arabesques. The doors are adorned with Indian and Chinese panels, but these as well as the gilded tiles have received no small damage from time and wear. We are all however surprised that the building has suffered so little considering the length of time the Government has been transferred to Tehran. Not a mirror is damaged nor is the gilding tarnished, tho' exposed to the air. Behind this Hall of Mirrors is the banquet room with its representations of battle and festive scenes, its 3 magnificent domes so exquisitely painted that they would require weeks to thoroughly examine and admire their beauties! And the treasured silken carpet of the great Abbas. Alas! this magnificent room on our arrival was become a workshop and tentmakers were employed in manufacturing a tent for the young Shah! The smaller rooms, which are few, are dirty, inconvenient and cold, but we soon spread our carpets and made ourselves comfortable. But if I have been surprised and delighted with the Chehel Sitoon, what shall I say of the smaller palaces, too numerous to name – perfect little gems of art. One of these (I have forgotten its name at present) is so tastefully decorated, the designs so exquisite and the colours so delicate and beautiful, that our party stood fairly enchanted. In it are 8 stained glass windows which have so taken my fancy that I am getting careful copies made by Persian artists. They are proceeding very well with them and it is just the style a Persian delights in. I hope to bring away with me a valuable reminiscence of this City of Palaces. They are to paint also for me the pattern of the roof and cornice of the same chamber. The people have been exceedingly polite and permitted us to examine the interiors of the mosques of Shah Abbas and of Lootf Oollah [Lotfollah] in the great square of the Maidan Shah. The first of these mosques has been lately newly decorated in so florid a style as to far surpass the mosque of Meshid Ali tho' it cannot boast of a gilded dome and minarets. That of Lootf Oollah is not so elaborate but more chaste in its decorations. I believe we shall go to visit that of Madre-i-shah [Madar-e Shah] this afternoon. From the top of the Ali Capi in the great square is obtained a magnificent view of the city (which the Persian in his enraptured praise calls "half the world"). It is certainly a beautiful sight especially at this season, with the variegated tints of the autumn foliage, but the extent is not so great as I had conceived. Travellers' tales usually delude us but it is likewise not to be forgotten that many portions of the ruins have melted into well cultivated fields, and the extent of Isfahan in its present state is much decreased. Three quarters of the houses are said to be unoccupied and the remainder said to contain about 80,000 inhabitants, but I am glad to say that the condition of the people is improving thanks to the viziership of Mirza Taqi Khan. The bazaars are all alive, old shops are being refitted and there is every indication of reviving prosperity. A few years of good government will do much for the country. The Persian is an industrious race as a sight of the bazaars here proves. You see no one with his pipe in his mouth as in Turkey but all are actively employed. What stock of goods each merchant possesses is very tastefully arranged and the quantity of English cottons tells what amount of traffic might be carried on with our Manchester looms if the Persian had but proper protection from his government. We arrived here from Hamadan (where I wrote to you) on the 9th performing our journey in 15 days by way of Khumayn [Khomeyn], Goolpaigan [Golpayegan], Khonsar [Khansar] and Nejjeff-a-bad [Najafabad] over a well cultivated country – beautiful valleys between serrated ranges of limestone having the same uniform character throughout. Most writers describe Persia as an utterly barren desert but I can say that I would not wish to see more fertile spots nor better cultivated fields in any country. The whole of the line of route is densely populated, the inhabitants living in villages each with its surrounding orchards. We have certainly chosen the best time for seeing these regions. The harvest was just over and the corn was being threshed and gathered in. The gardens were producing the most delicious fruit while the weather was delightful for travelling. At Khumayn [Khomeyn] we had a little incident. Two rascals of the town insulted the Colonel but they have paid dearly for their rashness. One was seized the same evening by a troop of horse sent by the Governor of Goolpaigan and his feet were touched up before the Colonel's tent next day and he is in prison for a month. The other escaped at the time but he is no doubt in limbo ere this with very little sensation in his toes [as] he was to receive 1,000 lashes, be fined £10, lose his horse and arms and be imprisoned for a month. Goolpaigan is celebrated for a coarse description of tobacco used by the Arabs of the plains of Susiana and the people of Shuster and Dizful who will smoke nothing else. Khonsar is noted for its apples. The utter absence of ruins throughout this portion of Media is rather remarkable. This is the great season of mourning for the death of Hossein and grand theatrical performances take place every day. We remain here to be present on the last when Ali is murdered and the enthusiasts cut their skins and throats to enable them to attain paradise! We met our old friends the Russians here [and] they proceed N. tomorrow. We proceed S. to Shiraz by way of the Tomb of Cyrus and Persepolis. Glascott and I have continued our work and have fixed the latitude of 31 places and find all the road laid down incorrectly. The Colonel has promised me that after our proposed excavations at Susa I shall carry out my design of once more invading Lower Chaldaea. I hope to cross the Tigris at Korma [sic], make my way thro' the Beni Lam to Wasut [Wasit] and thence to Warka once more and return by Kut el Amara. But it is long ere I can think about this journey. At Susa we purpose if possible working out our present route and if I am not asking too great a favour you would oblige me by sending (if not too long) a translation of Antigonus' march from Badaea across Mount Charban [?] to Khorram-abad [Khorramabad], contained in Diodorus Siculus Book XIX, Pliny [?] Book VI. In writing our paper I wish to make it interesting [from] an historical point of view by tracing this route. Also in the papers of the Geographical Society or else in the reports of the British Association, some rules are laid down by which the names of places in foreign countries are to be spelled. I refer to Eastern names, of course. Hancock most probably can direct you. We hear from Baghdad that all our English letters of Aug 9th and July 29th have been waylaid by the Arabs between Mosul and Baghdad and fears are entertained for the safety of our last packet from Mungerrah (Sept 23rd). From Constantinople Mr Stampa writes me that he has heard nothing of the boxes you sent. The Colonel tells me that Guarracino of Samsun [?] advises him of the arrival of two boxes but he does not say who for. Did you address them to the care of Stampa or not? I shall write to the agent of the company at Constantinople, Capt Ford [?]. Give my best regards to Mrs Radford, Edward and Mrs Mather, John Gray, Blacklock, Green, Charlton and all friends and

Believe me faithfully yours

Wm Kennett Loftus.

CHAPTER FOUR

Letter 50, Shiraz, 6 Dec 1850

My dear Edward,

I have only time to announce our arrival at this city of Persian wine and song. We arrived on the 4th and start, if the weather clears, for Dizful on the 8th. We have visited Pasargadae and Persepolis and spent nearly two days in wandering among the stately columns and vast ruins of the city of Xerxes. We searched in every hole and corner, surveyed over and over again the celebrated sculptures and cuneiform inscriptions, which by the bye are not so spirited as those of Nineveh and Nimrud. That the style of architecture was derived from Greece and Egypt I think there can be no doubt. The elegant fluted columns are of Grecian origin. The heavy doorways of Egyptian. Excavations would bring to light many architectural subjects but nothing else. The platform [on] which the ruins stand is a magnificent specimen of Cyclopean masonry. At Naksht Rustem [sic][119] we procured ropes and I was the first to scale to the tombs of the kings 43 feet from the ground. They are excavated in the face of the rock and the one we entered was 60 feet long and contained three recesses, each with three sarcophagi. Of course, they had long ago been broken into, the treasures stolen and the ashes of the kings scattered to [the] winds. At Pasargadae we visited the tomb of Cyrus, a solid building of enormous stones which the present race of Persians have no means of moving if they would. In form it much resembles the Lycian tombs in the British Museum. We visit Shapur on our way to Dizful, which we hope to reach before the beginning of the year, and whence I shall be heard from. In haste, I remain, with kind regards to Ellen [?], my cousin, Gray and all friends,

Ever yours truly,

Wm Kennett Loftus.

---

119 Naqsh-e Rustam.

THE LETTERS

Letter 51, Mohammerah, 4 March 1851

My dear Edward,

"Wonders never cease". Notwithstanding my positive assertion in my letter to you of January 20th that there was no chance of anything being done [on] the Boundary question this spring, here we are once more roasting in the fire of Mohammerah. Our steward returned to Susa without our stores, but with letters announcing that one of the contending parties had given way in its demand and that we were expected here without loss of time. So here we are once more. Before we can do anything, however, the other party must agree to the arrangement proposed, and I don't expect anything will be done besides drawing the base line for future triangulation. We shall cut and run in two months once more to the mountains and return early in the autumn. There is, I think, every prospect of our commencing work in earnest then, and I sincerely hope do xxx. I don't quite understand whether you purpose getting me a common pedometer or a Paynes' patent, what is the difference between them? I have to thank you for two penknives and a host of postage stamps, all valuable articles to me, as well as for your trouble about the Asiatic and Geological Societies' journals. There is one consolation, however. It appears my wants are productive of long and acceptable letters from you, for I had latterly denounced you as a bad correspondent. Sir Henry's (De la Beche) letter which you enclose is highly gratifying to me. For your satisfaction I quote part of his letter – "it has been with no slight interest that I have heard of your progress, not only from such letters of yours which have reached me, as from other sources. I have heard much of you, always with great credit for you, from Major Rawlinson. This is pleasant, tho' you may not have had good opportunities for much geological investigation, more's the pity. You have done right good service in various ways and have deservedly had credit for it in this country". I cannot do better than repeat his words "this is pleasant". He says he has written me twice before, but I have never received his letters. One written in July must have been in the post plundered by the Arabs between Mosul and Baghdad. I shall write him again by this post. The spectacles have not reached me and I fear they have been detained at the Foreign Office. I remember Mr Hammond's very particular instruction, "Nothing but letters will be sent".

CHAPTER FOUR

Perhaps they may cast up by next post. Regarding the Palaeontographical Society, I believe there are two nos published since I left home, King's monograph among them. I had no nos undistributed. The Society distributes them out of London as the subscribers direct the Secretary J.S. Bowerbank, Esq., 3 Highbury Grove, Islington, who will give Mr Carr or Mr Kele [?] all further information on the subject. I wrote to him from Isfahan to make some microscopic investigations for me. Can you send me out any papers (circulars) relating to the Society. Blackstock tells me that King has immortalized me! If I have time I will write Bowerbank on the subject of the enquiries made to you. By the bye, when you send me anything by way of Constantinople you should advise Stampa of it, or a parcel will lie for ever at the Customs House, if it is not robbed, xxx. I have since leaving Baghdad directed my labours to two subjects, antiquity and geography, which were not included in the duties of my appointment. I have no cause to regret having done so, but still the opportunities for geological investigation, which I so much desire, have not been afforded me to the extent which is necessary for me to do justice to my subjects, and I fear I shall have to wait long before I can send to Sir Henry such a paper on the geology of these regions as will prove that I have not been spending my time uselessly xxx. I have been suffering a good deal from my fall at Susa last June. The Dr passed the matter off as nothing of importance. I feel a constant gnawing at the lower ribs of my right side. The Colonel has been urging my return in autumn. I have obtained his permission to take a trip to Baghdad with Jones next voyage, under the idea that it will do me good, when I intend to consult my excellent friend Dr Hyslop at the Residency. With the exception of this constant annoyance when I exert myself my general health is first-rate and all I fear is that inattention may produce some confirmed internal disease. I think you will approve of the step I purpose taking. The Colonel said during our short conversation that by my past services I had a claim on the interest of the Foreign Office. I believe that Prof. Oldham has been appointed Director General of the Indian Geological Survey, which may probably cause an opening in the English staff? The Colonel also proposed in case my side is not better in autumn to send me off along the boundary to Erzeroum with facilities for prosecuting geological researches on my way. I would much rather prefer doing the work well with the Commission if there is any certainty of the line being proceeded with next autumn. Suleiman Khan at Dizful made each of us a present of a horse. Mine is a perfect little picture and thoroughbred, but rather too little, light and ladylike. The Dr got likewise £50 for his attention during the Suleimans illness. The khan made a similar present of horses to the Russian party. He is now about being turned out of his Governorship. On our sail up to Baghdad I shall write Charlton a short account of what has been done at Susa; at present I am packing up 38 casts of inscriptions for Rawlinson to go by post. I only wish you had seen my tent at Susa. It was the Record Office and I the Keeper of the said Records. The papers are full of your outcries against the "insidious" designs of the Pope. The Parliament must do something when it meets or you'll have precious rows. I am no bigot but defend us from further aggressions and the introduction of "Ave Marias", pater nosters and images among us. Liberty of conscience as at present but no surrender of our "reets" as Protestants. Layard was last heard of at Niffar where he has found coffins similar to mine, and it is presumed he is now at Warka. I don't think he will be able to throw much more light on the matter than I have done unless he digs into the Miffagjee [?], the great mound exterior to the walls of Warka. It is no doubt the tomb of a hero. I may possibly meet Layard at Baghdad. By the bye, from whom do you suppose I have received a letter, Valcenberg! – a very nice letter and which concludes having an eye to business among the Persian noblemen. Unfortunately for him wine is forbidden by the Koran and moreover isn't strong enough. "Raki" suits their tastes best.

Faithfully yours,

Wm Kennett Loftus

Letter 52, Mohammerah, 7 March 1851

My dear James,

You will learn from Mather the cause of our having flitted hither so unexpectedly. We all wish ourselves anywhere else, as we are without exception seized with the local complaint, want of appetite, indigestion and ennui. It is in fact a horrid place. Your letters of Oct 24th, Nov 5th [and] Dec 5th have reached me together with the copy of Arrian, your translation of Herodotus respecting Ardericca,[120] and Rawlinson's Cuneiform, for all of which my best thanks are due. Your prompt attention in executing my commissions I do not know how sufficiently to acknowledge. I find Arrian is not so difficult to make out as I had expected, as I have a little smattering left of school Greek. A copy of Rollin[121] is in the library (only fancy our peripatetic bookcase!) and he gives a very careful translation when he has occasion to quote ancient authors, still for actual reference the original is best. I think I have discovered a better site for Ardericca near Shuster, which would correspond more nearly with the "Royal Route". Rawlinson also refers to "Philostrat Apollon: [xxxx] book I c. 24 [?]". We have nearly all the papers of the Geogr. Soc. relating to these regions, except "Prof Long's remarks on the site of Susa, the Bakhtiyari, vol. 12"[122] and "De Bode's notes on Mal Amir etc. Vol 13".[123] These two as well as "Geo Long Esq on the site of Susa Vol 3"[124] would be very interesting to me. I have begun a letter to Charlton but doubt if I shall have time to finish it by this post, as I have received such a packet of letters. I have mentioned to Mather my purposed visit to old Baghdad. I shall endeavour to procure a brick for the sheriff. You highly amuse me with Albert Smith's account of his month's expenses at Constantinople.[125] He must have done it very "rough" for without exception it is the dearest place in Europe, and he would only [have been] able to judge of a certain class, for a traveller with a knapsack on his back would have some difficulty in getting into the society of the Pashas! Your remark regarding what I wrote for the Farmers Club is perfectly correct. I was not sufficiently explicit, and after it was enveloped I regretted having written such stuff, and from your letter I had hoped you had burned it, but Mather tells me it has been published!

---

120 Herodotus 1.165, 6.119.
121 Presumably Charles Rollin, *Ancient History of the Egyptians, Carthaginians, Assyrians, etc.*, (translated from the French).
122 A H Layard and Professor Long, 'Ancient sites among the Baktiyari Mountains, with remarks on the rivers of Susiana and the site of Susa', *JRGS* vol. 12 (1842), pp. 102–9.
123 Clement Augustus de Bode, 'Notes on a journey in January and February 1841 from Behbehan to Shuster with a description of the bas-reliefs at Tengi-Saulek and Mal Amir', *JRGS* vol 13 (1843), pp. 86–107.
124 G Long, 'On the site of Susa', *JRGS* vol. 3 (1833), pp. 257–67.
125 This is presumably a reference to Albert Smith, *A Month at Constantinople* (London 1850).

That was never intended, but can't be helped now. I certainly think the plan is very applicable to towns as well as country drainage, and it was intended partly to draw the attention of certain members of the Sanitary Committee! You see that Layard is aware of the importance of further discoveries in Chaldaea and has forestalled me in my proposed trip. He is at Warka we hear, and he will of course visit those sites I was so anxious to penetrate to. The French copy of Diodorus Siculus will be very acceptable and I thank you sincerely for the pains you have taken in hunting it up for me. I wonder when the two boxes are to make their appearance! If Jones does not bring them this trip I must positively get some things made at Baghdad, for I can wait no longer! How I get my shirts on and off is a difficult question! Glascott and myself have continued our route survey, and connected the whole of our work with Mohammerah across the desert from Susa. The Kerkhah and Hawiza are very incorrectly laid down on the best maps. We visited the celebrated bund which broke and caused the river to forsake its old channel and betake itself to the marshes, leaving the town destitute of water. They are about to lead the stream back into its old course, and to resume the cultivation of the district under the Wali. This will be one of the results of the Commission. We have no less than 70 latitudes fixed. When we shall have time to lay down our route on paper I scarcely know, but when done it will be the most correct of any. Susa was beginning to look green and beautiful, and we all regretted having to come to this barren desert. Our proposed movements are of course stumped, and I don't know if the Colonel has decided on any future plan. But this is quite certain, we shall be off before the middle of May into the cool mountains once more. I have been obliged to cast my flannels this morning as [they are] unbearable any longer! Delightful chine! Your kind letter of Xmas day has this moment reached me. I thank you sincerely for your remembrance. Our day of festivity was spent in pouring rain in the desert of Ram Hormouz. We sat down to a wretched dinner and tumbled into bed soaked with rain! Part of the pleasures of travel! The coffins <u>did</u> go to England by the Apprentice but I have heard no more of their arrival than of the paper describing them! It appears to me as very strange. Your letter came from Baghdad with the new French Consul, who has been 27 days on the road. We may therefore expect another post tomorrow or next day by Jones and the Nitocris. What a cargo of posts we have unanswered to be sure. It is fearful to contemplate. <u>March 9</u>. The Nitocris has just arrived with the post containing

CHAPTER FOUR

your and Mather's joint letter of January 4. The books sent by the "Jessie Gray" will be very acceptable, especially Diodorus Siculus. I shall write to Stampa about them. No news of the boxes. I fear they lie in the Custom House at Constantinople. I shall also enquire after them. We hear that Layard has failed in his attempt to reach Warka. His people were robbed, and he has gone off again to Mosul. So Chaldaea is still open to me, and I hope to avail myself of an opportunity in autumn. I shall be able to pass where he could not and if I were to go back to my old ground I should be laded [sic] with antiquities which the Arabs would retain for me. I want to dig into the great exterior mound of the Nuffagjee [?], the tomb of a king. However, we must be patient. I believe the Colonel's present plans for the summer are to quit this [place] about 2 months hence, visit Mal Amir and Mungerrah [?] and thence make our way to summer quarters at the pass of Kirrind which is said to be a delightful spot. But it is impossible to know at present where we shall go. The heat has set in very early this year. I am very anxious to follow [up on] our investigations [of] those rocks in the Bakhtiyari and Sir Henry too suggests that I should keep a sharp look out. The Nitocris starts for Baghdad tonight, so I beg you will excuse a longer scribble as I must strip my tent. With best regards to Mrs R. S. and all friends,

Yours sincerely

Wm Kennett Loftus

PS. I have just packed up my bricks etc. from Warka, and shall send them addressed to the Museum by a vessel of Lynch which is here. I have marked one for the Sheriff.

Letter 53, The Residency, Baghdad, 26 March 1851

My dear James,

Pray excuse a short scribble for I am not at all in writing trim. The trip hither has done me much good. In fact I do not feel any further effects of my fall. Hyslop tells me that he thinks I must have received a severe crush on a portion of the bowels near the liver, that the latter does not appear to be injured, as my general health bears most convincing testimony, for I never felt better in my life. He thinks I shall not suffer again, as the beautiful climate of this season has braced me up wonderfully. Capt Kemball and Capt Jones both wish me to remain till the end of next month, but I have no leave from the Colonel and I am undecided, tho' I know he would have no objection, as I can do no good down there and I am better out of the furnace of Mohammerah. We have excellent English society among the rest, two newly married couples, Mr and Mrs Stern (the missionaries), you probably met the former at Newcastle, and a Mr and Mrs Howard. Capt Kemball gave a picnic at Ctesiphon on Monday and Tuesday at which we heartily enjoyed ourselves. The ladies have much improved the tone of Baghdad society, they are two nice little bodies. Layard had gone off to Mosul before my arrival as he has not been successful in Chaldaea. He starts for England I understand directly, so the field is yet open for me, and if I don't again attack Warka it shan't be my fault. Capt Kemball declares I must, the Colonel has promised that I shall. Next November then, please the pigs, I shall be once more en route thro' the Muntefic. The Damascus post brought letters from Rawlinson to Jones of Feb 24 from which I find I am to figure once more in the Athenaeum. The tablets (on the value of which I have always laid great stress) prove to be government bank notes of the issue of Nabopolassar, Nebuchadnezzar, Nabonidus, Cyrus, Cambyses and others! Rawlinson writes a notice to the Athenaeum. I see I am figuring off too geologically as there is a notice of a paper by Mr W.K. Loftus "on the geology of the Zagros range of Western Persia"!! As I never wrote such a paper I can only presume it is an extract from my rough description to Sir Henry. Tho' I am annoyed that such an indistinct sketch should have been given to the public, I conclude from it that Sir Henry deems the subject worthy of being brought before the geological world. With opportunities I shall acquire I hope some KUDOS [written in Greek] in this matter, and a more worthy subject could not have come to my notice. I shall have to work like a diabolus next year in arranging my rough notes for a long geological paper. I sincerely hope I shall not be disappointed in getting to the Bakhtiyari this summer. No news of my antiquarian paper nor of the boxes. I wrote to Count Pisani about the former. The best plan to send out parcels in future will be by Messrs Lynch's vessels. [Xxxx] and Fisher will be able to give directions. Things sent in this way would be sure to reach me in 6 months. Pray tell

Charlton to excuse me not writing as I promised. I have been busy searching thro' the Residency library making notes. I have seen Chesney's book, it is a most decided failure, exceedingly incorrect and his maps as far as I can judge, humbug! If at any time you want to convey speedy tidings to me, there is a post via Marseilles and Damascus about the 24th of each month. Letters to the care of the British Residency would reach me here in 28 days.

Kind regards, etc,

Faithfully yours,

Wm Kennett Loftus.

Letter 54, Baghdad, 7 April 1851

My dear Cousin,

I scribble these few lines to say that I feel all right again. Ballingale the Dr on board the Nitocris (son of the eminent physician in Edinburgh) has I think most satisfactorily solved the question as to the cause of the late pain in my side. He thinks that the diaphragm and probably some of the integuments of the liver have received a severe strain. Perhaps over exertion may cause me to feel the pain again, but it will not affect my general health. We return to Mohammerah after a prolonged stay on the on the 10th or 12th. The Nitocris is to be changed at Busrah, and Capt. Jones does not want to wait there longer than actually necessary and he thus gives time for the relief to arrive from Bombay. There is a capital opportunity if you have anything to send to me. Mr Hector an English merchant has a vessel starting from England at the end of next month or the beginning of June, and has kindly promised that if Thomas Sterling Esq of Sheffield is communicated with a parcel may be forwarded by this means. I am very desirous of getting out one of those newly invented apparatus for taking sketches by means of the sun. There is one called Talbotype or Calotype? (I forget which) which produces an impression [in] a sort [of] sepia colour at once (without the aid of plates) on chemically prepared paper. I understand that Dr Keith [?] used one of these processes in Syria and has published a work lately with engravings from the impressions. If the process is simple and would succeed in the climate, if it is really applicable for landscapes, if the apparatus is portable, and above all if it is cheap, I should vastly like to try it. I apprehend that the apparatus is not expensive and the paper and acids cannot cost much. Directions for use and a sufficiency of paper and acids would be required and a box fastened by screws instead of glue (to stand the heat) would be requisite. I have a camera lucida but it is impossible to use it in such a climate, for one is scorched to death before the concern is all arranged and then you have to begin to sketch with your eyes almost torn out of your head. I have many times wished to get a few sketches with it, but have been obliged to desist. A few quires of thin writing paper of the size of this sheet, a case of carbonic paper, some tooth and nail brushes would also be very desirable as I don't know when the boxes you sent are going to cast up. I am very vexed at this because I have been absolutely obliged to get a new rig out here. We expect another post in tomorrow so that I shall on arriving at Mohammerah have the chance of receiving news by four packets, three having already gone down. I shall write to you by the first opportunity from that hot region. I dare say you wonder where I have got this carbonic paper! I set John Taylor (son of the late Resident) to hunt among his father's old papers, and wonderful to relate he found three sheets of it. Capt. Kemball with Dr Hyslop and Hector have gone off to see Nineveh so that I am sole Resident. I hope I shall be able to send you good news of our prospects of work. If the Persians will be persuaded, all will be right and we shall go ahead like wildfire. With kind regards to all friends.

I remain

Your affectionate cousin

Wm Kennett Loftus

CHAPTER FOUR

Letter 55, Kirrind, Persia, 24 May 1851
[a carbon copy of the original Loftus letter is pasted into the third notebook].

My dear Ben,

Many thanks for your letter of January 14th which reached me at Mohammerah on the 16th ult. and which I take the first possible opportunity of replying to. I had quite given you up as a correspondent, and trust you will keep your promise of better conduct for the future. I have written to the three friends, who so kindly and carefully attend to my interests at home, and have instructed them regarding the subject matter of yours in such manner, as, I trust, will meet with your wishes. I will not therefore take up more space on business matters, but give you, in this hasty letter, a short account of our last ramble over the hills, as you confess yourself interested in my proceedings. I fully believe that you are perfectly sincere in the sentiments your letter expresses, the knowledge that I have friends at home who watch my motions and operations, in this land of wonders so as closely as you are doing, is but an incitement to me to renewed exertion. Truly I have no ordinary subjects before me; let us see what will eventually be the result! On arriving from Baghdad on the 16th of April I found all my friends at Mohammerah exceedingly ill from the complaint we formerly had there, viz. constant sickness at the stomach. They had waited so long for our arrival with the "Nitocris" that all hopes of seeing us before their departure had ceased. I just joined them in time to set out once more on our travels on the following evening! The commencement of the preliminary matters had been began, when they were suddenly brought to a conclusion. I believe we shall not visit Mohammerah again, but that we shall fairly go to work, as soon as summer is over, at Zohab and [go] rapidly over the business without further impediments. Well, we travelled in two nights along the banks of the Karoon to Ismaili [?], where we struck across the desert to the Kurkhah, where we found Khouler Mirza encamped with a large number of troops, on what we term a skinning expedition! Our old friend Suleiman Khan the late Governor has been ousted and the Prince put in thro' the instrumentality of, it is supposed the Persian Commissioner. There are sad lamentations for the late Governor, tho' he was a Christian. Three days afterwards we once more encamped on the ruins of Susa and surveyed our former works there. We certainly have left our marks upon the mound. At Dizful we rested a couple of days and there I am sorry to say I was obliged to leave my poor lad Saleh, who I had brought from Baghdad, dangerously ill of fever. Another man too was left behind who fancied he could tame a serpent and nearly lost his life in consequence. I hope both the sick men will rejoin us in a few days. From Mohammerah to Dizful the heat was so intense that we were glad to sleep outside our beds, with our tents open at night. But as we got into the mountains and rose from the plains we were not sorry to encase ourselves once more in cloth clothes. Never was such a change and never did people so quickly revive as I saw my friends around me. We travelled along the Mah Sabadan[126] of Col. Rawlinson, the great high road of the ancient kings from their mountains to their abodes in the plains. A portion of this road we had formerly traversed on our journey from Mungerrah to Khorramabad. I call it a road, but it would somewhat puzzle you how it acquired the title. It is a continual scramble over huge blocks of stone and debris, and it is certainly more from good luck than good management that we all got over it with our legs and arms perfect! We visited the Pul-i-Tang "Bridge of the Gorge" which we had formerly passed without seeing. The Kerkah here forces its way thro' the solid limestone, cutting out a channel upwards of 100 feet in depth and excessively narrow. A bridge of a single arch has been thrown across, tho' the key of the arch is fallen, and an Illiyat [?] bridge of timber having been thrown across the gorge, presents a pretty sketch. We crossed the Kealin range and descended in to the Plains of Jaidar, where our sight was enlivened, after our eyes had been nearly burned out on the brown and barren desert, by the most beautiful meadows of deliciously green grass and herbage. I shall never forget the delight with which we rode thro' the first green field we had beheld for an age. It was worth journeying all the distance from Mohammerah to enjoy. We encamped that day on the Kashghan branch of the Kerkhah which here debouches from the mountains thro' a magnificent gorge, across the jaws of which once stood the fine bridge of Shapoor called "the bridge of the maid" or of Jaidar. It is now in ruins but the approaches are curious, being carried up

---

126 Rawlinson 1839: 47–49, 112.

the side of the river, under one of the arches on either side, and by an inclined plane doubling upon itself, reaching the roadway of the bridge. This is rather a novel way of doing the thing I conceive, the bridge being thus commanded from the rocks above on either side. We next day forded the Kashghan and the following day crossed the Kerkh river where ford there was none, floating across on these rickety contrivances called kelleks, inflated skins and sticks tied together. Our money chest [had] a preciously narrow escape from drowning. The Plain of Seimarrah is the great granary of Luristan, and certainly I never saw such crops of barley nor such heads of grain in even happy England. This plain is one vast cultivated field. The ruins of Seimarrah are curious, but not very interesting – a vast collection of roughly built arches of rubble work of the Sassanian age. Its situation at the head of a stream issuing from the Kebir Kuh range is very pretty. The Sassanians appear to have been very fond of the fountain heads of streams, especially if shade was to be obtained from trees or rocks near the spot. Their sculptures are usually found in these situations. We followed along the route of my learned friend Col Rawlinson to the ruins of Kaylan (Celonae of antiquity) and which he called Shirwan.[127] On our way my pet little horse Suleiman (the present of Suleiman Khan) fell down a precipice 400 feet high and was so damaged that I was obliged to have him shot on the spot. He was a great favourite of the groom's, who stood by wringing his hands and crying like a child. It is not often these natives shew such feelings; and Thaher [?] got a "baksheesh" for this show of his affection. Kaylan precisely resembles Seimarrah and therefore I need not say anything respecting it. The people along this road are excessively rude and treacherous, but they behaved exceedingly well, bringing everything for sale that we required. The Shah has little power in those portions of his dominions. We got here on the 17th inst. and are much delighted with Kirrind.[128] The snow rests on the summits of the high mountains, and the thermometer does not yet rise higher than moderate 85° Fahr in the shade! At night it falls to 54° and we sleep with our tents closed. We expect a visit from some of our Baghdad friends, who are only 5 good days' ride from us,

---

127   Rawlinson 1839: 53–56.
128   Kerend-e Gharb in Kermanshah province is at an elevation of 1588 m.

and we have a fine promise in the gardens of grapes and all kinds of delicious fruit to assist us in getting over the tedium of a long residence here. However long it may be Glascott and myself have enough to employ ourselves with, for all our map making has to be gone thru' as well as my rough geological notes to be put in order.

You must please excuse this scribble as I have such an infinity of letters to answer.

With best regards to all enquirers and a reminder that you have promised to make up for past bad conduct.

I remain, my dear Ben,

Yours ever sincerely,

Wm Kennett Loftus

Letter 56, Kirrind, Persia, 24 May 1851

My dear Blacklock,

I have such an accumulation of letters to answer and some of importance that I must beg you to excuse this short line in reply to yours of the 23rd Oct, 15th Nov, 15th Feb and 22nd March. In consequence of my absence at Baghdad I have received no less than 6 posts in a batch! I don't know how to get thro' my correspondence. I now hasten to acquaint you that I dispatched per the Brig "Fortitude", Capt. Brown, a large box addressed to the Museum, Newcastle. It contains bricks and spoils from Warka etc. which I propose placing in your safe custody. The vessel left Mohammerah at the end of March and the box is consigned to the care of Messrs S. Lynch & Co, 78 Great Tower Street, London. The box is padlocked but I cannot send the key. I enclose a list of the contents. I have marked one brick for the late sheriff of Newcastle, Ralph Dodds, Esq. You will oblige me by forwarding it to him with my best regards. There is one broken brick with inscriptions in relief (apparently rubbish) upon which I set great store. It might be carefully mended. In addition to the contents of the box there were two of my bricks placed by accident loose in the hold. Pray make particular enquiries after them as I would not lose them on any account. The vessel ought to arrive in August. Dr Charlton has made a proposition to me on behalf of the Antiquarian Society. I might probably some day or other have an opportunity of executing his commission, but I must beg of him to be somewhat more explicit with regard to expenses. Independently of the cost of excavation, there is to be considered the amount of expense for conveyance to Busrah, packing in substantial cases and finally freight home which costs £15–£20 per ton, tho' probably Messrs Lynch (who are most liberal in such matters) might charge less. As to sculptures two on an average weigh a ton. Tell him to inform me by next post if the Society would be disposed to pay so dearly for the piper. I would write to Charlton but really cannot by this post. Tell him "he owes me one" and that I shall send him another "Antiquity Letter" when he has replied to my last and he must be quick about it. Thanks for the extract from Edward's book; it is very interesting to me. I have seen similar tiles at Susa, and they appear to have been common in these early times. Many thanks also for the translations. I have been making an interesting discovery of fossil footsteps, rain and ripple arks in the sandstone near Dizful. They are in sandstone. The footsteps are casts of the impression which has originally been made on red clay. The sand probably brought by the retiring tide has covered up the impression and hence the cast. A portion of the clay adheres to it. I believe it to be that of the cheetah or hunting leopard, at any rate of some large feline animal. I believe this is the first occasion on which have been met the traces of any mammal, hence the interest of this late discovery. I am glad to hear that the Nat. Hist. Soc. is proceeding so favourably and that you purpose purchasing fossil plants to supply the hiatus when Mr Hutton's are removed. I once before proposed this to the Committee but the plan was not then approved of. Pray excuse this horrid scrawl and give my best regards to all.

Ever yours

Wm Kennett Loftus

THE LETTERS

Contents of box forwarded from Mohammerah per Brig "Fortitude" Capt. Brown, addressed to the Museum of the Nat. Hist. Soc. of Northumberland, etc.

From Warka   No. of articles

1 Brick marked No. 3 (small wedge)
1 Brick marked No. 3 (large wedge)
1 Brick marked No. 7 (broken; in relief)
1 Brick marked No. 4 (square, inscr)
1 Brick marked No. 6
2 Bricks, small   7

From Sinkara

3 Bricks marked (No.10) large inscrip   3

From Mugeyer

1 Brick marked No. 13   ___1___

Total No. of bricks   11

Vases from Warka 20, Sinkara 9		24 [sic]
Lamps Warka		3
Sepulchral figures	(W & S)	4
Lamp stands	W	7
Dishes & saucers	W & S	18
Cube stones	W	4
Phalloi? (written in Greek)	W	
Nails	W	
Flints	W	
Copper dish broken	S	

Appendix

Thanks to Elizabeth Frances Radford[1] the great-granddaughter of James Radford (1806-93) I have had sight of a folder with papers relating to the history of the Radford and Loftus families. Based on information in the folder and information found online I have put together a concise family tree showing W K Loftus's immediate contacts (pl. 32) with notes about a few individuals. I have also transcribed 10 letters in the folder which all have a bearing on the life and career of W K Loftus.

Letter 1 is about publication of his 1857 book.

Letters 2-4 are about a gift of Assyrian sculptures to the Literary and Philosophical Society in Newcastle.

Letters 5-6 are letters of condolence on the death of W K Loftus, from Sir Henry Layard and John George Dodson, 1st Baron Monk Bretton (1825-97), who was Loftus's travelling companion from Constantinople to Mosul in 1849.

Letters 7-10 relate to making provision for the surviving children of W K Loftus.

---

1   Elizabeth Frances Radford (always known as Frances) has edited the letters of two Radford kinsmen who were in the British army, James Radford (served 1794-1801) and his son John Radford (served 1804-16), the latter being lost at sea off the Irish coast. Her book is entitled *Two Military Men: the Letters of Father and Son 1794-1816* (Roundtuit Publishing 2006).

APPENDIX

Publication

Loftus's letter indicates that in 1853 both John Murray and Longman were being considered as possible publishers for his monograph, but in the event this was published in 1857 by James Nisbet & Co. with the title *Travels and Researches in Chaldaea and Susiana*. It is clear from this letter that Loftus kept detailed journals, but if they still exist their present whereabouts is unknown.

Letter 1: From W K Loftus to James Radford, written from 5 Clifton Road, and dated June 27, 1853 (pl. 30).

My dear James,

It is some time since I wrote to you, and I should not be annoying you now in the midst of your labours had I not devoted the day to the Stamboul Post and general correspondence.

Col. Williams has been and is very ill with a relapse of fever. I was to have met him last Tuesday week at dinner at Col. Sandham's (of the Ordnance Office) but he was too ill to attend and receive the congratulations of his assembled friends. I had to act as his lieutenant. Mr Gladstone, Cousin of the Chanc. of the Exchequer, sat next to me. The same evening I was at Norris'[2], Oriental Interpreter at the F.O. & Sec. of the Asiatic Society, where I met "Cilician" Barker[3], Fergusson[4], Latham[5] etc. I am not given to party going but could not resist these two invites for the same evening.

---

2   Edwin Norris (1795–1872) was a celebrated Orientalist.
3   This is probably William Burckhardt Barker (1810?–1856) who wrote (with William Ainsworth) *Lares and Penates or Cilicia and its Governors* (1853).
4   James Fergusson (1808–86) wrote *The Palaces of Nineveh and Persepolis Restored: an Essay on Ancient Assyrian and Persian Architecture*. It was published by John Murray in 1851.
5   Probably Robert Gordon Latham FRS (1812–88) who was a famous ethnologist and philologist.

You saw Murray's letter about publishing. On Col. W's return, Sir Henry[6] again urged me to see and try to get a more decisive answer from "his Lordship". Col. W. recommended me to follow Sir H.'s advice. I did so. His lordship was very shy, but said a small volume like Galton's[7] might take. He however proposed nothing, & only suggested that some discreet friend should read over the Journals and tell me what he considered most interesting points to dilate upon, I saw Sir H. again, and he seemed to consider this tantamount to Murray's declining anything to do with it. He is very anxious to get me before the public and insisted on my at once taking a note to Longman which he wrote. I shewed it to Col. W. & with his approbation went to Paternoster Row. Longman [was] exceedingly civil. I told him how matters stood with Murray. As my journals are lengthy, he suggested that his chief man Dr Cauvin [?] should step up on Saturday. The Dr came, spent three hours in overhauling, looking over Churchill's sketches and left me with high compliments on the subject matter & manner of keeping my journals. His opinion is that they will form a work of considerable interest, and that Longman must see them. Judge my surprise when I tell you that I saw Layard yesterday, who told me that Murray quite intended publication! This was a somewhat odd mode of shewing it! Sir H. now thinks he was not the man for me, and I am told that Murray has a very cute eye for £.s.d. I trust that you will shortly as the advertisements say, "hear something to my advantage".

Capt. Jones I.N.[8] arrived on Thursday from Baghdad on sick leave after an absence of 26 years! He is very much like a fish out of his element. We went on Saturday evening to see the beastesses [?] at the Zoological.

I sent Dr Richardson the Mineral Waters. If you should see him, will you explain to him that I shall not be down as I wrote [that] I should.

---

6   Sir Henry De la Beche (1796–1855), Director of the Geological Society of Great Britain.
7   This is probably a reference to *The Narrative of an Explorer in Tropical South Africa* by Francis Galton (1822–1911). It was published by John Murray in 1853.
8   Capt Felix Jones (1813/14–78) was an employee of the East India Company and celebrated surveyor. See also n. 28 on p. 21.

APPENDIX

Rawlinson wrote me a few days ago. Not very well. All his last papers plundered en route!

The weather looks somewhat unpropitious here today with a N.W. wind. I trust this will reach you tomorrow with a bright and sunny sky. I received the paper of last week with many thanks. I hope all is still favourable, and that you will early send me a good report.

With best regards to all friends,

Ever yours sincerely,

Wm Kennett Loftus

You have been very silent of late, owing I suppose to preparations.[9]

Donation of Assyrian Sculptures

It seems that while working in Assyria between June 1854 and March 1855 Loftus removed from Nimrud some Assyrian bas-reliefs which he subsequently offered to the Literary and Philosophical Society of Newcastle on condition that they paid for the cost of carriage (Harbottle 1973: 212). In the letter below Loftus tells James Radford that his offer has been accepted and that plans must be made for their transportation to Newcastle. The sculptures arrived in Newcastle in 1856 and were mounted on the principal staircase of the Lit and Phil building (Ermidoro 2020: 254, n. 31).

The sculptures, all of superb quality, come from the North-West Palace of Ashurnasirpal II at Nimrud, mostly excavated by Sir Henry Layard. They were first published by Ernst F. Weidner (1938). One shows an Assyrian king (Ashurnasirpal II) holding a bow with behind him a bearded figure holding a bucket in one hand and with the other upraised; another shows a four-winged bearded genie with a bucket in one hand and a pinecone in the

---

9 Presumably for Race Week at Newcastle Races, which in 1853 took place 19–21 July.

other; and a third shows an eagle-headed genie holding bucket and cone and administering to a "sacred tree". Lastly, there are two corner slabs which bear the joining halves of a "sacred tree". All the sculptures have long cuneiform inscriptions written across their central part, the so-called standard inscription of Ashurnasirpal II.

It is not quite clear what lies behind the two letters of Hormuzd Rassam enquiring about the provenance of the reliefs in the Lit and Phil. He himself had worked with Layard in Assyria and in 1852-54 he had taken over the running of the excavations at Nimrud and Nineveh. At Nineveh he worked in the South-West Palace of Sennacherib and the North Palace of Ashurbanipal, and was perhaps concerned that the slabs had come from one of those palaces. In his second letter, he acknowledges that they are from Nimrud.

Sadly, financial difficulties at the Lit and Phil combined with waning interest in the sculptures led in 1959 to a recommendation to sell them. In due course, they were sold by Spink & Son for £45,000, which after the deduction of expenses amounted to £35,275 for the Society (Ermidoro 2020: 253-255). After being exported to the USA, they were sold on in 1964 for $306,000 to Anna Bing Arnold who donated them to the Los Angeles County Museum of Art, where they are now (Mousavi 2012). One cannot resist making the comment that this matter was not well handled by the Lit and Phil. Not only did they let the sculptures go for a fraction of what they would be worth today, but they hardly acted in the spirit in which Loftus had donated the sculptures in the first place. Recognising their aesthetic quality and great importance for the study of antiquity, he wanted them to be on view in a place where they could be appreciated by the people of Newcastle, and he clearly went to some lengths to obtain them.

Letter 2: From W K Loftus to James Radford, written from Norwood, and dated Sept 23 1855.

My Dear James,

I received a letter the other day from the Lit. & Phil. accepting my offer. It is not I presume necessary to write further, but it would be well to prepare some plan of getting them to NC. They are somewhat ponderous cases, perfectly oriental! It will be well to allow them all to come to the B.M. together, or at least to London, unless the Committee can find an agent at Havre and get them shipped direct from thence to Ncastle [sic]. Care must be taken not to allow of their getting wet or the slabs will melt like lump sugar! I shall, of course, be glad to aid the Soc. here to the best of my ability.

You will be glad to hear that my fears as to having made an awkward blunder in the Geol. Memoir were groundless. I had with Prof Smyth of the M. P. G. [Museum of Practical Geology] a careful inspection of the rock specimens the other day, and find that, although Mr Witt pronounces the analysis of the Derik water to give nearly the whole of the solid contents as Carb. of Soda, there is not a particle of the same in the rock deposit which is, as I have said, travertin or Carb. of Lime. I can only account for it by supposing that the water carried off the Soda, a light substance, and deposited it further down the stream. But I think Mr Witt must have made an error in the matter, for it seems almost incredible that there should be no Soda in the rock specimens if the water is so saturated with it. This makes me the more anxious to see Dr Richardson's results.

James Radford has returned from his Irish trip looking very well. He & I went to the Crystal Palace on Monday and returned here to dinner.

Hoping you are all well at home. I am, my dear James,

Yours ever truly,

Wm Kennett Loftus.

We expect Mather up this or next week.

APPENDIX

Letter 3: From Hormuzd Rassam to James Radford, 50 Jesmond Road, Newcastle on Tyne, written from 10 Rochester Gardens, Hove, Brighton and dated 12 August 1892.

Dear Sir,

I regret that absence from home has prevented me from replying sooner to your former [?] of the 9th inst, and thanking you for your kindness in sending me two copies of the memoir of my lamented friend Mr Kenneth [sic] Loftus of whose sad demise I heard while I was at Aden.

I shall feel greatly obliged to you if you will kindly give me a short description of the four slabs which Mr Loftus presented to the " 'Lit. and Phil.' or the natural history society" of Newcastle, as I should like to find out from which palace in Nineveh they were excavated. They may belong to Sir Henry Layard's discoveries at Nimrud and belonging to Assur-Nazir-pal's palace. Pray forgive me for thus troubling you and

Believe me,

Yours very faithfully

H. Rassam

Letter 4: From Hormuzd Rassam to James Radford, written from 10 Rochester Gardens, Hove, Brighton and dated 21 August 1892.

My dear Sir,

Pray accept my best thanks for your kindness in sending me a description of the sculptures brought by my late friend W. Kennett Loftus from Assyria for the "Lit and Phil" Institute at Newcastle. They are, I perceive, from Nimrud, the ancient "Calah" of the Bible (Genesis X, 12), the engravings of which are found in Layard's "Nineveh and its Remains". No. 2 figure (eagle headed) is "Nisroch" or "eagle" deity mentioned in II Kings XIX, 37. These sculptures were discovered by Sir Henry Layard in 1846.

APPENDIX

Amongst my old letters I found one from Mr Loftus written to me on 8th January 1853 and as he was a relative of yours and his communication is interesting I have the pleasure to send it to you to read. Please return it to me after you have perused it.

With kind regards,

Believe me,

Yours very faithfully,

H. Rassam

Condolences

Loftus died at sea on 27 November 1858 on the SS 'Tyburnia', the day after embarking for England from Calcutta. He was three days short of his 38th birthday. The letters of condolence here are to James Radford (?) from Sir Henry Layard and from John George Dodson, 1st Baron Monk Bretton (1825–97), who was Loftus's travelling companion from Constantinople to Mosul in 1849. Both letters were written on 11 March 1859, showing that it took more than three months for the news of Loftus's death to reach England, the time of the sea voyage from Calcutta.

Letter 5: From Sir Henry Layard to James Radford (?), written from 130 Piccadilly and dated 11 March 1859 (pl. 31).

Dear Sir,

I was sincerely grieved to hear from you that Mr Loftus, your relative, had died on his passage home to England. I saw him when at Calcutta last year and feared then from his account of himself that his health was giving way under the influence of the climate and much disappointment and vexation. I am truly sorry that he did not then, as I urged him to do, return to England.

His friends – and indeed all those who knew him – will deeply regret his early death. I had some opportunities of knowing him and my opinion of his character and abilities agree entirely with that expressed in your letter. I had a high esteem for him and believe with you that had he been spared he would have distinguished himself even more than he has done. His memory will, however, be connected with a very interesting and important branch of Eastern research, in which he made many important discoveries, and showed great judgement and skill. It grieves me much to hear that he has left a widow & five children in very modest circumstances. I need only say that if at any time you think I could be of assist to them you need have no hesitation in applying to me.

I find that his death was already known the day before yesterday to some of his friends in London. Those to whom I have communicated the intelligence of it yesterday [?] over [?] lunch expressed very sincere regret, for he was very genuinely liked and esteemed.

Begging to assure you of the sympathy I feel for his relatives.

I am,

Yours truly,

A.H. Layard

Letter 6: From John George Dodson, 1st Baron Monk Bretton (1825–97) to James Radford (?), written on House of Commons notepaper and dated 11 March 1859.

Sir,

I am deeply grieved to learn [of] the death of your relative and my good friend and travelling companion Mr W. K. Loftus. From the day on which we were first thrown together in an Hotel at Constantinople I conceived a high esteem for him, and that esteem on becoming more intimately acquainted ripened into a sincere friendship. I was with him for many months in the Eastern parts of Asia Minor & in Mesopotamia under circumstances under which months enable one to know and appreciate a man's character and value better that the same number of years would at home. I am afraid from the account you give me of his illness and death, that besides the melancholy reflection of dying away from England and far from all those nearest & dearest to him, his end must have been preceded by considerable physical suffering.

Were I not afraid that it might be felt obtrusive on the part of one almost a ... [part of letter cut out]...sincere sympathy with her in her sad bereavement. I have recently suffered a heavy loss in my own family and can the more enter into the feelings of others.

Pray accept my condolences on the loss of your relative, and let me assure you of the pleasure it will afford me to be of any service to Mrs Loftus if I can ... [end of letter and signature cut out].

Making provision for widow and children

It seems that following the news of Loftus's death his friends petitioned the East India Company for a pension to be given to Charlotte, but this was rejected, apparently on account of his short length of service. Those who attempted to help included General Sir William Fenwick Williams, who had been leader of the British team in the Turco-Persian Boundary Commission, on which Loftus had served as geologist and naturalist, and Sir Roderick Murchison,[10] the famous British geologist. Letters 9–10 from J G Dodson and an unknown writer to James Radford are rather obscure, but as Letter 9 mentions F L Loftus (presumably Fanny Laura Loftus, b. 17 Feb 1855), and both letters were pasted on a sheet alongside those from Williams and Murchison, they probably have something to do with making provision for the children. The last letter (no. 10), of 16 April 1862, was written some 3 years after the news was received of Loftus's death, so if our interpretation of

---

10 Sir Roderick Murchison FRS (1792–1871) became Director-General of the British Geological Survey in 1855.

APPENDIX

the intent of the last two letters is correct, efforts to make provision for the children continued for some time.

Letter 7: From Colonel William Fenwick Williams to James Radford, dated 15 March 1859.

My dear Sir,

The moment I get the petition, I will use every effort to bring the matter before Lord Stanley, and will write to Sir H. Rawlinson & speak to Sir Roderick Murchison.

Yours in great haste,

W.F. Williams

Letter 8: From Sir Roderick Murchison to James Radford, Gateshead, written from 16 Belgrave Square, and dated 13 April 1859.

Sir,

I ought to have replied before now to your letter of the 2nd in reference to the case of the late Mr W.K. Loftus & his widow & children. I found, on moving in the matter, that the authorities of the India Board <u>had</u> absolutely decided against the possibility of granting anything to the widow. Further, I found from Sir Henry Rawlinson, that owing to the very short term of service of his old assistant [?] there was no chance of assisting his widow & children <u>in that quarter</u>. I have also talked with Sir Fenwick Williams on the subject who is disposed to do anything he can if there be a chance of success in any other quarter – say the Foreign Office. But I confess that I see small hope of success.

Again I apprehend that you are quite misinformed if you suppose that in virtue of being a Trustee of the British Museum [I can help]. I am also a Governor of the Police Cadet [?] School! I regret to say that I have no more influence in that establishment [the British Museum] than any other gentleman wholly unconnected with it.

If however I can [help] through my geological or geographical friends … [part of letter cut out]…it would give me much pleasure as I respected Mr Loftus though I was slightly acquainted with him only.

Yours … [end of letter and signature cut out, but noted to be Sir Roderick Murchison].

Letter 9: From John George Dodson to James Radford, written from 'Danny, Hurstpierpoint', and dated 2 Nov 1859.

Sir,

If you can send me some of the canvassing cards on behalf of F.L. Loftus (from 18 to 24) it will be of service to me in writing to persons to solicit votes. I am afraid it is too late for me to do anything this election as everybody must have promised by this time, but I have made some attempts. For next time I might succeed in obtaining some votes.

Yours faithfully,

J.G. Dodson.

Letter 10: From [xxxx] (signature undeciphered) to James Radford (?), written from 'Southend, Eltham, Kent' and dated April 16 1862.

My dear Sir,

I shall be very glad to give you a vote for the poor child – and will continue to do so, till he is provided for. If you can send me any more papers, we will send them to many of our friends, and I doubt not, we shall be able to obtain a good many. To save trouble, I will send mine to either of the two clergymen on the card, without [sic] you would like to have the vote yourself.

APPENDIX

Should you see Mr Charlton, pray remember me kindly to him ... and to Adamson [?], and any other of my Newcastle friends...

Believe me,

Yours truly,

Etc.

Notes to accompany concise genealogical tree (see pl. 32) showing children of W K Loftus and his relationship with James Radford

(1) William Loftus (1760–1834), the grandfather of William Kennett Loftus, was proprietor of the Turf Hotel, Newcastle, owner of an extensive coaching business, and for many years clerk of Newcastle Racecourse (Harbottle 1973: 195). He also built and owned the grandstand at Newcastle Races (Obituary of James Radford, *Newcastle Daily Chronicle* [?], 7 January 1893). He married in succession three sisters, Ann, Frances and Winifride Harvey.

(2) Ann Harvey (1760–87), the grandmother of William Kennett Loftus, was the third daughter of Thomas Harvey (*c.* 1725–1806) and Margaret Harvey (*c.* 1731–73). Their children were Elizabeth (Champney) (1758–1814), Frances (1759–1830), Ann (1760–87), and Winifride (1762–1837). The family is commemorated in a brass plaque in Newcastle Cathedral.

(3) William Loftus (1787–1860), the father of William Kennett Loftus, was an army officer (Harbottle 1973: 195–6). According to Welford (1895: 66–7), after leaving the army he 'lived a quiet and retired life, first in the south of England, then near Newark, and lastly, in the county town of Lancaster, where he passed away'. However, according to a newspaper article by F J Radford, *Newcastle Weekly Chronicle*, 4 December 1915, he was at some point clerk of the course at Newcastle Races.

APPENDIX

(4) James Radford (1806-93) was the nephew by marriage of William Loftus (1760-1834),[11] the proprietor of the Turf Hotel Newcastle. He was the son of James Radford (d. 1812) who had married Winifride Harvey, sister of Ann and Frances, William's 1st and 2nd wives. He was therefore the 1st cousin of William Loftus (1787-1860) and the 1st cousin once removed of William Kennett Loftus (1820-58). James Radford was born in Manchester, qualified as a solicitor in 1830, and moved to Newcastle in *c.* 1834 after the death of his uncle to manage the coaching business based at the Turf Hotel. He was much involved in Newcastle Racecourse, and was the secretary and treasurer of the race committee and clerk of the course 1831-41. He was also concerned with local politics and schools administration. He had an only son, Francis John Radford. (See obituary in *Newcastle Daily Chronicle* [?], 7 January 1893).

(5) Captain Alfred John Loftus, FRGS (1836-99), the half-brother of William Kennett Loftus, was a naval adventurer who became hydrographer to the King of Siam 1871-91 and was a Knight Commander of Siam.

(6) Alfred Kennett Loftus (1845-1905), the eldest son of William Kennett Loftus, emigrated with his family to Canada in 1884, having previously worked in Canada as a locomotive engineer on the old European and North American Railway. See also Letter 13.

(7) William Kennett Loftus (1849-), the 2nd, the third son of William Kennett Loftus, became a royal court photographer in Siam. Some of his prints are in the Pitt Rivers Museum, Oxford. See also Joachim K. Bautze, *Unseen Siam: Early Photography 1860-1910* (Bangkok 2017).

---

11   In the will of William Loftus he is described as 'the nephew of my late dear wife'.

Bibliography

Ateş, S 2013. *The Ottoman – Iranian Borderlands: Making a Boundary 1843–1914*, Cambridge, Cambridge University Press.

Barnett, R D 1975. *A Catalogue of the Nimrud Ivories in the British Museum*, 2nd ed., London, British Museum Publications.

Barnett, R D 1976. *Sculptures from the North Palace of Ashurbanipal at Nineveh (668–627 B.C.)*, London, British Museum Publications.

Barnett, R D 1987. 'Loftus, William Kennett', *Reallexikon der Assyriologie und Vorderasiatischen Archäologie* 7: 102–03.

Barnett, R D, Bleibtreu, E, and Turner, G 1998. *Sculptures form the Southwest Palace of Sennacherib at Nineveh*, text and plates, London, British Museum Press.

Boulger, G S 1893. 'Loftus, William Kennett (1821? –1858)', *Dictionary of National Biography* 34: 80–81.

Brereton, G 2021. 'Gift of an artist: An Assyrian relief fragment from Ashurbanipal's palace at Nineveh, *The British Museum Middle East Newsletter* 6: 42–6.

Curtis, J E 1979. 'Loftus' Parthian cemetery at Warka', *Akten des VII. Internationalen Kongresses für Iranischen Kunst und Archäologie, München, 7.–10. September 1976* (Berlin): 309–17.

Curtis, J E 1983. 'Some axe-heads from Chagar Bazar and Nimrud', *Iraq* XLV: 73–81.

Curtis, J E 1986. 'A basalt sculpture found at Warka', *Baghdader Mitteilungen* 17: 131–4.

Curtis, J E 1992. 'The dying lion', *Iraq* 54: 113–17.

Curtis, J E 1993. 'William Kennett Loftus and excavations at Susa', *Iranica Antiqua* XXVIII: 1–55.

Curtis, J E 2004. 'Maceheads from Tell Mohammed in the British Museum', in Frame, G (ed.), *From the Upper Sea to the Lower Sea: Studies on the History of Assyria and Babylonia in Honour of A.K. Grayson*, Leiden, Peeters, 57–66.

Curtis, J E 2010. 'A Victorian artist in Assyria', *Iraq* 72: 175–82.

Curtis, J E and Reade, J E (eds.) 1995. *Art and Empire: Treasures' from Assyria in the British Museum*, London, British Museum Press.

Curtis, J E 2018. 'More figurines from Susa', in Gondet, S., and Haerinck, E. (eds.), *L'Orient est son Jardin: Hommage à Rémy Boucharlat*, Acta Iranica 58: 129–35.

Ermidoro, S 2020. 'The William Kennett Loftus legacy to the North: Near Eastern materials in Newcastle upon Tyne', in I L Finkel and S J Simpson (eds.), *In Context: the Reade Festschrift*, Oxford, Archaeopress, 245–57.

Firouz, E 2005. *The Complete Fauna of Iran*, London, I.B. Tauris.

Gadd, C J 1936. *The Stones of Assyria*, London, Chatto and Windus.

Harbottle, S T L 1973. 'W.K. Loftus: an archaeologist from Newcastle', *Archaeologia Aeliana Fifth Series*, vol. 1: 195–217.

Larsen, M T 1996. *The Conquest of Assyria: Excavations in an Antique Land 1840–1860*, London and New York, Routledge.

Layard, A H 1849. *Nineveh and its Remains*, 2 vols., London, John Murray.

Layard, A H 1853. *Discoveries in the Ruins of Nineveh and Babylon*, London, John Murray.

Layard, A H 1887. *Early adventures in Persia, Susiana, and Babylonia including a residence among the Bakhtiyari and other wild tribes before the discovery of Nineveh*, 2 vols., London: John Murray.

Loftus, W K 1851. 'On the geological structure of the mountain range of Western Persia', *Quarterly Journal of the Geological Society* 7: 263.

Loftus, W K 1854. 'On the geology of portions of the Turko-Persian Frontier, and of the districts adjoining', *Quarterly Journal of the Geological Society* 10: 464–69.

Loftus, W K 1854a. *Report of the Assyrian Excavation Fund* in Barnett 1976: 71–73.

Loftus, W K 1855. 'On the geology of portions of the Turko-Persian Frontier, and of the districts adjoining', *Quarterly Journal of the Geological Society* 11: 247–344.

Loftus, W K 1855a. *Report of the Assyrian Excavation Fund II* in Barnett 1976: 73–75.

Loftus, W K 1856. 'Notes of a journey from Baghdad to Busrah, with descriptions of several Chaldaean remains', *Journal of the Royal Geographic Society* 26: 131–53.

Loftus, W K 1856–57. 'On the excavations undertaken at the ruins of Susa in 1851–52', *Transactions of the Royal Society of Literature* 5 (2nd series): 422–53.

Loftus, W K 1857. *Travels and Researches in Chaldea and Susiana; with an account of excavations at Warka, the "Erech" of Nimrud, Shush, "Shushan the palace" of Esther, in 1849-52*, London, James Nisbit and Co.

Loftus, W K 1857a. 'On the determination of the River "Eulœus" of the Greek Historians', *Journal of the Royal Geographical Society* 27: 120-33.

Loftus, W K 1859a 'Warkah: its ruins and remains', *Transactions of the Royal Society of Literature* 6: 1-64.

Loftus, W K 1859b. *Lithographic Facsimiles of Inscriptions in the Cuneiform Character from the Ruins of Susa*, London.

Malley, S 2012. *From Archaeology to Spectacle in Victorian Britain: the Case of Assyria, 1845-1854*, Farnham, Ashgate.

Mitchell, T C and Searight, A 2008. *Catalogue of the Western Asiatic Seals in the British Museum: Stamp Seals III*, Leiden, Brill.

Moorey, P R S 1971. 'The Loftus hoard of Old Babylonian tools from Tell Sifr in Iraq', *Iraq* 33: 61-86.

Moorey, P R S, Curtis, J E, Hook, D R and Hughes, M J 1988. 'New analyses of Old Babylonian metalwork from Tell Sifr', *Iraq* 50: 39-48.

North, R 1957. 'Status of the Warka excavations', *Orientalia* N.S. 26: 185-256.

Potts, D T and Basello, G P 2022. 'The "Black Stone of Susa": a lost *kudurru*, an unpublished drawing and a line of Middle Elamite copied in the 1820s', *East and West* N.S. 3 (62): 98-116.

Rawlinson, H C 1839. 'Notes on a march from Zoháb, at the foot of Zagros, along the mountains to Khúzistán (Susiana), and from thence through the province of Luristan to Kirmánsháh, in the year 1836', *Journal of the Royal Geographical Society* 9: 26-116.

Reade, J E 2022. *Design and Destruction: the Palace of Ashurbanipal at Nineveh*, Archiv für Orientforschung 34, Vienna.

Simpson, S J 2005. 'Making their mark: foreign travellers at Persepolis', *Arta 2005.001*.

Smail, R 2004. 'Loftus, William Kennett (1820–1858)', *Dictionary of National Biography* 34: 310–11.

Thompson, D 1979. 'Parthian stucco from Warka in the British Museum', *Akten des VII. Internationalen Kongresses für Iranischen Kunst und Archäologie, München, 7.-10. September 1976* (Berlin): 294–308.

Turner, G 2001. 'Sennacherib's Palace at Nineveh: the drawings of H.A. Churchill and the discoveries of H.J. Ross', *Iraq* 63: 107–38.

Turner, G 2021. *The British Museum's Excavations at Nineveh, 1846–1855*, Leiden and Boston (edited by J. Russell).

Waterfield, G 1963. *Layard of Nineveh*, London: John Murray.

Weidner, E F 1938. 'Die Reliefs der assyrischen Könige, IV. Die assyrischen Reliefs in England (II. Teil)', *Archiv für Orientforschung* 23: 206–37.

Welford, R 1895. 'William Kennett Loftus', in R Welford, *Men of Mark 'twixt Tyne and Tweed*, London and Newcastle vol.3: 66–72.

Index

Abdi Pasha 152
Abu Shahrain (Eridu) 33, 188
Ahvaz 35, 182–5, 189
Ainsworth, William Francis 19–20, 28, 69–70, 231
Al Hadhr (Hatra) 19, 28, 64–5, 69–73, 83, 119, 125, 129, 160, 180, 182
Aneiza Arabs 156, 166, 169, 175
SS Apprentice 10, 172, 219
Aqar Quf (Akker Koof) 13, 32–3, 42, 154–5, 160
Ardericca 194, 218
Ardeshir Mirza 36, 202
Assad Khan 139
Babylon 15–16, 30–2, 74, 78, 89, 116, 121, 131–2, 139–47, 155, 157–8, 162–3, 167, 180, 183, 191, 201, 208, pl. 10
Baghdad 10, 14, 20, 25, 28–30, 32–3, 35, 38–41, 46–7, 49, 51–2, 54, 65–6, 70–8, 80, 82–7, 89–91, 116–19, 124, 126, 128–9, 135–6, 138–9, 142, 145, 147–8, 152, 154, 156–8, 160–1, 163–4, 168, 171, 175, 177–8, 187, 190, 192, 196, 203, 205, 213, 215–22, 224–7, 232
Bahr al-Najaf 151
Ballingale, Dr 39, 222
Basheikhah 27–8, 63
Basra (Busrah) 16, 29, 33–4, 74, 77, 80, 87, 121, 126, 135, 142, 156, 159, 162, 164, 166, 169, 172, 175, 177, 184–5, 187, 228
Beder Khan Bey 28, 64
Behbehan 198, 202, 209, 218
Beni Lam Arabs 126, 138, 181, 213
Birs Nimrud (Borsippa) 31–3, 89, 141, 146–7, 152, 155, 158
Bisitun (Bisutun, Behistun) 14, 36–7, 200, 202–3, 206–8
Blacklock, Joseph 11, 39, 72, 81, 135, 154, 157, 179, 185, 189, 195, 213, 227
Borujerd 197–8, 200
Botta, Paul-Émile 27, 29, 63
Bowerbank, James Scott 79, 88, 216
British Museum 15, 17–20, 24, 29, 33, 41, 62, 64, 80, 121, 132, 135, 159, 162, 240–1, pls 12–27
Bushire 78, 154, 198
Canning, Sir Stratford 9, 22, 25, 33, 45, 50, 55, 160, 177, 187
Charlton, Dr Edward 11, 39, 81, 136–7, 139, 147, 179, 187, 192, 195, 199, 201, 205, 213, 217–18, 222, 228, 242
Chesney, General Francis Rawdon 20, 222
Churchill, Henry A 13, 15–18, 27, 31, 33–7, 40–1, 51, 62–3, 66, 69, 138, 141, 143, 153, 162, 165, 175, 177–8, 181, 185, 188, 199, 202, 204, 232
Constantinople 9–10, 13, 18, 22, 25–7, 45, 48–57, 61–3, 74, 76, 84, 87, 117–18, 127, 132, 136, 154, 157, 191, 213, 216, 218, 220, 230, 237–8
Ctesiphon 13, 30, 32, 39, 90, 116, 129, 142, 153, 221

INDEX

De la Beche, Sir Henry 9, 14, 22, 45, 88–9, 123, 159, 169, 185, 215–16, 220–1, 232
Deliktaş 26, 59, 61, 66.
Delli Abbas 156
Dervish Pasha 13, 29–30, 87, 117, 120, 125, 139, 143, 162, 188
Diwaniyah (Diwanieh) 164
Diyala, River 137–8, 156
Diyabakir 26–7, 55, 57, 62, 67, 84, 116, 121
Dizful 11, 35–6, 38–9, 163, 176, 178, 180–1, 183–5, 188–9, 192–3, 195–9, 209, 212, 214, 216, 225, 228.
Dodson, John George, 1st Baron Monk Bretton 21, 25–6, 52–4, 56, 58, 69, 89, 121, 124–5, 131, 133, 230, 237–9, 241
El Heimar 141, 156, 158, 174
SS Erin 13, 25, 46–7, 49, 51, 53, 88
Erzerum 45, 55, 120, 216.
Euphrates, River 19–20, 26, 29, 33, 61, 70, 131, 134, 141–8, 151, 153, 155, 157, 163–4, 166–7, 170–1, 174–5, 184, 187, 191
Ezekiel, Tomb of 31, 146, 148
Fahed, Sheikh of Montefic Arabs 169
Fath-Ali Shah 202
Ferhan, Sheikh of Shammar Arabs 160
SS Fortitude 39, 227, 229

Fraser, James Baillee 89, 161, 169
Garey, Mr (commissariat?) 13, 27, 62, 66, 119
Gherrara 14, 30, 32, 35, 90, 116, 120, 124, 128, 133–4, 137, 139, 147, 153–4, 178
Glascott, Lieut. A G 13, 15, 27, 29, 36, 38–9, 51, 62–3, 65, 69, 73, 88, 125, 134, 138, 145, 197–9, 201, 203, 205, 213, 219, 227
Gray, John 11–12, 45–8, 57, 61–2, 68, 72, 82, 84, 89, 123–4, 128, 139, 179, 190, 213–4
Green, Benjamin 6, 11, 44, 57, 61–2, 84, 90, 116, 119, 121, 124, 169, 192, 213, 224, 227
Guarracino, Frederick 26, 56, 58, 213
Haffar, River 176
Hamadan (Ecbatana) 11, 37, 199, 203, 206–7, 209, 212, pl. 5
Hammam Ali 28, 73.
Hammond, Rt Hon Edmund 48, 136, 190, 215
Hancock, Albany 10–11, 15, 57, 65, 76, 81–3, 90–1, 119, 135, 137, 192, 213
Hancock, John 11, 90–1, 137
Hector, Aexander 37, 163, 222–3
Hillah 31, 33, 78, 83, 124–5, 131, 141, 144–6,
149–50, 152, 155–6, 158, 160, 163, 188
Hit 25, 131, 134, 153
Hudson, George 123, 127
Hyslop, Dr James McAdam 38, 86, 216, 220, 223
Ikbal-id-Doula, Nawab of Oude 75, 81
Imam al-Dur (shrine) 73
Isfahan 11, 37–8, 198, 200, 202, 206, 209–10, 212, 216
Jabba, Sheikh 176
Jones, Capt Felix 21, 30, 32, 85, 119, 137, 154, 175, 177, 187, 216, 219, 221–2, 232
Kalaat Debbi 33, 166, 175
Kalah Shergat (Assur) 73
Kangavar 37, 208
Karakosh 28, 63
Karbala (Kerbala) 29, 32–3, 83, 87, 117, 122, 140, 142, 146–7, 149–53, 158–9, 169
Karkheh, River 35, 178, 182, 219, 225.
Karun, River 35, 39, 176, 178, 182–3, 194, 224
Kaylan 226
Keffil 31–2, 146–8.
Kemball, Capt Arnold Burrowes 39, 154, 221, 223
Kermanshah 11, 36, 39, 200–1, 205–7
Khorramabad 11, 36, 193, 197–9, 202, 213, 225
Khorsabad 27, 29, 63–4, 121
Khouler Mirza 224
Khuzeyl Arabs 158

250

INDEX

Kirrind (Kerend) 220, 224, 226, 227
Kouyunjik 27–8, 62–5, 83, 129, 173, 186
Kufa 32, 142, 149
Kut al Amara 137, 213
Layard, Austen Henry 8–10, 16–20, 22–3, 25, 27–8, 35, 40, 45, 48, 50–1, 55, 63, 70, 73, 83, 88–9, 121, 123, 125–6, 132, 136, 156, 159–60, 165–8, 170, 172–3, 176–9, 181–4, 194, 198, 205–6, 208, 217, 219–21, 230, 232–4, 236–8, pl. 31
Lynch, Lt Henry Blosse 126, 135, 188, 220–1, 227–8
Madan Arabs 173, 175, 182
Malamir 218, 220
Masjid-e Soleiman 200.
Mather, Edward 11, 22, 47–50, 54, 57, 61–2, 68, 72, 89, 116, 119, 123–4, 127–8, 134, 137, 139, 154, 160–1, 166, 169, 172, 192, 199, 213–15, 217, 235
Mirza Jafar Khan 13, 29, 87, 117, 120, 125, 181, 190, 202, 204
Mirza Sultan Ali Khan 35, 183
Mirza Taqi Khan 120, 212
Mitford, Edward Ledwich 20, 70
Mizrakji Khan 140, 153
Mohammad Ai Mirza 36, 202, 204

Mohammad Shah Qajar 78
Mohammerah (Khorramshahr) 8, 10–11, 30, 32–6, 38–9, 76, 118, 132, 159, 161, 163, 166, 168, 172, 174, 176–8, 180, 182, 186, 188, 190, 192–4, 197, 200–1, 203, 209, 215, 217, 219, 221, 223–5, 227
Mohawil Khan 140
Montefic Arabs 126, 158, 166, 169
Mosul 9, 12, 19, 25–9, 42, 52, 54, 56, 61–74, 76, 79, 81, 83, 87, 121–2, 125, 129, 136, 154, 165, 167, 213, 215, 220–1, 230, 237
Mungerrah (Mungirah) 15, 36, 186, 189–90, 192, 196–7, 199, 202, 204–5, 207, 213, 225.
Murray, John 56, 231-2
Musseib 147, 153, 158
Nahrawan Canal 30, 127, 137
Najaf (Meshed Ali) 32, 140, 142, 146, 149–51, 167
Naqsh-e Rustam 38, 214
Nasser al-Din Shah 120
Nebbi Yunus 32, 149.
Nedjib Pasha 58, 126, 136–7, 152, 160
Newbold, Capt Thomas John 32, 154, 158, 160, 201
Newcastle upon Tyne 6, 8–12, 14–15, 21–2, 34, 39, 43–4, 49–50,

52, 76, 80–2, 84, 90–1, 123, 128, 135–9, 157–8, 168, 195, 221, 227, 230, 233–4, 236, 242–3, pls 1,32
Nil, River 34, 174.
Nimrud 8, 18, 28, 31, 35, 42, 64, 73, 179, 205, 214, 233–4, 236
Nineveh (see also Kouyunjik) 8, 18, 23, 27, 31, 35, 42, 45, 50, 63–5, 72, 88–9, 117, 129, 132, 143, 148, 159, 179–80, 191, 205, 208, 214, 223–4, 236.
Nippur (Niffar) 16, 162–3, 174–5, 217
SS Nitocris 29–30, 39, 116–17, 119, 124, 127, 137, 139, 172, 175, 178, 219–20, 222, 224.
Norris, Edwin 191, 231
Olquin, Dr Joseph 13, 27, 37–8, 51, 62, 66, 124, pl.29
Pasargadae 38, 213–14
Palmerston, Lord 9, 33, 167, 187
Persepolis 38, 118, 132, 176, 198, 200, 202–3, 209, 213–14
Pisani, Count Alexandre 50, 54, 221
Pol-e Tang 197, 225
Qadisiyyah 73.
Radford, James (solicitor) 11, 43, 45, 49, 62, 68, 71–2, 76, 81, 87, 116, 119, 128, 133–4, 136, 157, 160, 163, 177, 179–80, 189, 196, 198, 205–7, 217, 220, 222,

INDEX

230–1, 233–4, 236–43, pls 5, 30–2
Radford, James (artist) 11, 128, 201, 205, 235
Ram Hormuz 194, 219.
Rolland, Capt Stewart Erskine 179
Rassam, Christian 20, 27–8, 62–5, 67, 70–1, 121, 163
Rassam, Hormuzd 41–2, 234, 236
Rawlinson, Major Henry Creswicke 10, 14, 17, 20–2, 28–32, 35, 37, 39, 40–2, 71, 73, 83, 85, 89, 118–19, 121, 125, 129, 132–3, 146, 153–5, 162–3, 166, 168, 176–8, 181, 183–4, 186–7, 189–90, 194–5, 200, 202–3, 205, 208, 215, 217–18, 221, 225–6, 233, 240
Redhouse, Sir James 51, 55
Rennell Major James 143
Rich, Claudius James 31, 72, 141–3
Ross, Dr John 29, 70, 73, 75, 87, 119, 125, 161
HMS St Vincent 48
Samarra 28, 73, 137
Samava 172
Samsun 26, 52, 54, 56–7, 66, 73, 213
Seimarrah (Seimare) 226
Seleucia-on-the-Tigris 29–30, 90, 116, 119, 142
Shahabad 184
Shammar Arabs 28, 64–5, 68, 71, 80, 125, 136, 160
Shaour, River 182

Shatt al-Arab, River 176, 201
Shiraz 11, 38, 78, 118, 200, 202, 209, 213–14
Shushtar (Shuster) 178, 181–4, 191, 205, 212, 218
Sinkara (Larsa) 16, 21, 23, 34, 41–2, 171, 174, 177, 187, 195, 205, 210, 229, pl. 21
Sofuk, Sheikh of Shammar Arabs 71, 125, 136, 160
Sopwith, Thomas 12, 161, 179–80, 185–6, 190, 201
Stevens, Frances Iliff 58
Suleiman Khan 178, 183–4, 194, 216, 224, 226
Suk-es-Sheioukh 161, 166, 169, 184
Susa (Shush) 11, 14, 16–19, 23, 35, 38–40, 43, 174, 176, 178–84, 186, 190–4, 200, 203, 205–6, 209–10, 213, 215–19, 225, 228, pls 22–7.
Susan, Khuzestan 178, 186
Suttum, Sheikh of Shammar Arabs 15, 28, 68, 70–1, 80, 160
Tahir Bey 145, 163
Takht-e Shirin 37, 203, 208
Taq-e Bustan 13, 36–7, 206–7, pls 28–9
Taurus Mountains 12, 26, 59, 122, 132
Taylor, John George 33, 42, 135, 223
Taylor, Col Robert 30, 135, 142, 152, 223

Tcherikoff, Colonel Yegor Ivanovitch 13, 26, 29, 54, 61, 156, 176
Tekrit 28, 73
Tell Ede 33, pl. 12
Tell Hammam 33, 164, pl. 11
Tell Ibrahim al-Khalil 31, 146
Tell Mohammed 127
Tigris, River 12, 20, 26, 28–9, 52, 61–2, 71–2, 77, 91, 116, 122, 126–7, 129, 134, 137, 139, 154, 156–7, 191, 210, 213
Topham, Capt W 46
Ukhaydir 159
Ur (Tell Mugeyer) 33, 42, 166, 171, 177, 187–8, 229, pl. 20
Victoria, Queen 14, 23, 29, 60, 80, 84–6, 177
Warka 11, 15–19, 21–3, 33–5, 41, 164–9, 172, 174–5, 177–80, 182, 186–7, 189–90, 192, 194, 196, 200, 205, 213, 217, 219–21, 227, 229, pls 13–19
Wasit 157, 159, 161–2, 178, 187, 190, 213
Williams, Lieut Col W F *passim*
Wolff, Joseph 55, 90
Wood, Algernon 13, 27, 36, 51, 62, 66, 68, 88, 125, 134, 156, 193, 197–9, 204, 207
Yenihan 26, 59, 66
Yezidis 27–8, 63–4